Cash and Credit Information for Teens

Second Edition

TEEN FINANCE SERIES

Second Edition

Cash and Credit Information for Teens

Tips For A Successful Financial Life

*Including Facts about Earning Money, Paying Taxes,
Budgeting, Banking, Shopping, Using Credit, And
Avoiding Financial Pitfalls*

◆

Edited by Karen Bellenir

Omnigraphics

P.O. Box 31-1640, Detroit, MI 48231-1640

Bibliographic Note

Because this page cannot legibly accommodate all the copyright notices, the Bibliographic Note portion of the Preface constitutes an extension of the copyright notice.

Edited by Karen Bellenir

Teen Finance Series

Karen Bellenir, *Managing Editor*
Elizabeth Collins, *Research and Permissions Coordinator*
Cherry Edwards, *Permissions Assistant*
EdIndex, Services for Publishers, *Indexers*

* * *

Omnigraphics, Inc.

Matthew P. Barbour, *Senior Vice President*
Kevin Hayes, *Operations Manager*

* * *

Peter E. Ruffner, *Publisher*

Frederick G. Ruffner, Jr., *Chairman*

Copyright © 2009 Omnigraphics, Inc.

ISBN 978-0-7808-1065-5

Library of Congress Cataloging-in-Publication Data

Cash and credit information for teens : tips for a successful financial life
including facts about earning money, paying taxes, budgeting, banking,
shopping, using credit, and avoiding financial pitfalls / edited by Karen
Bellenir. -- 2nd ed.
    p. cm.
Includes bibliographical references and index.
Summary: "Provides information for teens about earning and managing money,
spending and using credit wisely, and avoiding fraud. Includes index,
resource information, and a list of online money management tools"--Provided
by publisher.
    ISBN 978-0-7808-1065-5 (hardcover : alk. paper) 1. Teenagers--Finance,
Personal. I. Bellenir, Karen.
HG179.C346 2009
332.0240083'5--dc22

                                                        2009012105

$$\infty$$

Table of Contents

Preface ix

Part One: Earning Money

Chapter 1—Facts About The Money In Your Wallet 3

Chapter 2—Do You Get An Allowance? 19

Chapter 3—Jobs For Teens 23

Chapter 4—Finding A Summer Job Or Internship 31

Chapter 5—Want To Be Your Own Boss? 37

Chapter 6—Tax Information For Students 51

Part Two: Managing Your Money

Chapter 7—Making Your Money Grow 67

Chapter 8—Preparing A Budget 77

Chapter 9—Banking Basics 85

Chapter 10—Electronic Banking 93

Chapter 11—Avoiding Costly Banking Mistakes 101

Chapter 12—Managing Your Savings Account 113

Chapter 13—What You Should Know About
            Checking Accounts 121

Chapter 14—Insurance: Protecting Your Assets 145

Chapter 15—Another Good Use Of Your Money:
            Helping Others 153

Part Three: Being A Savvy Consumer

Chapter 16—Shopping And Impulse Buying 165

Chapter 17—It's On Sale, But Is It A Good Deal? 171

Chapter 18—Online Shopping: A Guide For E-Consumers 179

Chapter 19—Payment Options For Purchases 183

Chapter 20—Facts For Consumers: How To Right A Wrong 191

Chapter 21—What You Should Know About Warranties
            And Service Contracts 201

Chapter 22—Shopping For A Cell Phone Plan 215

Chapter 23—Buying A Computer 221

Chapter 24—Buying Jewelry 229

Chapter 25—Buying Your First Car 237

Chapter 26—CD, Book, And Video Buying Clubs 243

Part Four: Using Credit And Credit Cards

Chapter 27—What You Need To Know About Credit 253

Chapter 28—Borrowing Basics 273

Chapter 29—Choosing A Credit Card 283

Chapter 30—Other Plastic: Debit Cards, Prepaid Cards,
            Gift Cards, And More 295

Chapter 31—Installment Loans 301

Chapter 32—Car Loans.. 305

Chapter 33—Education Loans 309

Part Five: Avoiding Financial Pitfalls

Chapter 34—Avoid Out-Of-Control Debt 321

Chapter 35—Watch Out For Predatory Lending Practices 329

Chapter 36—If Your Credit, ATM, Or Debit Cards Are
         Lost Or Stolen 337

Chapter 37—Identity Theft And Identity Fraud 341

Chapter 38—Con Artists Want Your Money:
         Avoid These Scams And Schemes 351

Chapter 39—Avoid Modeling Scams 373

Chapter 40—Travel Fraud: Avoiding A Spring Break Bust 377

Chapter 41—Gambling: Don't Bet On Winning 385

Part Six: If You Need More Information

Chapter 42—Online Money Management Tools 391

Chapter 43—Resources For Financial Information 397

Index 409

Preface

About This Book

According to a recent survey of teen attitudes about money conducted by the Charles Schwab Corporation, most teens want to learn about budgeting, saving, avoiding debt, and achieving financial independence. Efforts to reach these goals are often thwarted, however, because young adults are unfamiliar with the tools used in money management and they lack hands-on experience. Fewer than one in four teens reported knowing how to use a credit card responsibly, only one in three understood the financial decisions made by their parents, and a mere 14 percent reported any involvement in the process of bill paying or other tasks related to managing their family's household finances.

Cash and Credit Information For Teens, Second Edition provides an updated look at how teens can earn and manage money. It provides practical information about receiving income, paying taxes, and budgeting. It also discusses choosing appropriate banking services, managing a checking account, using credit and debit cards, making informed shopping decisions, and borrowing money for education or major purchases. A section on avoiding financial pitfalls provides facts about debt-related problems, identity theft, and common financial scams. The book concludes with a list of online money management tools and a directory of resources for additional information.

How To Use This Book

This book is divided into parts and chapters. Parts focus on broad areas of interest; chapters are devoted to single topics within a part.

Part One: Earning Money begins with facts about the history, manufacturing, and value of coins and currency. It continues with information about the most common ways teens can acquire money, including allowances, jobs, internships, and even starting their own businesses. Information about taxes on income and other earnings is also included.

Part Two: Managing Your Money discusses ways to monitor the use of money, save for specific goals, and increase personal wealth. It describes the importance of budgeting, explains different types of banks and the services they offer, and discusses the use of insurance for risk management. The part concludes with a chapter about using personal resources, including time and money, to help others.

Part Three: Being A Savvy Consumer provides tips about shopping and spending money wisely. It discusses ways to evaluate purchase decisions and describes the benefits and risks of various payment options, including cash, checks, credit cards, and debit cards. It offers suggestions for resolving problems when things go wrong, especially with online, telephone, and mail-order shopping. Several individual chapters discuss some of the purchase challenges many teens encounter, including shopping for cell phone plans, buying computers, buying a car, or joining a club to purchase music, books, or videos.

Part Four: Using Credit And Credit Cards explains how credit works and the importance of building a good credit history. It discusses the factors lenders consider when making decisions about loaning money, and it describes the types of loans teens may encounter most frequently, including credit cards, car loans, and loans for education.

Part Five: Avoiding Financial Pitfalls explains some of the most common problems that threaten financial well-being, including spiraling debt, predatory lending practices, and identity theft. It also offers cautions about the risks associated with sweepstakes frauds, lottery scams, bogus fundraising activities, fraudulent work-at-home and internet schemes, pyramid and Ponzi schemes, modeling scams, travel offer fraud, and gambling.

Part Six: If You Need More Information includes a list of online money management tools and a directory of resources for additional information about personal finance.

Bibliographic Note

This volume contains documents and excerpts from publications issued by the following government agencies: Federal Bureau of Investigation (FBI); Federal Deposit Insurance Corporation (FDIC); Federal Reserve Board of Governors; Federal Trade Commission; Internal Revenue Service (IRS); National Network of Libraries of Medicine, South Central Region; U.S. Department of Justice; U.S. Department of Labor; and the U.S. Small Business Administration.

In addition, this volume contains copyrighted documents and articles produced by the following organizations: Bank of America; CastleWorks, Inc.; Federal Reserve Bank of Atlanta; Federal Reserve Bank of Chicago; Federal Reserve Bank of Dallas; Investopedia, ULC; Making It Count; Motley Fool; National Consumer League; Nemours Foundation; Northwestern Mutual Foundation; Office of Attorney General, State of Idaho; Planned Parenthood Federation of America, Inc.; Securities Industry and Financial Markets Association Foundation for Investor Education; and ultimatemoneyskills.com.

Full citation information is provided on the first page of each chapter. Every effort has been made to secure all necessary rights to reprint the copyrighted material. If any omissions have been made, please contact Omnigraphics to make corrections for future editions.

Acknowledgements

In addition to the organizations who have contributed to this book, special thanks are due to research and permissions coordinator, Liz Collins; permissions assistant, Cherry Edwards; editorial assistant, Nicole Salerno; and prepress technician, Elizabeth Bellenir.

Part One
Earning Money

Chapter 1

Facts About The Money In Your Wallet

U.S. currency, recognized and valued by people everywhere, is the most widely held currency in the world. This chapter gives some basic information about U.S. currency and coin: how they are made, their design and features, how they circulate, and how to spot counterfeit currency.

Types Of U.S. Paper Money

Currency In Circulation

More than 99 percent of the total dollar amount of paper money in circulation in the United States today is made up of Federal Reserve notes. The other small part of circulating currency consists of U.S. notes or legal tender notes still in circulation but no longer issued.

Federal Reserve notes are printed and issued in denominations of $1, $2, $5, $10, $20, $50, and $100. The $500, $1,000, $5,000, and $10,000 denominations have not been printed since 1946.

The Federal Reserve Act requires that adequate backing be pledged for all Federal Reserve notes in circulation. U.S. Treasury securities, acquired through open market operations, are the most important form of collateral

About This Chapter: "Dollars and Cents," reprinted with permission from the Federal Reserve Bank of Atlanta, www.frbatlanga.org. © 2006.

and provide backing for most of the value of the currency in circulation. Some other types of collateral the Federal Reserve holds are gold certificates and certain eligible instruments such as notes, drafts, and bills of exchange.

The Federal Reserve System, established by Congress in 1913, issues Federal Reserve notes through its twelve Federal Reserve Districts. Every district has its main office in a major city, and all but two have branches in other large cities. Each district is designated by a number and the corresponding letter of the alphabet.

The Bureau of Engraving and Printing, a division of the U.S. Treasury Department, produces currency for the Federal Reserve System to replace damaged or worn notes or to support economic growth. Federal Reserve Banks issue currency according to the need in their districts. The district letter and number on the face of a note identify the issuing Reserve Bank.

♣ It's A Fact!!
Federal Reserve Districts And Their Designations

Boston	A	1
New York	B	2
Philadelphia	C	3
Cleveland	D	4
Richmond	E	5
Atlanta	F	6
Chicago	G	7
St. Louis	H	8
Minneapolis	I	9
Kansas City	J	10
Dallas	K	11
San Francisco	L	12

Types No Longer Issued

Besides the denominations of U.S. notes, from $1 to $10,000, that were issued before 1929, several other types of U.S. paper money no longer issued have circulated within the past 75 years. National Bank notes were issued by national banks from 1863 to 1929. Gold certificates, authorized in 1865 and issued by the Treasury Department in exchange for gold coin and bullion, circulated until 1933. Silver certificates, authorized in 1878 and issued in exchange for silver dollars, accounted for nearly all of the $1 notes in circulation until November 1963, when the first $1 Federal Reserve notes were issued.

Currency Features

All U.S. currency is produced by the Bureau of Engraving and Printing, which also designs, engraves, and prints items such as postage stamps.

Since 1862 all U.S. currency had been printed in Washington, D.C., but to help meet increasing demand, a second printing facility was opened in Fort Worth, Texas, in 1991. Fort Worth now produces about half the nation's currency.

Security Features

Because U.S. currency is universally accepted and trusted, it is widely counterfeited. The U.S. Secret Service was created in 1865 to curtail counterfeiting.

U.S. currency has traditionally had a number of features that deter counterfeiters. One is the cotton and linen rag paper, which has a distinctive, pliable feel and has tiny red and blue fibers embedded in it. Though a commercial company produces the paper, it is illegal for anyone to manufacture or use a similar type except by special authority. Inks manufactured according to secret formulas by the Bureau of Engraving and Printing also help prevent counterfeiting.

♣ It's A Fact!!

How Currency Is Printed

U.S. currency is printed by the engraved intaglio steel plate method, a complicated procedure that gives notes an embossed feel and other distinctive features difficult to counterfeit.

For security reasons each feature of a note—the portrait, vignette, ornaments, lettering, script, and scrollwork—is the work of a separate, specially trained engraver. A geometric lathe is used to produce the intricate lacy design and borders.

A steel die is made of each feature. Rolls made from these dies are put together into a master die of the complete note. The master die is then used in the first of a series of operations leading to the making of press plates from which the notes are printed.

As advances in technology have made digital counterfeiting easier, more advanced security features have been added to deter counterfeiting. Two advanced features—a security thread and microprinting—were first added in series 1990 notes, and several additional ones were incorporated into 1996 series notes. Most of these features were retained and others were added to the series 2004 redesign, which debuted in October 2003 with the $20 note. The redesigned $50 note was introduced in 2004 and the redesigned $10 note in early 2006. A redesigned $5 note [was] issued in early 2008, with the $100 note to follow. No redesign is planned for the $2 and $1 notes.

To stay ahead of counterfeiters, the Treasury plans to introduce new designs every seven to ten years. Redesigned and existing notes will circulate at the same time, with the new notes replacing the older ones as they wear out. Of course, all U.S. money, whether old or new, retains its full value because the United States never recalls any of its currency.

The security features added to notes in the 1990s and in the 2004 redesign were recommended by an extensive study of counterfeit deterrence methods.

Features In The 2004 Redesign

Color: The most noticeable change in the 2004 series notes is the addition of subtle background colors, which differ for each denomination. On the $20 note, the background colors are green, peach, and blue. "TWENTY USA" is printed in blue in the background to the right of the portrait. On the back of the note, small yellow numeral 20s are printed in the background. Although consumers shouldn't use color to check notes' authenticity, the use of more colors makes the notes more complex and more difficult to counterfeit.

Portrait: Another noticeable change is a larger portrait from which the border and surrounding fine lines have been removed. The portrait has been moved up and the shoulders have been extended into the borders. The portrait is off-center to reduce wear on the portrait and to provide more room for the watermark and security thread.

Watermark: A watermark, created during the paper-making process, depicts the same historical figure as the portrait. It is visible from both sides when held up to a light.

Security Thread: An embedded polymer strip, positioned in a unique spot for each denomination, guards against counterfeiting. The thread itself, visible when held up to a bright light, contains microprinting—the letters USA, the denomination of the bill, and a flag. When viewed under ultraviolet light, the thread glows a distinctive color for each denomination.

Color-Shifting Ink: The ink used in the numeral in the lower right-hand corner on the front of the bill looks copper when viewed straight on but green when viewed at an angle.

Microprinting: Microprinting, which can be read only with a magnifier and becomes blurred when copied, appears in unique places on each denomination. On the $20 bill, it appears around the borders of the first three letters of the "TWENTY USA" ribbon to the right of the portrait and in the border below the Treasurer's signature.

Low-Vision Feature: A large dark numeral in the lower right corner on the back of the note makes it easier for people with low vision to identify the note's denomination.

Federal Reserve Indicators: A seal to the left of the portrait represents the Federal Reserve System. A letter and number below the left serial number identifies the issuing Federal Reserve Bank.

Symbols Of Freedom: The 2004 series features American symbols that will differ for each denomination. On the $20 note, a large blue eagle appears in the background to the left of the portrait. A smaller eagle printed in green metallic ink appears to the lower right of the portrait.

Other Design Features

Series: The series identification shows the year the note design was first used. If a slight change is made in the note that does not require a completely new engraving plate—for example, a change in signature when the Secretary of the Treasury or the Treasurer of the United States changes—the year remains the same and a letter is added to show that the design differs slightly from previous printings. A "C" suffix, for example, as in "Series 1935C," means that the original design has been changed slightly three times.

♣ It's A Fact!!
The Great Seal
Of The United States

The first currency note to have the Great Seal of the United States as part of the design was the $1 Silver Certificate, Series 1935. The seal has appeared on the reverse (green) side of all $1 notes since then.

In 1776 the Continental Congress appointed Benjamin Franklin, Thomas Jefferson, and John Adams to arrange for the preparation of a seal for the United States of America. This committee and two other committees labored over the design for six years. The third committee enlisted the aid of William Barton, the son of a Philadelphia Episcopal clergyman and an authority on heraldry. Barton created two designs, one of which was simplified by Charles Thompson, Secretary of Congress. Congress adopted the design in 1782.

The face of the seal, on the right-hand side of the bill, shows the American bald eagle with wings and claws outstretched. Above the eagle's head is a glory, or burst of light, containing 13 stars. (The number 13 represents the original 13 states.) The right claws hold an olive branch with 13 leaves, representing peace, and the left, a bundle of 13 arrows, symbolizing war; the eagle's head is turned toward the olive branch, indicating a desire for peace. The shield (with 13 stripes) covering the eagle's breast symbolizes a united nation. A ribbon held in the eagle's beak bears the Latin motto *E Pluribus Unum* (13 letters), which means "out of many, one."

The back of the Great Seal, on the left-hand side of the bill, depicts a pyramid, a symbol of material strength and endurance. The pyramid is unfinished, symbolizing a striving toward growth and a goal of perfection. Above the pyramid a glory, with an eye inside a triangle, represents the eternal eye of God and places the spiritual above the material. At the top edge is the 13-letter Latin motto *Annuit Coeptis*, meaning "He has favored our undertakings." The base of the pyramid bears the roman numerals MDCCLXXVI (1776). Below is the motto *Novus Ordo Seclorum*, "a new order of the ages."

Serial Number: Beginning with the 1996 series, serial numbers consist of two prefix letters (except on $1 and $2 notes, which have one prefix letter), eight numerals, and a one-letter suffix. The serial number appears twice on the front of the note. No two notes of the same kind, denomination, and series have the same serial number. This fact can be important in detecting counterfeit notes; many counterfeiters make large batches of a particular note with the same number.

Notes are numbered in lots of 100 million. Each lot has a different suffix letter, beginning with A and following in alphabetical order through Z, omitting O because of its similarity to the numeral zero.

Because serial numbers are limited to eight numerals, a "star" note is substituted for the 100 millionth note. Star notes also replace notes damaged in the printing process. Made up with independent runs of serial numbers, star notes are exactly like the notes they replace except that a star is substituted for one of the serial letters.

Size: Until July 1929 U.S. currency was 7.42 inches by 3.13 inches. Currency printed since 1929 is 6.14 inches by 2.61 inches, a size easier to handle and less expensive to produce.

Portraits And Emblems: The seven denominations of notes now produced by the Bureau of Engraving and Printing feature portraits of American statesmen on the face and emblems and monuments on the back.

Bank tellers and others who frequently handle currency use the portrait in assembling and counting it. They assemble each denomination separately and uniformly—face up and top up. This practice also helps handlers detect counterfeit and altered notes. All Reserve Banks require banks to arrange their currency for deposit in this way.

"In God We Trust": Secretary of the Treasury Salmon P. Chase first authorized use of "In God We Trust" on U.S. money—on the two-cent coin in 1864—after receiving a number of appeals from citizens urging that the deity be recognized on U.S. coins. In 1955, Congress mandated the use of this phrase on all currency and coins. All denominations of paper money now being issued carry the motto.

♣ **It's A Fact!!**

Faces And Backs Of Currency

Denomination	Face	Back
$1	George Washington	Great Seal of the United States
$2	Thomas Jefferson	The Signing of the Declaration of Independence
$5	Abraham Lincoln	Lincoln Memorial
$10	Alexander Hamilton	U.S. Treasury Building
$20	Andrew Jackson	White House
$50	Ulysses S. Grant	U.S. Capitol
$100	Benjamin Franklin	Independence Hall

U.S. Coins

U.S. coins have changed many times since the Coinage Act of 1792, which adopted the dollar as the standard monetary unit.

Silver dollars have been minted and issued at various times since 1794. Dollar coins were discontinued in 1935, then resumed in 1971 with the introduction of the silverless Eisenhower dollar. The silverless Susan B. Anthony coin, honoring the famed women's suffrage advocate, replaced the Eisenhower dollar in 1979. The current dollar coin, which replaced the Susan B. Anthony coin in 2000, depicts Sacagawea, the Native American woman whose presence was essential to the success of the Lewis and Clark expedition. The coin has a copper core clad in an alloy of copper, zinc, manganese, and nickel, which gives the coin a golden color.

Half-dollars virtually disappeared from circulation following the introduction, in 1964, of the Kennedy half-dollar. Despite the fact that huge quantities were produced, the half-dollar remained scarce in general circulation through 1970. Silverless halves first appeared in 1971.

Other coin denominations in common use today are the 25-cent, 10-cent, five-cent, and one-cent pieces, familiarly known as the quarter, dime, nickel, and penny.

The composition of U.S. coins has changed considerably since the 1960s. Because of a growing worldwide silver shortage, the Coinage Act of 1965 authorized a change in the composition of dimes, quarters, and half-dollars, which had been 90 percent silver. Silver was eliminated from the dime and the quarter. The half-dollar's silver content was reduced to 40 percent and after 1970 was eliminated altogether.

In 1981 Congress authorized a change in the penny's composition, abandoning the 95 percent copper and 5 percent zinc alloy used for decades. The one-cent piece is now copper-plated zinc—97.5 percent zinc and 2.5 percent copper. The old and new pennies look virtually identical, but the new coin is about 19 percent lighter.

U.S. coin denominations used in the past were the half-cent, two-cent, three-cent, and 20-cent pieces, as well as a small silver coin called a half-dime. Gold coins in denominations of $1, $2.50 ("Quarter Eagle"), $3, $5 ("Half Eagle"), $10 ("Eagle"), and $20 ("Double Eagle") were used from 1795 until 1933.

The Mint

The U.S. Mint, which makes all U.S. coins, was established by Congress in 1792 and became an operating bureau of the Treasury Department in 1873.

The Philadelphia Mint has been in continuous operation since 1792. The Denver Mint began its coinage operations in 1906. The West Point, New York, and San Francisco Mints gained official Mint status in 1988. Originally an assay office, the San Francisco Mint is the primary production facility for proof coins. The West Point Mint, once used exclusively as a bullion depository, is now the Mint's chief producer of gold coins.

U.S. coins typically bear a mint mark showing which mint produced them. Coins minted in Philadelphia bear a P or no mint mark; those minted in

Denver, a D; in San Francisco, an S; and in West Point, a W. Although the Coinage Act of 1965 specified that no mint marks would be used for five years, Congress authorized in late 1967 that mint marks be resumed. The marks reappeared on regular coinage in 1968.

Several branch mints are no longer in operation. These mints were located in Carson City, Nevada (mint mark, CC); Charlotte, North Carolina (C); Dahlonega, Georgia (D); and New Orleans, Louisiana (O).

Design

The Director of the Mint selects designs for U.S. coins with the approval of the Secretary of the Treasury, although Congress may prescribe a coin design. A design may not be changed more often than every 25 years unless Congress determines otherwise.

Emblems: All of the U.S. coins currently minted

♣ It's A Fact!!
How Coins Are Made

The first step in minting coins is the production of strips of metal in the proper thickness. (The U.S. Mint buys these strips, for all coins except pennies, from commercial suppliers.) Strips for pennies are zinc. Strips for nickels are an alloy of 75 percent copper and 25 percent nickel. Clad dimes, quarters, half-dollars, and dollars are produced from three layers of metal fused together; the outer layers are the same alloy used for nickels, and the core is copper.

The metal strips are fed into blanking presses, which cut round blanks (planchets) the approximate size of the finished coin. (The blanks for pennies, made of zinc, are coated with copper before going on to the next step. Commercial companies provide the planchets for pennies to the Mint.) The blanks are run through annealing furnaces to soften them and then through tumbling barrels, rotating cylinders that contain chemical solutions to clean and burnish the metal. Next, the blanks are washed and put into drying machines. Then the blanks go through milling or "upsetting" machines, which produce the raised (upset) rim.

Blanks next proceed to the stamping or coining press. The blank is held in place by a ring, or collar, as it is struck under tremendous pressure. Pennies require about 40 tons of pressure, and the larger coins require proportionately more. Upper and lower dies stamp the design on both sides of the coin at the same time. Grooves inside the ring holding the blank form the "reeding" or ridges on the rim of finished coins, except for pennies, nickels, and the Sacagawea dollar, which have smooth rims.

portray past U.S. Presidents. They are the Lincoln one-cent piece, adopted in 1909; the 25-cent piece portraying Washington, first minted in 1932; the five-cent piece honoring Jefferson, adopted in 1938; the Franklin D. Roosevelt dime, introduced in 1946; and the Kennedy half-dollar, which appeared in 1964.

The 50 States Quarters Program Act of 1997 provided for the redesign of the reverse side of quarters to feature designs created by each of the 50 states. Each year from 1999 through 2008, coins commemorating five states were issued in the order in which the states signed the Constitution or joined the Union. These quarters are in general circulation, but the Mint also sells sets of collector edition proof, uncirculated, and silver proof coins.

Two new designs for the nickel, issued only in 2004 and 2005, depict images commemorating the Louisiana Purchase and the Lewis and Clark expedition; the designs appear on the reverse side while the obverse still depicts Thomas Jefferson.

♣ It's A Fact!!

Commemorative Coins

Coins to commemorate American people, places, events, and institutions are authorized by special acts of Congress and manufactured in limited quantities. Commemorative coins, which may be gold, silver, or clad, usually sell at a premium, so they seldom circulate as regular coin.

Legislation specifies that commemorative coin programs must operate at no net cost to taxpayers. Surcharges raised from the sale of commemorative coins are designated for a specific purpose or for reducing the national debt.

The first commemorative coin was minted in 1892 to help finance the World's Columbian Exposition in Chicago. Since that time many other commemorative coins have been issued.

Recent commemorative coins include 2004 coins marking the Lewis and Clark expedition bicentennial and the 125th anniversary of Thomas Edison's invention of the light bulb and 2005 coins honoring John Marshall, fourth Chief Justice of the United States, and the Marine Corps' 230th anniversary.

♣ **It's A Fact!!**

Faces And Backs Of Coins

Coin	Face	Back
1¢	Abraham Lincoln	Lincoln Memorial
5¢	Thomas Jefferson	Monticello
10¢	Franklin D. Roosevelt	Torch
25¢	George Washington	50 States Design
50¢	John F. Kennedy	Presidential Coat of Arms
$1	Sacagawea	Bald Eagle

"**In God We Trust**": The phrase was first used on the U.S. two-cent coin in 1864. It appeared on the nickel, quarter, half-dollar, and silver dollar and on the $5, $10, and $20 gold pieces in 1866, on the penny in 1909, and on the dime in 1916. Dropped from the nickel in 1883, the phrase reappeared on the nickel in 1938. All U.S. coins now issued bear the motto.

Circulation Of Money

The amount of U.S. currency and coin in circulation increased dramatically during the 20th century (see Table 1.1. Figures are from statements published by the Treasury Department.)

How Money Circulates

The Treasury Department ships new paper money and coins to the Federal Reserve Banks; the Reserve Banks pay it out to commercial banks, savings and loan associations, and other depository institutions. Customers of these institutions withdraw cash as they need it. Once people spend their cash at department stores, grocery stores, and so on, most of this money is eventually redeposited in depository institutions. As notes wear out or become dirty or damaged, depository institutions redeposit them at the Reserve Banks.

When Money Wears Out

Money wears out from handling and is sometimes accidentally damaged or destroyed. The average life span of a $1 bill, for example, is about 21 months. The $10 bill has a life span of about 18 months; the $5 bill, 16 months; and the $20, two years. The $50 and $100 notes don't circulate as often as the smaller denominations, so they last longer—the $50 bill, about four and a half years, and the $100, seven and a half years. The average life of a coin is 25 years.

Banks send old, worn, torn, or soiled notes to a Federal Reserve Bank to be exchanged for new bills. The Reserve Banks sort the money they receive from commercial banks to determine if it is "fit" or "unfit." Fit (reusable) money is stored in their vaults until it goes out again through the commercial banking system. Reserve Banks destroy unfit currency and return damaged and worn coins to the Treasury.

Table 1.1. Money In Circulation

Date	Amount of Cash in Circulation	Amount of Cash Per Capita*
June 30, 1910	$ 3,148,700,000	$ 34.07
June 30, 1920	$ 5,698,214,612	$ 53.18
June 30, 1930	$ 4,521,987,962	$ 36.74
June 30, 1940	$ 7,847,501,324	$ 59.40
June 30, 1950	$ 27,156,290,042	$ 179.03
June 30, 1960	$ 32,064,619,064	$ 177.47
June 30, 1970	$ 54,350,971,661	$ 265.39
June 30, 1980	$ 127,097,192,148	$ 570.51
June 30, 1990	$ 266,902,367,798	$ 1,062.86
June 30, 2000	$ 571,121,194,344	$ 2,075.63

*In the United States

♣ It's A Fact!!
Redeeming Damaged Money

Paper money that has been mutilated or partially destroyed may in some cases be redeemable at full face value. Any badly soiled, defaced, torn, or worn-out currency that is clearly more than half of the original note can be exchanged at a commercial bank, which processes the note through a Federal Reserve Bank. More seriously damaged notes—those with clearly less than half of the original surface or those requiring special examination to determine their value—must be sent to the Department of the Treasury for redemption.

The redemption value of mutilated coins depends on their type, denomination, and the extent of their mutilation. Redemption of mutilated coins is handled by the U.S. Mint in Philadelphia. Coins that are merely bent or worn slick through natural wear are not considered mutilated and are exchangeable at full face value.

Spotting Counterfeit Currency

The amount of counterfeit currency in circulation in the United States is very small—only 3/100ths of one percent of total currency. About 75 percent of all known counterfeit currency is seized before it reaches the public.

But it is in your interest always to examine any currency you receive because you must assume the loss for any counterfeit note you accept. Perhaps the following suggestions from the U.S. Secret Service will help you spot one.

Study genuine currency. In series 1996 or later currency, the security features described earlier will be present. In addition, look closely at the workmanship of several features. On genuine notes, the portrait and the picture on the back of the note stand out sharply from the background, and the eyes in the portrait appear lifelike. Numbers are firmly, evenly printed and well spaced, and the fine criss-crossing lines of the scrollwork borders are sharp and unbroken.

On counterfeit notes, the portrait and picture may merge with the background, the eyes or other features on the portrait may be dull or smudgy, or the face may seem unnaturally white. Numbers may be out of line, poorly spaced, and printed too light or too dark, and the lines in the scrollwork borders may be blurred or broken.

The paper used for genuine notes is of very high quality. The tiny red and blue fibers embedded in the paper of genuine notes may not be visible if the bill is badly worn or dirty; on counterfeit bills, these threads may be imitated by fine red and blue lines printed or drawn on the paper. Counterfeit currency paper may feel different or be whiter than genuine paper.

Rubbing a bill on a piece of paper is not a good test. Ink can be rubbed off genuine as well as counterfeit notes.

If you're not sure whether a note is counterfeit, consult an experienced money handler—a bank teller, for example.

Rules About Reproducing Money

The law places strict limitations on photographs or other printed reproductions of U.S. and foreign paper currency, checks, bonds, stamps, and securities.

U.S. Currency: The Counterfeit Detection Act of 1992 permits color illustration of U.S. currency provided that

- the illustration is less than three-quarters or more than one and one-half times the size, in linear dimension, of any part of the bill;

✔ Quick Tip

If you get a counterfeit bill,

- Write your initials and the date on the back of the bill so that you can identify it later.

- Record on a separate sheet of paper all the details about how you got the bill: Who gave it to you? Where and when did you get it?

- Handle the bill as little as possible to preserve any fingerprints. Put the bill in a protective cover such as an envelope.

- Contact the nearest U.S. Secret Service office or local police. Surrender the bill only to these agencies.

Anyone convicted of passing a counterfeit bill may be fined as much as $5,000 or imprisoned for up to 15 years.

✔ **Quick Tip**
Visit the Federal Reserve Bank of Atlanta's website,
http://www.frbatlanta.org, to find out more about the Federal Reserve Bank of Atlanta and its publications, which cover
economic and financial topics.

- the illustration is one-sided; and

- any negatives, positives, plates, or digital, magnetic, or optical files used
  in making the illustration are destroyed, deleted, or erased after their
  final use.

Other Obligations: Similar restrictions apply to photographs or printed
reproductions of foreign currency as well as U.S. and foreign checks, bonds,
stamps, and securities. In addition, these items may be reproduced only in
black and white.

Color or black and white motion picture films, microfilms, videotapes,
and slides of U.S. and foreign paper currency, securities, and other obligations may be made for projection or telecasting. But prints may not be made
from these media unless the prints conform to size and color restrictions.

Coins: There are no restrictions on printed or motion picture reproductions of U.S. or foreign coins. But the law prohibits, with few exceptions, the
manufacture, sale, or use of any token or device that is meant to resemble a
U.S. or foreign coin and that is issued as money.

For more information on the rules about reproducing money, contact the
U.S. Secret Service office nearest you; office locations are available on the
internet at www.treas.gov/usss or by contacting the U.S. Secret Service, Office
of Government Liaison and Public Affairs, 950 H Street, N.W., Suite 8400,
Washington, DC 20001-4518, 202-406-5708.

Chapter 2

Do You Get An Allowance?

Let's Talk Allowances

The idea behind allowances is to give kids and teens money of their own so that they can learn to manage it. The idea is great, but putting it into play is sometimes frustrating on both sides.

The Parent Side

Parents want to guide their kids' spending, so the kids don't make foolish mistakes. Yet the whole reason for an allowance is to let kids make mistakes and learn from them. Making mistakes while living at home is much safer than at college, where mistakes in spending and with credit cards carry big consequences. So parents, if they are playing by the rules, have to zip their lips, and let their kids learn the hard way during those early years.

And to make the whole allowance strategy work, parents must hold their ground when their child spends too much and runs short. The very worst thing a parent can do is bail a kid out of his or her financial trouble. Parents shouldn't cave. If parents rescue a child, he or she doesn't have to deal with the impact of the mistake. It loses its punch and its lasting effect. (Bailing

About This Chapter: "Let's Talk Allowances," © 2007 Northwestern Mutual Foundation. Reprinted with permission. For additional information, visit www.themint.org.

kids out is like giving them an easy "undo" button. Unfortunately, real life doesn't provide "undo" buttons.)

The Kid Side

Kids want the freedom to use their money. They'll tell you, "What's the good of an allowance if I don't get to choose what do with it?" Besides, Mom and Dad don't understand about being a kid. The teenage wish list is endless—each week another really cool thing pops up. While Mom and Dad think this stuff is unnecessary, a teen can list all of the advantages of these purchases to any adult who will listen.

So typically teens have a problem. There's never enough money to do everything kids are supposed to do with an allowance. Some families insist that a part of the allowance should be saved or donated. "It's not enough," teens will say.

Both Sides

For allowances to work, both sides have to keep to their side of the playing field. The terms of the allowance are clear. Parents can't criticize their kid's spending. Kids can't ask for help when they get in trouble. But the beauty of this system is that the two sides no longer argue over purchases: their cost, their necessity, or their value. Each side stays on its side of the line.

Kids Learn To Negotiate

Here's a possibly unexpected benefit of allowances. When kids get older, they may "petition" their local allowance-giver to increase their weekly pay.

♣ It's A Fact!!

About Chores: Many parents tie allowances to doing chores to give kids a work-world experience. But what happens when the chores don't get done? What if this happens repeatedly? If parents withhold the allowance, they also remove the opportunity for the child to learn to manage money. Parents may want to consider imposing a different consequence for not doing chores—no movie, no telephone—to make the point.

Petitions should be allowed, but the responsibility for building a persuasive case falls squarely on the child's shoulders. If the allowance is tied to chores, what tasks will be added to the chore list to prompt the increase?

If the allowance is not tied to chores, why does the teen need more money? Simply saying that he or she cannot live within the bounds of the allowance won't cut it unless expenses are really growing.

If so, why? Are they reasonable expenses? Will the teen now take on more or total responsibility for them? If the case doesn't persuade, parents have every right to deny the request. It will be a great opportunity for kids to build a real-world skill. They may have to negotiate a salary with an employer someday.

What's Value?

Whenever anybody spends money—whether it's an allowance or a paycheck—they want to know they're getting their money's worth. In other words, are they getting value in return for their money? What exactly does that mean?

It means that you should understand what you're paying for. If you're going to pay more than the item's worth, you should know why.

For example, you can buy a five-pound bag of potatoes in the grocery store for $2.50. Why, then, would you spend $2.09 on a few ounces of fries at a fast-food restaurant? *Because they taste great!* you say. That's one reason, but you could also put some frozen fries in the oven at home. They'd crisp up in about 20 minutes, and you have fries enough for a family of four for about $2.00. So what gives those fast food fries value? Try another answer.

Okay. I've just finished sports practice. I've got to hustle to my music lesson. I'm starving after practice, I don't have time to go home and grab a sandwich, and I didn't pack one this morning, so I've got nothing to eat. If I don't get some food soon, I'll never be able to concentrate during my lesson. How's that?

Closer. You're saying that you're really paying for more than a box of skinny spuds. You're paying for convenience. The right food (something you like) in the right place (on your way to your lesson) when you need it (you're starving.) What good will five pounds of raw potatoes do you at this moment?

But if you had rolled out of bed right away this morning, you would have had time to make a sandwich and throw in a drink, an apple, and a couple of granola bars.

So what you're really paying for is your disorganization! You're hungry—buying fries is your best way to solve your problem. This story would not be a good one to use when negotiating the need for a larger allowance.

But this is only one example of what people buy and why they buy it. There are many ways to judge value—you can find another at themint.org. Go to Spending, and click on What's It Worth? It will give you a totally different view.

Then There's Donating

For many families, giving is as important as earning. If that's your family's philosophy, then you may need to learn early that a certain part of your allowance goes to help others.

How much to give? It depends. Kids with generous allowances and not many expenses can afford to give more. Kids who must use most of their allowance to pay expenses may have to give less. Another option is to give time instead. Kids have lots of energy that organizations can use. Whether you contribute money, time, or both, requiring kids to involve themselves in the community gives them the satisfaction that comes with helping others. It will also teach them that sometimes they might have to delay their own desires to help someone else with a more serious need.

Giving can be a family decision: the family chooses from several causes, listing pros and cons. Then everyone gives to the chosen organization.

Or, you can make giving more individual. What is important to you? Ask your parents to help you find an organization that furthers this cause. Be sure that the organization you choose is legitimate. givespot.com or guidestar.org might be places to start.

Sometimes causes can be quite personal. Kids who lose a grandparent to a disease may decide that their money should go toward finding a cure. Others may want to connect with kids their own age at holiday time through programs like "Toys for Tots." Still others may want to donate food at Thanksgiving.

Chapter 3

Jobs For Teens

Making Money

The most common way that most young people get money is through an allowance. Not every teen gets one, of course, and your parents' beliefs or financial situation might mean you get little or nothing. According to various surveys, the average allowance for teens is anywhere from $20 to $50 per week. If yours is a lot lower, perhaps try negotiating a raise.

Here are some more ways to get money:

From Your Family: Your parents might pay you for getting good grades in school, or for reading a certain number of books, or for doing various jobs around the house. You might even earn some money from siblings, if you offer to do some of their chores.

Selling Things: If your closet or basement is full of belongings that you no longer need or want, consider selling them. (These might include toys, games, comics, and clothes. Don't get rid of things you have a strong attachment to, though, such as your old Furby or your Teenage Mutant Ninja Turtles lunchbox.) You could hold a yard sale in your neighborhood. You might even

> ♣ It's A Fact!!
>
> ## Age Requirements For Working
>
> The Fair Labor Standards Act (FLSA) sets wage, hours worked, and safety requirements for minors (individuals under age 18) working in jobs covered by the statute. The rules vary depending upon the particular age of the minor and the particular job involved. As a general rule, the FLSA sets 14 years of age as the minimum age for employment, and limits the number of hours worked by minors under the age of 16.
>
> Also, the FLSA generally prohibits the employment of a minor in work declared hazardous by the Secretary of Labor (for example, work involving excavation, driving, and the operation of many types of power-driven equipment). The FLSA contains a number of requirements that apply only to particular types of jobs (for example, agricultural work or the operation of motor vehicles) and many exceptions to the general rules (for example, work by a minor for his or her parents). Each state also has its own laws relating to employment, including the employment of minors. If state law and the FLSA overlap, the law which is more protective of the minor will apply.
>
> Source: Excerpted from "Youth and Labor," U.S. Department of Labor (www.dol.gov), 2008.

offer to sell other people's knickknacks, for a small fee or a percentage of the price. Another option is selling items online, such as on eBay.

A Job: This is perhaps the most obvious way to earn money, and teens frequently land part-time or full-time summer jobs.

Jobs For Teens

Believe it or not, there are many, many jobs you can find or create. You have more choices than just working at McDonald's or babysitting. Here are lots of ideas, a few of which might appeal to you.

- **Pet-Sitting:** When someone in your neighborhood goes on vacation, there's often a pet that needs looking after. Also, with people working longer and longer hours these days, some will pay you to visit their pets during the day and take them for a walk.

- **Working For Your Parents:** If mom or dad owns a business, they might be able to use your help. Even if they work for a company, they may be able to hook you up with a part-time job there. (Check with your parents' friends, too.)

- **Tutoring:** Some teens report that they earn anywhere from $5 to $20 per hour tutoring. If you're good at a subject, you may be able to earn money by helping others to understand it.

- **Lifeguard:** In some parts of the country, there are shortages of lifeguards. Some have been earning $10 per hour or more. If you have the skills needed, consider this option.

- **Camps:** If you look into it early enough, you can line up a job at a summer camp—you might work with kids, tend the grounds, prepare food, or do any of a number of things.

- **Jobs Matching Your Interests:** If you enjoy working with young children, see if any daycare centers near you need help. If you like the great outdoors, check with your local parks department. If you like movies or recreation, look into movie theaters or amusement parks.

- **Mowing Lawns, Raking Yards, Shoveling Snow, Gardening:** These can all be part of the same job. Once your customers know you and the good work you do, they may use your services doing other jobs in other seasons.

- **Department Stores:** A big perk with these jobs is that you often get to enjoy employee discounts (which can be substantial, often 20–30% off) and commissions on items you sell.

- **Create Websites:** If you know enough about computers to create well-designed websites, you can make some good money. Many small companies and organizations pay thousands of dollars to have websites built for them. You might charge very little at first, but once you have a few impressive websites to show potential customers, you can hike your rates. Some small companies might also pay you to help maintain their sites, adding content, and solving problems that arise.

- **Be Crafty:** If you enjoy arts and crafts, you might make jewelry or other items and sell them—perhaps on eBay, where you'll have instant access to a large customer base. Some painters and photographers are making money selling their work online, too, although that can be harder to do.

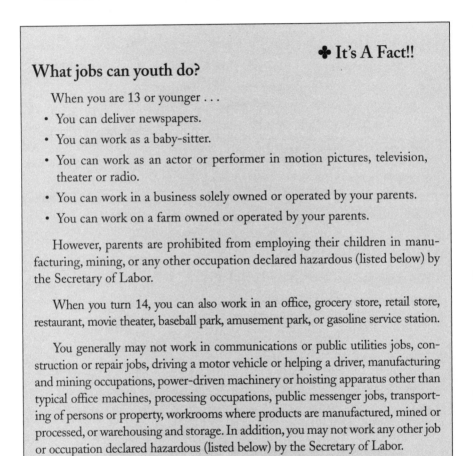

♣ **It's A Fact!!**

What jobs can youth do?

When you are 13 or younger . . .
- You can deliver newspapers.
- You can work as a baby-sitter.
- You can work as an actor or performer in motion pictures, television, theater or radio.
- You can work in a business solely owned or operated by your parents.
- You can work on a farm owned or operated by your parents.

However, parents are prohibited from employing their children in manufacturing, mining, or any other occupation declared hazardous (listed below) by the Secretary of Labor.

When you turn 14, you can also work in an office, grocery store, retail store, restaurant, movie theater, baseball park, amusement park, or gasoline service station.

You generally may not work in communications or public utilities jobs, construction or repair jobs, driving a motor vehicle or helping a driver, manufacturing and mining occupations, power-driven machinery or hoisting apparatus other than typical office machines, processing occupations, public messenger jobs, transporting of persons or property, workrooms where products are manufactured, mined or processed, or warehousing and storage. In addition, you may not work any other job or occupation declared hazardous (listed below) by the Secretary of Labor.

When you turn 16, you can work in any job or occupation that has not been declared hazardous by the Secretary of Labor.

Hazardous Occupations

You generally may not work in any of the following hazardous occupations:
- Manufacturing and storing of explosives
- Driving a motor vehicle and being an outside helper on a motor vehicle

- **Serve The Elderly:** Not only might you find work in a nursing home or retirement community, but you might also serve older people in your neighborhood. Many older people can't get around much. They may welcome your services delivering groceries, running errands, or doing odd jobs around their home.

- Coal mining
- Logging and sawmilling
- Power-driven woodworking machines
- Exposure to radioactive substances
- Power-driven hoisting apparatus
- Power-driven metal-forming, punching, and shearing machines
- Mining, other than coal mining
- Meat packing or processing (including the use of power-driven meat slicing machines)
- Power-driven bakery machines
- Power-driven paper-product machines
- Manufacturing brick, tile, and related products
- Power-driven circular saws, band saws, and guillotine shears
- Wrecking, demolition, and shipbreaking operations
- Roofing operations and all work on or about a roof
- Excavation operations

There are some exemptions for apprentice/student-learner programs in some of these hazardous occupations.

When You Turn 18

When you turn 18, you can work any job for any number of hours. The child labor rules no longer apply to you.

Note: Different rules apply to farms, and individual states may have stricter rules.

Source: "What Jobs Can Youth Do?" U.S. Department of Labor (youthrules.dol.gov), 2008.

- **Be A Computer Guru:** Many people buy computers and have a lot of trouble setting them up and trying to use them. Even if you have an intermediate familiarity with computers, you might offer your services as a local computer consultant. You can set things up, solve problems, answer questions, teach programs, and show people how to send and organize e-mail, upload digital photos, buy something on Amazon.com, use Instant Messaging, and conduct online searches (with Google or other search engines).

- **Caddy At A Golf Course:** This not only helps you learn more about a sport you might enjoy, it also gives you the chance meet a lot of adults from whom you might learn more about the business world. They could be turn out to be valuable connections that help you land other jobs.

- **Delivering Newspapers:** If you sign up to deliver a lot (which may be more possible in areas with apartment buildings), you can make a good bit of money. Some teens make $100 or $200 per week or more.

- **Use Your Skills:** Think about what you're good at and try to teach others—adults or children. You might offer piano lessons, horseback riding lessons, or Spanish lessons.

♣ **It's A Fact!!**

What is the youngest age at which a person can be employed?

The Fair Labor Standards Act (FLSA) sets 14 as the minimum age for most non-agricultural work. However, at any age, youth may deliver newspapers; perform in radio, television, movie, or theatrical productions; work in businesses owned by their parents (except in mining, manufacturing, or hazardous jobs); and perform babysitting or perform minor chores around a private home. Also, at any age, youth may be employed as homeworkers to gather evergreens and make evergreen wreaths.

Different age requirements apply to the employment of youth in agriculture.

Source: From "What Is the Youngest Age at which a Person Can Be Employed?" U.S. Department of Labor (www.dol.gov), 2008.

Maybe you can juggle and entertain at children's birthday parties. If you play an instrument, perhaps you could play at weddings or other events. If you write, you could try to sell articles to magazines or newspapers.

- **Volunteer:** If all else fails, or even as a first choice, consider volunteering. Don't just do the first thing that pops into your mind, though. Be a strategic volunteer. Think of a field or company you'd like to learn more about. If you're really concerned about hunger in the world, volunteer at a food bank. If you're thinking about becoming a doctor (perhaps one who treats the elderly), consider volunteering at a hospital (or a nursing home).

♣ It's A Fact!!
What hours can youth work?

If you are 14 or 15, you can work outside school hours after 7 a.m. and until 7 p.m., except from June 1 through Labor Day, when you can work until 9 p.m.

You can work no more than:

- 3 hours on a school day,
- 18 hours in a school week,
- 8 hours on a non-school day, and
- 40 hours in non-school week.

If you are 16 or older, you can work any day, any time of day, and for any number of hours. There are no restrictions on the work hours of youth age 16 or older.

Different rules apply to farms, and individual states may have stricter rules.

Source: "What Hours Can Youth Work?" U.S. Department of Labor (youthrules .dol.gov), 2008.

Once You've Made Some Money, Save Some

How much should you save? You actually may be able to save 100% of your money. Does that mean you should? Not at all. The best way to develop good saving habits is to make saving a regular part of your life, along with spending.

Here's a few ways you can save:

- **Save Before Spending:** Whenever some money gets into your hands, from a job or your allowance or whatever, take your savings out immediately, before spending any of the money. The beauty of this system is that once you've removed your savings, you're free to spend the rest.

- **Negotiate With Your Parents:** This may or may not work for you, but it's worth a shot. See if they'll "match" your savings, in order to encourage good saving habits. If they match your savings dollar-for-dollar, for example, that would mean that for every $25 you plunk into savings, they'd plunk an additional $25.

- **Consider The "Opportunity Cost" Of Purchases:** Opportunity cost is an economic term that applies to many parts of our lives. It essentially refers to the cost of giving up one alternative in order to act on another. Imagine that you can either buy concert tickets for $50 or you can invest the money. If you invest for 10 years, and your investment grows by an average of 11% per year, your original $50 will become $142. So your decision can be framed like this: "Would I rather have these tickets now, or $142 in 10 years?" If you're thinking of buying a pair of shoes for $75, consider whether it's worth the opportunity cost of $600 in 20 years. Perhaps it is. If so, then by all means, buy the shoes.

Chapter 4

Finding A Summer Job Or Internship

Every year the race begins again. You slip on your best shoes and your most responsible attitude and hit the streets running. The countdown's on to find the best summer employment available.

Why Get A Summer Job Or Internship?

Summer jobs and internships have lots of terrific benefits. Working is a great way to prepare for life after high school or for college. The skills you learn early on will help you develop the professional talents you'll need throughout your life. These include basic but important skills like customer service, caring for children—and even learning to work with a boss!

Work experience can also help people feel good about themselves. The self-esteem and self-confidence you can develop at a job or internship will come in handy when you're ready to interview for college or a job after high school.

What's The Right Job For Me?

Take the first step in landing the right job before you even start looking: Think about what's motivating you to get the job. Is it because you need money, want to build your work experience, or want a job that looks good on your résumé or will help you get into college? Knowing what you want will help bring job satisfaction.

Next, make a list of your interests and strengths, as well as your weaknesses, and keep them in mind as you look for a job. For example, you may be in love with books or gifted when it comes to animals—a job in a bookstore or pet store would be perfect for you. On the other hand, if looking after little kids drives you crazy or if you burn in the sun, then you'll know to avoid babysitting or lifeguard jobs.

A job or internship should not only be enjoyable, it should be a learning experience too. Because working demands so much of your time, try to find a job or internship that may help guide you toward your long-term goals. For example, if you want to study veterinary science in college, finding a job in a vet's office, animal shelter, or even a pet store may be better choices for you than working in a restaurant.

> ✔ **Quick Tip**
> **Start Early**
>
> In the past few years the tight job market has meant fewer jobs available for high school students. Start your job search early to beat the competition and land the job you want.

Where Should I Start?

Begin by putting together a résumé. A good résumé is your best job-hunting tool. Unlike an application form, which you only fill out when you're applying for a particular job opening, you can hand résumés out to relatives, friends of the family, teachers, and other people you know. Ask them to pass it on to anyone who might be interested in hiring you. Hundreds of job-related sites on the internet offer advice on preparing a résumé.

The most common way to find a job opening is by reading the classified ads section of your local newspaper. Of course, some of the jobs listed—usually those that appear under "sales" and claim you can work for yourself and make thousands of dollars a week—may be too good to be true. So make sure the job ad mentions what the work entails (e.g., "server, evenings and weekends" or "day camp counselor").

Some people also get job leads from their school counselors, whereas others fill out applications or drop off résumés at prospective employers and temporary employment agencies. If you're interested in working at a restaurant, bookstore, garden center, or other service business in your area, the best approach is to go there and fill out an application form.

If you can afford to work on a short-term basis without pay, volunteering can be a great way to get quality experience that looks good on a resume. Check out the volunteer center in your area (or online) for ideas, or head over to your local YMCA [Young Men's Christian Association], YMHA [Young Men's Hebrew Association], or JCC [Jewish Community Center] and offer to coach soccer or help out with a summer camp. Help your favorite teacher tutor summer-school students. Walk dogs at your local animal shelter. Work with a local environmental organization on river cleanup or help the National Park Service maintain hiking trails in your area. Volunteering means you'll be working for a good cause—something that future employers or colleges like to see on an applicant's résumé—while investing time in your career goals.

Your school counselor may be able to help open other doors of opportunity via internships. Some companies and businesses offer bright students short-term, hands-on training (and sometimes even a modest rate of pay) in exchange for a willingness to learn and work hard. If you perform well at your internship, you may be offered a full-time job next summer or even an ongoing part-time job. Internships can also provide you with valuable references that can help you to land future jobs.

If traditional job opportunities don't appeal to you, consider more creative opportunities. Be your own boss by starting a pet sitting, dog walking, lawn care, computer services, or cleaning business. Print up flyers advertising the services your business offers, your rates, and your phone number or e-mail address, then drop one off at every house in your neighborhood.

Some enterprising people recognize opportunities in an existing business that the business owner may not see. For example, Amalia frequently heard her aunt complain that she never had time to take care of the accounting in her small graphic design firm because she and her partner were too busy. Although Amalia knew that she couldn't handle the business's finances, she offered to help her aunt after school by answering phones and handling the mail and copying, giving her aunt time to do other tasks.

Other Things To Consider

Keep these practical limitations in mind when you apply for the job of your dreams:

Safety First: Some jobs just aren't right for teens. For example, jobs that involve working alone late at night put anyone at risk for muggings or assaults, particularly people who are young and inexperienced.

> ### ♣ It's A Fact!!
>
> The National Consumers League warns about these **five worst jobs** for teens:
>
> 1. Agricultural field work or processing
>
> 2. Construction jobs and jobs that involve working at heights, such as on ladders and scaffolding
>
> 3. Landscaping, lawn service, and other outdoor work
>
> 4. Jobs that involve driving or operating everything from delivery trucks to forklifts
>
> 5. Jobs that involve door-to-door sales, such as selling magazine subscriptions

Know The Law: Federal and state laws limit the number of hours teens can work. For summer employment (when school is not in session), the federal government does not allow 14- and 15-year-olds to work before 7 a.m. or after 9 p.m., and they cannot work more than 8 hours a day or 40 hours a week. You can find out your state's laws and curfews (times when teens are not allowed to work) by calling your state department of labor. If you know your curfews and mention them when interviewing for or starting a job, your boss can keep them in mind when he or she schedules your start or quitting time.

Getting There: Be sure your job location is within walking distance or on a regular bus route if you don't have your driver's license or access to a car. If you do drive, it's usually a good idea leave a few minutes early—especially on the first couple of days you're working—to be sure you arrive on time without out feeling pressured.

The Interview

It's not just previous job history or unique skills that matter at the interview. Both your attitude and your appearance affect your chances of getting the job you want. You've probably heard your parents talk about making a good first impression with what you wear (it may sound like a lecture, but in this case they're right!). Here are some other strategies to help make your interview a success:

Appear Confident: Look your potential employer in the eye, shake his or her hand, and remember another parental mantra: good manners.

Be Prepared: Find out what you can about the position or company in advance and show your knowledge during the interview. Doing a little research on the job or field in which you're applying—so easy to do on the internet—shows the interviewer that you're smart and eager to learn. Knowing what a position involves also allows you to think in advance about which specific skills you have that fit well with the job.

Answer (And Ask!) Questions: You'll no doubt be asked typical interview questions, such as why you're interested in the position, what types of skills you offer, and the hours you're available to work. Prepare your answers before the interview. And don't be afraid to ask questions. Asking questions doesn't make you look stupid. In fact, it's the reverse. Questions show the interviewer that you're thoughtful and that you're not afraid to interact with other people—a particularly good interview strategy if the position involves dealing with people, such as a guide or salesperson.

☞ Remember!!

Looking for a job, preparing for a job interview, and even getting to work are all areas in which a parent or older sibling can offer good advice. So don't hesitate to ask for help on everything from putting together your résumé to choosing an interview outfit. Chances are, you'll be interviewing and working for people their age anyway so a little insight can't hurt.

Follow Up: Send your interviewer a brief e-mail or letter thanking him or her for spending time with you. Repeat your interest in the position. This is a particularly good strategy if you're interviewing for an internship or office position. Your future employer will be impressed by your determination.

Chapter 5

Want To Be Your Own Boss?

Frequently Asked Questions

What is an entrepreneur?

An entrepreneur is a person who organizes and manages a business, assuming the risk for the sake of profit. An entrepreneur sees an opportunity, makes a plan, starts the business, manages the business, and receives the profits.

What are some ideas for a teen business?

Always be on the lookout for ideas, because they can come from anywhere: your work experience, a hobby; your perceptions or experiences as a consumer, when an existing product or service doesn't work as well as you think it should; or when there is no product or service where you believe one should exist.

Learn everything you can about the business you want to start and the marketplace in which you'll be operating. That means getting work experience in and collecting information about your marketplace so that you know

About This Chapter: This chapter includes the following documents produced by the U.S. Small Business Administration (www.sba.gov) in 2005: "Frequently Asked Questions," "Ideas for Your Business," "Putting It in Writing," "$$$ Cha-Ching: Money Matters," "Avoiding Legal Business Hassles," and "Your Business Buddy List."

it inside and out. Make sure that your idea is so focused that you can express it clearly in fifty words or less.

There is a world of ideas that you can turn into a business. You're the best judge of what most appeals to you however. Businesses include: starting a production company for visual arts or music; starting a paper or journal to be circulated within your town, creating web pages for companies, after-school writing workshops, editing papers, tutoring services, and pet sitting services. Once you determine what product or service interests you, identify a specific niche within the market that may arouse customers' interest in purchasing your product or service.

What is a mentor and how can I find one?

A mentor is a caring, experienced individual who volunteers to be your guide. Your mentor can help you focus your talents and create a successful business. You can have more than one mentor. The National Mentoring Association (http://www.mentoring.org) can assist you with finding a mentor in your community or online.

What are the benefits of owning a business?

If you are actively considering going into business for yourself, you probably have already thought about the potential advantages of owning your own business. These advantages include, but are not limited to, the following:

- Being your own boss and not having to report to a superior

- Creating and developing your own idea, product, or service

- Having the independence and authority to make your own business decisions

- Receiving personal satisfaction and the sense of achievement that comes with being a success, plus the recognition that goes with it

- Having the opportunity to create substantial wealth and job security for yourself

- Making a living doing something you truly enjoy

♣ It's A Fact!!

What is a business plan and why do I need one?

A business plan is a written document which precisely defines your business, identifies your goals, and serves as your road map for your business. Its basic components include a current and pro forma balance sheet, an income statement, and a cash flow analysis. It helps you make the right decisions. Because it provides specific information about your company and how you will repay borrowed money, a good business plan is crucial if you need to borrow money. If you manage your business processes well, with a bit of luck you will be able to convert your product or service into a profit large enough to repay you for all the time, energy, and money you will have put into your business venture.

Source: "Frequently Asked Questions," SBA, 2005.

• Doing something that contributes to the well-being of others, whether it is providing a product or service, providing employment, or doing something else useful that creates value

What legal issues do I need to know about as I start my business?

Before choosing the legal form of your business, you may want to meet with a qualified business adviser, tax and accounting professional or lawyer. Information on patents, copyrights, business structures, and other legal issues can be found later in this chapter under Avoiding Legal Business Hassles.

What do I need to do to set up my business?

The importance of structuring your business is for both legal and tax purposes. Your business can be classified under the following business structures:

• **Sole Proprietorship:** One individual owns and manages the business. As the sole owner, you make all the business decisions and assume all the risk. There is no formal legal structure that separates you as the owner from the business.

- **Partnerships:** All partners may be actively involved with the business or they may designate one person to run the business and make day-to-day decisions.

- **Corporations:** A formal business structure that protects business owners from legal and financial liability, and is created according to your state's laws. Corporations may be owned by one or more people. Decisions are made by a board of directors that may appoint one person to be president of the company.

- **Franchises:** May be sole proprietorships, partnerships, or corporations whereby the business is operated as part of a large chain.

What type of insurance do I need to protect my business?

You should research and consider the following types of insurance when starting your business:

- Business interruption
- Product, property, and personal liability
- Property insurance (for example: Fire)

How do I know when my business is in trouble?

You can't pay your bills on time. You are not keeping good business records. You are selling products and services for less money than you normally would and you need to keep borrowing money just to get through the day.

Where can I meet other entrepreneurs in my community?

Many national youth groups have local chapters in your community where you can meet other teens with interests similar to yours.

How do I protect my business idea, product or name from being stolen?

There are several ways to protect your business. They include the following:

- **Patents:** A property right granted by the government to the inventor to make, use and sell his/her invention for a given period of time.

- **Copyrights:** Protect your literary or artistic work and, allows you to sell, give away or show your work. For more information on copyright, please visit http://www.copyright.gov.

- **Trademarks:** Name, mark, symbol, or motto that identifies your company and/or its product and is legally restricted to the use by the owner or manufacturer.

- **Trade Secrets:** Is information that you do not want known by your competition because your business may lose significant business advantages.

Please visit http://www.uspto.gov for more information on patents, trademarks, and trade secrets.

Ideas For Your Business

Where do great ideas come from?

- Personal experiences—hobbies, interests
- Work-related experiences
- Friends, family, teachers, coaches
- The internet
- Library research

As you think about your idea consider these questions:

- What do I like to do with my time?
- What technical skills have I learned or developed?
- What do others say I am good at?
- How much time do I have to run a successful business?
- Do I have any hobbies or interests that are marketable?

Aha! The great idea—now what?

Before starting out, list your reasons for wanting to go into business. Some of the most common reasons for starting a business are as follows:

- You want to be your own boss

- You want financial independence

- You want creative freedom

- You want to fully use your skills and knowledge

Then identify the niche your business will fill. Conduct the necessary research to answer these questions:

- Is my idea practical, and will it fill a need?

- What is my competition?

- What is my business advantage over existing firms?

- Can I deliver a better quality service?

- Can I create a demand for my business?

Consider the time it takes to run a business:

- Do I really want to give up baseball, hockey, soccer, basketball, football, dance, piano and voice, or hanging out with or going to the mall with my friends to run this business?

- Will I have to run my business every day or just sometimes?

- Will running my business have an effect on school?

- Will my family help me out?

> ✔ **Quick Tip**
>
> To help you generate creative ideas visit these websites:
>
> - Creative Education Foundation: http://www.creativeeducationfoundation.org/youthwise.shtml
>
> - National Collegiate Inventors and Innovators Alliance: http://www.nciia.org
>
> - Junior Achievement: http://www.ja.org
>
> After you have developed your idea, here are websites to keep your business moving along:
>
> - JA Titan—test your skills in running a business in this ultimate business simulation: http://titan.ja.org
>
> - Entrepreneurship Education: http://eweb.slu.edu/youth_entrepreneurship.htm
>
> - Entrepreneur.com: http://www.entrepreneur.com/tsu/archivesba/0,6835,298716,00.html
>
> Source: "Ideas For Your Business," SBA, 2005.

What is a pre-business check list?

The final step before developing your plan is the pre-business checklist. You should answer these questions:

- What services or products will I sell? Where will I be located?
- What skills and experience do I bring to the business?
- What will I name my business?
- What equipment or supplies will I need?
- What insurance coverage will be needed?
- How much money, if any, will it cost to start my business? Will I need financing?
- What are my resources?
- How will I compensate myself?

Your answers will help you create a focused, well-researched business plan that will serve as a blueprint. The plan will detail how the business will be operated, managed, and financed.

Put It In Writing

Developing your business plan is your road map to success in the business world. A business plan is a written document that outlines measures and actions to define where you want to go and how you will get there. Without a business plan, you have no written goals or objectives to measure your success. Starting a business is a full of uncertainties. Developing a thorough business plan helps minimize those uncertainties.

Before you begin writing your business plan, consider these questions:

- What service or product does your business provide, and what need does it fill?
- Who are the potential customers for your product or service, and why will they purchase it from you?
- How will you reach your potential customers?

- Where will you get the financial resources to start your business?

- Do you really want to give up baseball, hockey, soccer, basketball, football, dance, piano and voice, or hanging out with or going to the mall with your friends to run this business?

- Will you have to run your business every day or just sometimes?

- Will running your business have an effect on school?

- Will your family help you out?

The business plan is your guide. You can adapt it to your specific business. Dividing the plan into several components helps make drafting it a more manageable task.

Introduction

- Give a detailed description of the business and its goals.

- Discuss the ownership of the business and the legal structure.

- List the skills and experience you bring to the business.

- Discuss the advantages you and your business have over your competitors.

Marketing

- Discuss the products/services offered.

- Identify the customer demand for your product/service.

- Identify your market, its size, and locations.

- Explain how your product/service will be advertised and marketed.

- Explain the pricing strategy.

Financial Management

- Explain your source and discuss the amount of initial equity capital you'll need.

- Develop a monthly operating budget for the first year.

- Develop an expected return on investment and monthly cash flow for the first year.

- Provide projected income statements and balance sheets for a two-year period.

- Discuss your break-even point.

- Explain your personal balance sheet and method of compensation.

- Discuss who will maintain your accounting records and how they will be kept.

✔ **Quick Tip**

For a more in-depth look at writing a business plan go to: http://www.sba.gov/starting_business/planning/writingplan.html

Source: "Put It In Writing," SBA, 2005.

- Provide "what if" statements that address alternative approaches to any problem that may develop.

Operations

- Explain how the business will be managed on a day-to-day basis.

- Discuss hiring and personnel procedures.

- Discuss insurance, lease, or rent agreements, and issues pertinent to your business.

- Account for the equipment necessary to produce your products or services.

- Account for production and delivery of products and services.

Concluding Statement

Summarize your business goals and objectives and express your commitment to the success of your business.

Cha-Ching: Money Matters

Let's face it. Money matters. You can't start, grow or simply exist in business without sufficient money to pay the bills and provide some income.

Here are some questions you should answer as you consider starting or growing your business.

- How much do I need to either get started or grow my business?

- Will I use my personal money?

- Should I ask someone else for a loan?

- Can I apply for a credit card?

- Will a vendor or a supplier be willing to give me trade credit? (This usually means that you have an extended period of time to pay your bill usually 30 days from time of invoice.)

- To minimize costs, should I start my business in my home?

- If I use someone's money, will my business generate enough money to be able to repay the loan (principal and interest)?

Funding Your Business

Many entrepreneurs start businesses at home using their own personal funds. Some ask friends and family to provide the initial or ongoing capital. When your business has been established for a while, you may want to go to your local bank for a loan.

You Can Bank On It

Developing a relationship with your bank and your personal banker is important. If you decide to seek a loan from your bank, your personal banker serves as your advocate supporting your application before the bank's loan committee. When you apply for a loan, you and your parents must co-sign the papers.

Before asking for a loan, you need to establish a savings or checking account. Banks generally prefer to lend to their existing clients who will bring the bank additional business—other new clients or establish a number of accounts both personal and business. Once you have demonstrated that your business is successful, a bank may consider a line of credit or possibly a small commercial loan if you and/or your parents bank there.

Your Credit History Is Your Rep

Finally, establishing and maintaining a good credit history is critical to getting money for your business. Always pay your bills on time and make sure that you periodically check your credit history. A credit report contains information on where you live, how you pay your bills, and whether you've been sued, arrested or filed for bankruptcy. Nationwide consumer reporting companies sell the information in your report to creditors who use it to evaluate your applications for credit. Your credit is like your name—do not abuse it.

♣ **It's A Fact!!**
Free Credit Reports Available

The Fair Credit Reporting Act requires each of the nationwide consumer reporting companies to provide you with a free copy of your credit report, at your request, once every 12 months, from http://www.annualcreditreport.com.

Source: "Cha-Ching: Money Matters," SBA, 2005.

Avoiding Legal Business Hassles

Do the Right Thing! Yes, it's not just director Spike Lee's first movie nominated for an Academy Award®, but also a best practice for everyone—especially entrepreneurs. Having a successful enterprise means being aware of relevant legal issues when organizing and growing your small business.

Below is a selection of resources which can help you manage common legal issues:

Organize Your Business

• http://www.business.gov: Get access to resources and services to help you start, grow, and succeed in business. The site gives you information on business laws, financing, government relations, taxes and much more.

Protect Your Ideas

- U.S. Patent & Trade Office (http://www.uspto.gov) and U.S. Copyright Office (http://www.copyright.gov): Assist in protecting your investments, promoting goods and services, and safeguarding against confusion and deception in the marketplace.

Be Aware Of Labor Laws

- Department of Labor (http://www.dol.gov/dol/topic/youthlabor): Find information on teen employment, wage and hour requirements, and providing a safe and healthy work experience.

- Internal Revenue Service: http://www.irs.gov

Your Business Buddy List

Similar to a buddy list on an instant message site, here is a compilation of organizations for you to access at the touch of a button. These resources will assist you in counseling, training, and leadership development. Use this list—in addition to other sources on the internet—to guide you on your path to business ownership.

Counseling And Training

National Academy Foundation (http://www.naf.org): The National Academy Foundation (NAF) sustains a national network of career academies to support the development of America's youth toward personal and professional success in high school, in higher education, and throughout their careers. NAF Academies represent business/school partnerships that prepare young people for future careers through a combination of school-based curricula and work-based experiences.

The W.E.B. Dubois Scholars Institute (http://www.webduboisscholars.org): The Institute cultivates scholarship, leadership potential, and community service among high-achieving African-American and Latino-American adolescents.

Mentoring (http://www.mentoring.org): The National Mentoring Partnership is a resource for mentors and mentoring initiatives nationwide.

Leadership Development And Business Resources

Junior Achievement (http://www.ja.org): JA educates and inspires young people to value free enterprise, business and economics to improve the quality of their lives.

Future Business Leaders Of America (http://www.fbla-pbl.org): Future Business Leaders of America brings business and education together in a positive working relationship through innovation, leadership, and career development programs.

Distributive Education Clubs Of America (http://www.deca.org): Distributive Education Clubs of America (DECA) is the association for students of marketing, management, and entrepreneurship. DECA sponsors a competitive awards program; provides scholarships, leadership training, and classroom support; and hosts conferences.

Students In Free Enterprise (http://www.sife.org): Students in Free Enterprise (SIFE) offers students the opportunity to develop leadership, teamwork and communication skills through learning, practicing and teaching the principles of free enterprise, thereby improving the standard of living for millions in the process.

Boy Scouts Of America (http://www.scouting.org): Boy Scouts of America prepares young people to make ethical and moral choices over their lifetime by instilling in them the values of the scout oath and law. Leadership training focuses on character development and values.

Boys And Girls Clubs Of America (http://www.bgca.org): Boys and Girls Clubs of America teach young people the skills they need to succeed in life. The Education and Career programs, for ages 13–18, expands knowledge of money management and teaches skills that lead to financial independence.

Girl Scouts Of America (http://www.girlscouts.org): Girl Scouts of America teaches the importance of personal responsibility, the value of goal-setting, teamwork and accomplishment. For girls 11–17, scouting provides an opportunity to practice decision-making skills and how to relate to others with understanding and respect.

Association Of Young Latino Entrepreneurs (http://www.ayle.org): The association promotes the business development of young Latino entrepreneurs with economic programs designed to strengthen and expand the income potential of its members and affiliates in the trade area.

4-H (http://www.4husa.org): 4-H is a community of young people across America who are learning about leadership, citizenship, and life skills.

Entrepreneur Magazine (http://www.teenstartups.com)

Entrepreneur U (http://www.entrepreneuru.org): This site was created for the purpose of informing students, administrators, and parents about the opportunities for studying entrepreneurship beyond high school.

Young America's Business Trust (http://www.ybiz.net): Believing The talents and prospects of young entrepreneurs of the Americas and the Caribbean today will determine the Hemisphere's potential for future economic growth and democratic stability. Young Americas Business Trust combines the energy of talented young people with the experience and prestige of the Organization of American States, an international organization of the 34 countries of the Americas.

Chapter 6

Tax Information For Students

The following kinds of income often received by students are generally taxable:

- Pay for services performed

- Self-employment income

- Investment income

- Certain scholarships and fellowships

Pay For Services Performed

When figuring how much income to report, include everything you received as payment for your services. This usually means wages, salaries, and tips.

Wages And Salaries: The amount of wages (including tips) or salaries you received during the year is shown in box 1 of Form W-2, Wage and Tax Statement. Your employer will give you Form W-2 soon after the end of the year.

Tips: All tips you receive are income, and subject to income tax. This includes tips customers give you directly, tips customers charge on credit cards that your employer gives you, and your share of tips split with other employees.

About This Chapter: "Taxable Income for Students," Internal Revenue Service (IRS), December 3, 2007.

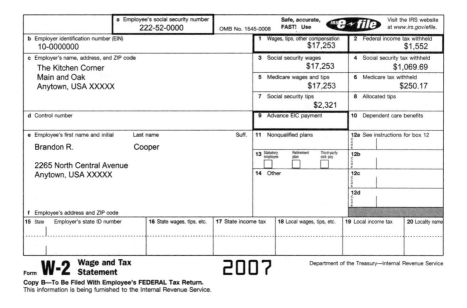

Figure 6.1. A Sample W-2 form. (Source: From "Tax Tutorial: Module 2—Wage and Tip Income," Internal Revenue Service (IRS), December 12, 2007.)

Keep a daily record or other proof of your tips. You can use Form 4070A, Employee's Daily Record of Tips. Your daily record must show your name and address, your employer's name, and the establishment's name. For each day worked, you must show the amount of cash and charge tips you received from customers or other employees, a list of the names and amounts you paid to other employees through tip splitting, and the value of any noncash tips you get, such as tickets, passes, or other items of value. Record this information on or near the date you receive the tip income.

Reporting Tips To Your Employer: If you receive cash, check, or credit card tips of $20 or more in any one calendar month while working for one employer, you must report the total amount of your tips to your employer by the 10th day of the next month. If the 10th falls on a Saturday, Sunday, or legal holiday, give your employer the report on the next day that is not a Saturday, Sunday, or a legal holiday.

To report your tips, you can use Form 4070, Employee's Report of Tips to Employer. To get a year's supply of this form, ask your employer or call the IRS for Publication 1244, Employee's Daily Record of Tips and Report to Employer. Fill in the information asked for on the form, sign and date the form, and give it to your employer. If you do not use Form 4070, give your employer a statement with the following information:

- Your name, address, and social security number

- Your employer's name, address, and business name (if it is different from the employer's name)

- The month (or the dates of any shorter period) in which you received tips

- The total tips required to be reported for the period

Withholding On Tips: Your employer must withhold social security tax and Medicare taxes or railroad retirement tax, and any income tax due on the tips you report. Your employer usually deducts the withholding due on tips from your wages. If your wages are too small for your employer to withhold taxes, you may give him or her extra money to pay the taxes up to the close of the calendar year. Your employer should tell you how much is needed.

Any taxes that remain unpaid may be collected by your employer from your next paycheck. If withholding taxes remain uncollected at the end of the year, you may be subject to a penalty for underpayment of estimated

---

♣ It's A Fact!!

Employers withhold taxes from employees' pay.

- Gross pay is the amount the employee earns.

- Net pay, or take-home pay, is the amount the employee receives after deductions.

The difference between gross pay and net pay is accounted for by the following:

- Social Security taxes

- Medicare taxes

- Income tax withheld

- Other amounts withheld

Employers send the withheld taxes to the taxing authorities.

Source: Excerpted from "Tax Tutorial: Module 1—Payroll Taxes and Federal Income Tax Withholding." Internal Revenue Service (IRS), December 12, 2007.

❧ What's It Mean?

Medicare Tax: Used to provide medical benefits for certain individuals when they reach age 65. Workers, retired workers, and the spouses of workers and retired workers are eligible to receive Medicare benefits upon reaching age 65.

Payroll Taxes: Include Social Security and Medicare taxes.

Social Security Tax: Provides benefits for retired workers and their dependents as well as for the disabled and their dependents. Also known as the Federal Insurance Contributions Act (FICA) tax.

Source: Excerpted from "Tax Tutorial: Module 1—Payroll Taxes and Federal Income Tax Withholding." Internal Revenue Service (IRS), December 12, 2007.

♣ It's A Fact!!

Payroll Tax Rates

- Social Security tax rate: 6.20%

- Medicare tax rate: 1.45%

- Total payroll taxes: 7.65%

If an employee earns $1,000, the payroll taxes are:

- Social Security tax $62.00

- Medicare tax $14.50

- Total payroll taxes $76.50

The employer sends the $76.50 to the federal government.

Tax Tip: There is a maximum annual amount of Social Security tax withheld per employee. Social Security taxes are not withheld on amounts over the earnings limit. In 2008, the earnings limit was $97,500, and the maximum Social Security tax was $6,045 ($97,500 x 6.2%).

Source: Excerpted from "Tax Tutorial: Module 1—Payroll Taxes and Federal Income Tax Withholding." Internal Revenue Service (IRS), December 12, 2007.

taxes. See IRS Publication 505, Tax Withholding and Estimated Tax, for more information.

Form W-2: The tips you reported to your employer will be included with your wages in box 1 of Form W-2. Federal income tax, social security tax, and Medicare tax withheld on your wages and tips will be shown in boxes 2, 4, and 6, respectively.

Your Form W-2 may show an amount in box 8, "Allocated tips." This is an additional amount allocated to you if tips you reported to your employer were less than the minimum amount expected to be earned by employees where you work.

If you do not have adequate records of your actual tips, you must report at least the amount of allocated tips shown in box 8 on your Form W-2.

If you have adequate records, report your actual tips on your return. For more information on allocated tips, see IRS Publication 531, Reporting Tip Income.

If you did not report tips to your employer as required, you may be charged a penalty in addition to the tax you owe. If you have reasonable cause for not reporting tips to your employer, you should attach a statement to your return explaining why you did not.

♣ It's A Fact!!

Employees complete Form W-4, Employee's Withholding Allowance Certificate. Employers use Form W-4 to determine how much federal income tax to withhold. The amount of federal income tax withholding depends on the employee's marital status, the number of withholding allowances claimed by the employee, any additional amount the employee wants to withhold, and any exemptions from withholding that the employee claims.

Source: Excerpted from "Tax Tutorial: Module 1—Payroll Taxes and Federal Income Tax Withholding." Internal Revenue Service (IRS), December 12, 2007.

Reserve Officers' Training Corps (ROTC): Subsistence allowances paid to ROTC students participating in advanced training are not taxable. However, active duty pay, such as that received during summer advanced camp, is

Cut here and give Form W-4 to your employer. Keep the top part for your records.

Form **W-4** — Department of the Treasury, Internal Revenue Service

Employee's Withholding Allowance Certificate

▶ Whether you are entitled to claim a certain number of allowances or exemption from withholding is subject to review by the IRS. Your employer may be required to send a copy of this form to the IRS.

OMB No. 1545-0074 — **2007**

1 Type or print your first name and middle initial.	Last name	2 Your social security number
Alicia	Myers	222 00 5476

Home address (number and street or rural route)	3 ☑ Single ☐ Married ☐ Married, but withhold at higher Single rate. Note. If married, but legally separated, or spouse is a nonresident alien, check the "Single" box.
462 Main Street	
City or town, state, and ZIP code	4 If your last name differs from that shown on your social security card, check here. You must call 1-800-772-1213 for a replacement card. ▶ ☐
Anytown, US xxxxx	

5 Total number of allowances you are claiming (from line **H** above **or** from the applicable worksheet on page 2) — 5: 1

6 Additional amount, if any, you want withheld from each paycheck . . . . — 6: $

7 I claim exemption from withholding for 2007, and I certify that I meet **both** of the following conditions for exemption.

- Last year I had a right to a refund of **all** federal income tax withheld because I had **no** tax liability **and**
- This year I expect a refund of **all** federal income tax withheld because I expect to have **no** tax liability.

If you meet both conditions, write "Exempt" here . . . . ▶ 7

Under penalties of perjury, I declare that I have examined this certificate and to the best of my knowledge and belief, it is true, correct, and complete.

Employee's signature (Form is not valid unless you sign it.) ▶ **Date** ▶

8 Employer's name and address (Employer: Complete lines 8 and 10 only if sending to the IRS.)	9 Office code (optional)	10 Employer identification number (EIN)

For Privacy Act and Paperwork Reduction Act Notice, see page 2. Cat. No. 10220Q Form **W-4** (2007)

Figure 6.2. A sample Form W-4 for Alicia Myers. Note that Alicia is single and claims one withholding allowance. (Source: Excerpted from "Tax Tutorial: Module 1—Payroll Taxes and Federal Income Tax Withholding." Internal Revenue Service (IRS), December 12, 2007.)

taxable. For example, Jim Hunter is a member of the ROTC who is participating in the advanced course. He received a subsistence allowance of $100 each month for 10 months and $600 of active duty pay during summer advanced camp. He must include only the $600 active duty pay in his gross income.

Self-Employment Income

Earnings you received from self-employment are subject to income tax. These earnings include income from baby-sitting and lawn mowing. These earnings are not self-employment income if you provided these services as an employee.

You are taxed on your net earnings (income you received minus any business expenses you are allowed to deduct). For information on what expenses can be deducted, see IRS Publication 535, Business Expenses. As a self-employed person, you are responsible for keeping records to show how much income you received and how many expenses you had. Your income and expenses are reported on Schedule C or C-EZ (Form 1040).

Self-Employment Tax: If you had net earnings of $400 or more from self-employment, you also will have to pay self-employment tax. This tax pays for your benefits under the social security system. Social security and Medicare benefits are available to individuals who are self-employed the same as they are to wage earners who have social security tax and Medicare tax withheld from their wages. The self-employment tax is figured on Schedule SE (Form 1040).

Newspaper Carriers And Distributors: Special rules apply to services you perform as a newspaper carrier or distributor. You are a direct seller and treated as self-employed for federal tax purposes if you meet the following conditions.

- You are in the business of delivering/distributing newspapers or shopping news, including directly related services such as soliciting customers and collecting receipts.

- Substantially all your pay for these services directly relates to sales or other output rather than to the number of hours worked.

- You perform the delivery services under a written contract between you and the service recipient that states that you will not be treated as an employee for federal tax purposes.

Carriers And Vendors Under Age 18: Carriers or distributors (not including those who deliver or distribute to any point for subsequent delivery or distribution) and vendors (working under a buy-sell arrangement) under age 18 are not subject to self-employment tax.

If you were self-employed, you can deduct half of your self-employment tax and part of your health insurance premiums. See the Form 1040 instructions for lines 27 and 28 for more information.

Investment Income

This section explains whether you have to report income from bank accounts and certain other investments. Various types of investment income are treated differently. Some of the more common ones are discussed here.

Interest: Interest you get from checking and savings accounts and most other sources is taxable.

Bank Accounts: Some credit unions, building and loan associations, savings and loan associations, mutual savings banks, and cooperative banks call what they pay you on your deposits "dividends." However, for tax purposes, these payments are considered interest, and you should report them as interest.

U.S. Savings Bonds: Interest on U.S. savings bonds is taxable for federal income tax purposes, but exempt from all state and local income taxes. The most common bonds are series EE and series I bonds. Series EE bonds are issued in several different denominations and cost one-half the amount shown on the face of the bond. For example, a $100 bond costs $50. The face value of the bond is paid only when the bond matures. The difference between what you paid for the bond and the amount you get when you cash it is taxable interest.

Series I bonds are inflation-indexed bonds issued at their face value. The face value plus accrued interest is payable to you at the bond's maturity.

You can report all interest on these bonds when you cash them, or you can choose to report their increase in value as interest each year. IRS Publication 550, Investment Income and Expenses, explains how to make this choice.

Under certain circumstances, the interest on U.S. savings bonds (series EE and series I) issued after December 31, 1989, is exempt from tax if the bonds are used for educational purposes. See IRS Publication 550 for further information.

Other Interest From The U.S. Government: Interest on U.S. Treasury bills, notes, and bonds is taxable for federal income tax purposes. This interest is exempt from all state and local income taxes.

Tax-Exempt Bonds: Generally, interest from bonds issued by state and local governments is not taxable for federal income tax purposes.

Interest Statements: Your bank, savings and loan, or other payer of interest will send you a statement if you earned at least $10 in interest for the year. You should receive these statements sometime in January for the previous tax year. Banks may use Form 1099-INT, Interest Income. However, they may include your total interest on the statement they send you at the end of the year. Do not throw these statements away.

✎ What's It Mean?

<u>Bonus:</u> Compensation received by an employee for services performed. A bonus is given in addition to an employee's usual compensation.

<u>Commission:</u> Compensation received by an employee for services performed. Commissions are paid based on a percentage of sales made or a fixed amount per sale.

<u>Salary:</u> Compensation received by an employee for services performed. A salary is a fixed sum paid for a specific period of time worked, such as weekly or monthly.

<u>Tip Income:</u> Money and goods received for services performed by food servers, baggage handlers, hairdressers, and others. Tips go beyond the stated amount of the bill and are given voluntarily.

<u>Wages:</u> Compensation received by employees for services performed. Usually, wages are computed by multiplying an hourly pay rate by the number of hours worked.

Source: Excerpted from "Tax Tutorial: Module 2—Wage and Tip Income," Internal Revenue Service (IRS), December 12, 2007.

Dividends: Dividends are distributions of money, stock, or other property paid to you by a corporation. You may also get dividends through a partnership, an estate, a trust, or an association that is taxed as a corporation. Ordinary dividends, the most common type, are paid out of the corporation's earnings. You must report these as income on your tax return.

Dividend Statements: Regardless of whether you receive your dividends in cash or additional shares of stock, the payer of the dividends will send you a Form 1099-DIV, Dividends and Distributions, if you earned at least $10 in dividends for the year.

Other Investment Income: If you received income from investments not discussed here, see IRS Publication 550. Also, the payer of the income may be able to tell you whether the income is taxable or nontaxable.

Taxable Scholarships And Fellowships

If you received a scholarship or fellowship, all or part of it may be taxable, even if you did not receive a Form W-2. Generally, the entire amount is taxable if you are not a candidate for a degree.

If you are a candidate for a degree, you generally can exclude from income that part of the grant used for tuition and fees required for enrollment or attendance, or fees, books, supplies, and equipment required for your courses. You cannot exclude from income any part of the grant used for other purposes, such as room and board.

A scholarship generally is an amount paid for the benefit of a student at an educational institution to aid in the pursuit of studies. The student may be in either a graduate or an undergraduate program.

A fellowship grant generally is an amount paid for the benefit of an individual to aid in the pursuit of study or research.

- **Example 1:** Tammy Graves receives a $6,000 fellowship grant that is not designated for any specific use. Tammy is a degree candidate. She spends $5,500 for tuition and $500 for her personal expenses. Tammy is required to include $500 in income.

- **Example 2:** Ursula Harris, a degree candidate, receives a $2,000 scholarship, with $1,000 specifically designated for tuition and $1,000 specifically designated for living expenses. Her tuition is $1,600. She may exclude $1,000 from income, but the other $1,000 designated for living expenses is taxable and must be included in income.

Payment For Services: All payments you receive for past, present, or future services must be included in income. This is true even if the services are a condition of receiving the grant or are required of all candidates for the degree.

- **Example:** Gary Thomas receives a scholarship of $2,500 for the spring semester. As a condition of receiving the scholarship, he must serve as a part-time teaching assistant. Of the $2,500 scholarship, $1,000 represents payment for his services. Gary is a degree candidate, and his tuition is $1,600. He can exclude $1,500 from income as a qualified scholarship. The remaining $1,000, representing payment for his services, is taxable.

Fulbright Students And Researchers: A Fulbright grant is generally treated as any other scholarship or fellowship in figuring how much of the grant can be excluded. If you receive a Fulbright grant for lecturing or teaching, it is payment for services and subject to tax.

Pell Grants, Supplemental Educational Opportunity Grants, And Grants To States For State Student Incentives: These grants are nontaxable scholarships to the extent used for tuition and course-related expenses during the grant period.

Reduced Tuition: You may be entitled to reduced tuition because you or one of your parents is or was an employee of the school. If so, the amount of the reduction is not taxable so long as the tuition is for education below the graduate level (but see Graduate student exception, next.) The reduced tuition program must not favor any highly paid employee. The reduced tuition is taxable if it represents payment for your services.

Graduate Student Exception: Tax-free treatment of reduced tuition can also apply to a graduate student who performs teaching or research activities at an educational institution. The qualified tuition reduction must be for education furnished by that institution and not represent payment for services.

Contest Prizes: Scholarship prizes won in a contest are not scholarships or fellowships if you do not have to use the prizes for your education. If you can use the prize for any purpose, the entire amount is taxable.

Qualified State Tuition Program: If you receive distributions from a qualified state tuition program, only the amount that is more than the amount contributed to the program is taxable. Part of the benefits may qualify as a nontaxable scholarship or fellowship (for example, matching-grant amounts paid under the program to a degree candidate). Other benefits are partly a nontaxable return of the contributions made to the program on your behalf (for example, by your parents). You must include in your income the part of the benefits that is neither a nontaxable scholarship or fellowship nor a return of contributions. For more information about qualified state tuition programs, see IRS Publication 525, Taxable and Nontaxable Income, but for more information on a specific program, contact the state or agency that established and maintains it.

Other Grants Or Assistance: If you are not sure whether your grant qualifies as a scholarship or fellowship, ask the person who made the grant.

✔ **Quick Tip**

Keeping Good Records

You can avoid headaches at tax time by keeping track of your receipts and other records throughout the year. Good recordkeeping will help you remember the various transactions you made during the year, which in turn may make filing your return a less taxing experience.

Records help you document the deductions you've claimed on your return. You'll need this documentation should the IRS select your return for examination. Normally, tax records should be kept for three years, but some documents—such as records relating to a home purchase or sale, stock transactions, IRA and business or rental property—should be kept longer.

In most cases, the IRS does not require you to keep records in any special manner. Generally speaking, however, you should keep any and all documents that may have an impact on your federal tax return:

- Bills

- Credit card and other receipts

- Invoices

- Mileage logs

- Canceled, imaged or substitute checks or any other proof of payment

- Any other records to support deductions or credits you claim on your return

Good recordkeeping throughout the year saves you time and effort at tax time when organizing and completing your return. If you hire a paid professional to complete your return, the records you have kept will assist the preparer in quickly and accurately completing your return.

For more information on what kinds of records to keep, see IRS Publication 552, Recordkeeping for Individuals, which is available on IRS.gov or by calling 800-TAX-FORM (800-829-3676).

Remember that for the genuine IRS website be sure to use .gov. Don't be confused by internet sites that end in .com, .net, .org or other designations instead of .gov. The address of the official IRS governmental website is www.irs.gov.

Source: "Keeping Good Records," IRS, December 8, 2008.

Additional Information: See IRS Publication 970, Tax Benefits for Education, for more information on how much of your scholarship or fellowship is taxable.

How To Report

If you file Form 1040EZ, include the taxable amount of your scholarship or fellowship on line 1. Print "SCH" and any taxable amount not reported on a W-2 form in the space to the right of the words "W-2 form(s)" on line 1.

If you file Form 1040A or Form 1040, include the taxable amount on line 7. Print "SCH" and any taxable amount not reported on a W-2 form in the space to the left of line 7 on Form 1040A or on the dotted line next to line 7 on Form 1040.

Other Income

If you are not sure whether to include any item of income on your return, see IRS Publication 525.

Part Two

Managing Your Money

Chapter 7

Making Your Money Grow

How Your Money Can Grow

Making regular payments to yourself, even in small amounts, can add up over time. The amount your money grows depends on the interest earned and the amount of time you leave it in the account.

Interest: Interest is an amount of money banks or other financial institutions pay you for keeping your money on deposit with them. Interest is expressed as a percentage and is calculated based on the amount of money in your account.

If you have $1,000 stashed away under your mattress for a year, it will still be $1,000 at the end of the year, providing that it has not been lost or stolen. Your mattress is not paying you interest for keeping your money under it.

Compound Interest: Compounding is how your money can grow when you keep it in a financial institution that pays interest. When the bank compounds the interest in your account, you earn money on the previously paid interest, in addition to the money in your account. But not all savings accounts are created equal. This is because interest can be compounded daily, monthly, or annually.

About This Chapter: Excerpted from "Module 4: Pay Yourself First," *Money Smart for Young Adults*, a CD-based curriculum developed by the Federal Deposit Insurance Corporation (FDIC), March 2008.

Annual Percentage Yield (APY)

APY reflects the amount of interest you will earn on a yearly basis. It is expressed as a percentage.

- The APY includes the effect of compounding. The more often your money compounds, the higher the APY and the more interest you will receive.

- When comparing different accounts, you should compare the APYs of the savings products, not the interest rates.

♣ It's A Fact!!
How To Calculate Annual Percentage Yield (APY)

APY = 100 [(1 + Interest/Principal)(365/Days in term) − 1]

- Principal is the amount of funds assumed to have been deposited at the beginning of the account.

- Interest is the total dollar amount of interest earned on the principal for the term of the account.

- Days in term is the actual number of days in the term of the account.

When the days in term is 365, the annual percentage yield can be calculated by use of the following simple formula:

APY = 100 (Interest/Principal)

For example, if a bank pays $61.68 in interest for a 365-day year on $1,000 deposited into an account, using the general formula above, the annual percentage yield is 6.17%:

APY = 100[(1 + 61.68/1,000)(365/365) − 1]

APY = 6.17%

Or, using the simple formula above since, as an account without a stated term, the term is deemed to be 365 days:

APY = 100(61.68/1,000)

APY = 6.17%

If you are planning on opening a savings account or want to get more out of the one you already have, ask your bank's customer service representative for the "Truth in Savings" disclosures. These disclosures list the APY and other important information that you should know about the accounts you are interested in.

Savings And Investing

There are two basic ways to save money. You can open a savings account at a federally insured bank or credit union or you can invest your money. An important difference between the two is that savings accounts are federally insured and investments are not.

Open A Savings Account: We have already seen that, with a savings account, you make money by earning interest. The bank pays you interest for the opportunity to use your money. A savings account also ensures that your money is safe and that you have easy access to it.

The Federal Deposit Insurance Corporation (FDIC) guarantees your money in insured financial institutions up to the maximum allowed by law. Likewise, the National Credit Union Administration or NCUA insures your money at insured credit unions. This means that if your financial institution goes out of business, the FDIC or NCUA will make sure that you get your money.

The FDIC has an online tool called Electronic Deposit Insurance Estimator (EDIE) available at www.fdic.gov/EDIE. EDIE lets you calculate the insurance coverage of your accounts at each FDIC insured institution.

Buy An Investment: You've probably heard a lot about investing and how sometimes it can be good or bad. It is important to be well-informed before making an investment. You probably do not have the extra money to begin investing now, but you will soon and this information is very important for your financial success and stability.

An investment is a long-term savings option that you purchase for future income or financial benefit. Many banks now sell investment products, such as mutual funds.

- While some investment products are sold at banks, they are not the same as deposit accounts because the money you invest is not federally insured.

- When you invest money, there is also a greater risk of losing it than if you put your money in a savings or other deposit account. In fact, there is a possibility that you might lose the entire amount you invest if the investment does not perform well.

- Because of the risk, your investment may earn and grow more than a regular savings account. In general, the higher the risk, the higher the expected rate of return on the investment.

You make money on investments by selling them for more than you paid for them, or by earning dividends and interest. The money you earn is considered income; therefore, you may have to pay taxes on it.

Before You Invest

If you are interested in learning more about investment products, talk to your bank, a reputable financial advisor, or an investment firm. When you become employed, ask your employer about any retirement accounts that are offered through your job.

♣ It's A Fact!! Rule Of 72

The Rule of 72 is a formula that lets you estimate how long it will take for your savings to double in value. This calculation assumes that the interest rate remains the same over time and interest is compounded once a year.

Here is how you use the Rule of 72:

72 ÷ interest rate = number of years

- Divide 72 by the current interest rate to determine the number of years that it will take to double your initial savings amount.

- For example, if you invest $50 in a savings account at a 4 percent interest rate, it will take 18 years for your initial savings of $50 to double.

$$72 \div 4 = 18$$

You can also find the interest rate you need to have when you know how many years you want your initial savings amount to double. Here is an example of how this works:

- If you put $500 in an account that you want to double in 12 years, you will need an interest rate of 6 percent.

- $72 \div 12 = 6$

Retirement accounts, such as a 401(k), typically require you to be a full-time employee so you may not be eligible until after college or when you have a full-time job. You can also do your own research on investments. A public library or the internet is a good place to start.

Investment Products

Some more popular types of investment products that you can buy include bonds, stocks, mutual funds, and retirement investments. Most financial advisors recommend that, before you buy any of these investment products, you should have a savings cushion that will allow you to pay your expenses for two to six months. Any money you have saved beyond this amount can be used for investing. Because of this, you will want to wait until you are financially stable before investing. In case of an emergency, sudden illness, or job loss, you always want to be able to support yourself.

> ✔ **Quick Tip**
> **How To Choose**
> **The Best Investments**
>
> Investments can benefit you financially, but you need to be well prepared and ready to take on the responsibility. Do not rush into any investment. Make sure you know all things to consider when choosing an investment.

Other Investments

Owning a home or business are two additional ways to invest. Why do you think owning a home is an investment?

When your home increases in value and your debt decreases as you pay the mortgage, your equity increases. Equity is the difference between how much the house is worth and how much you owe on the house. For example:

Value of home $250,000

Minus Debt (how much you owe) − $200,000

Equity = $ 50,000

✎ What's It Mean?

Annual Percentage Yield (APY): APY is the amount of interest you will earn on a yearly basis expressed as a percentage. The APY includes the effect of compounding. When comparing different accounts, you should compare the APYs of the savings products, not the interest rates. The higher the APY, the higher the interest you will receive.

Bonds: When you purchase a bond, you are essentially loaning money to a corporation or to the government for a certain period of time, called a "term." The bond certificate promises the corporation or government will repay you on a specific date with a fixed rate of interest.

Certificates Of Deposit (CDs): CDs are accounts where you leave your money for a set period of time called a term, such as six months or one, two, or five years. You usually earn a higher rate of interest than in a regular savings account. The longer you promise to keep your money in a CD, the higher the interest rate. Be sure to think about your cash needs before opening a CD because you will pay a penalty if you withdraw your money early.

Club Account: A club account is a type of savings account you join to save money for a special reason, such as holidays or family vacations. Club accounts usually require you to make regular deposits.

Diversification: Diversification means you spread the risk of loss in a variety of savings and investment options. It is the concept of "don't put all your eggs in one basket."

401(k) And 403(b) Retirement Plans: 401(k) plans are retirement plans that some private corporations offer their employees. A 403(b) plan is similar to a 401(k), but is offered to employees of some non-profit organizations. In both types of plans, you choose to deduct part of your paycheck and place it into the investment strategy you design. The plans allow you to choose different types of investments, depending on how much risk you want to take. The money you place into the account lowers your taxable income. The employer usually matches a portion of your contribution, sometimes up to 50 percent. The funds grow tax-free until the money is withdrawn during retirement.

Equity: When referring to a home, equity is the difference between how much the house is worth and how much you owe on the house.

Investment: A savings option purchased for future income or financial benefit.

Individual Retirement Account (IRA): An IRA is a retirement account that lets you save and invest money tax-free until you withdraw it when you retire. There are different types of IRAs, including traditional and Roth IRAs. Visit www.irs.gov for current regulations regarding contributions.

Liquidity: Liquidity refers to the ease with which an asset (a thing of value) can be turned into cash without losing its value. For example, cash is the most liquid; a certificate of deposit (CD) may be liquidated, but you pay an early withdrawal penalty; a house might be your least liquid asset because it takes time to sell.

Money Market Accounts: A money market account is one that usually pays a higher rate of interest than a regular savings account. Money market accounts usually require a higher minimum balance to earn interest, but they also pay higher rates for higher balances.

Mutual Funds: A mutual fund is a professionally managed collection of money from a group of investors. A mutual fund manager invests your money in some combination of various stocks, bonds, and other products. The fund manager determines the best time to buy and sell the products in the fund. By combining your resources with other investors in a mutual fund, you can diversify even a small investment, which should reduce risk.

Risk _versus_ Return: This means that the more risk you take in your investment, the higher the expected return on that investment. However, there is also a higher risk that you might lose the entire amount you invested.

Statement Savings: A statement savings account is an account that earns interest. If you have a statement savings account, you will usually receive a quarterly statement that lists all of your transactions (withdrawals, deposits, fees, and interest earned).

Stocks: When you buy stocks (shares), you become part owner of the company. If the company does well, you might receive periodic dividends. Dividends are part of a company's profits given back to you when you own stock in the company. If the company does poorly, you might lose your money.

Owning a business is an investment as well. Starting a business can be risky. If planned and managed correctly, however, the business has the potential to increase your future financial security.

These are things to think about as you become adults. Purchasing a home and opening a business may be things you want to think about after college or when you enter the work force.

How To Create A Savings Action Plan

Decision Factors

You need to consider three decision factors when selecting the best savings and investment options.

- How much money do you want to accumulate over a certain period of time? You can figure this out by using the Rule of 72. This rule tells you how long it will take for your savings to double in value. It also tells you what interest rate you will need when you know in how many years you want your money to double.

✎ What's It Mean?

U.S. Bonds: Savings bonds are one type of Treasury securities. They are a long-term investment option backed by the full faith and credit of the U.S. government. Purchasing these bonds is an easy way to save small amounts of money, and they are often purchased for a child's education; however, they may be used for any purpose. Savings bonds can be purchased at a financial institution for as little as $25 or through payroll deductions.

U.S. Treasury Securities: U.S. Treasury securities are debt instruments. When you purchase a Treasury security, you are loaning money to the government. Treasury securities are backed by the full faith and credit of the U.S. government, which means the government guarantees interest and principal payments will be made on time. Treasury securities include:

- Savings bonds, which can earn interest for up to 30 years, but can be cashed after six months.

- Treasury bills, which mature in one year or less from their issue date.

- Treasury notes, which mature in more than a year, but not more than 10 years from the issue date.

- Treasury bonds, which mature in more than 10 years from the issue date.

- Treasury bills, notes, and bonds are transferable, which means you can buy or sell them in the securities market. You can buy Treasury bills, notes, and bonds for a minimum of $1,000.

☞ **Remember!!**

Pay Yourself First: Paying yourself first means that when you get a paycheck, you put some of that money in a savings account before you pay your bills or buy things that you want. There are many reasons to pay yourself first. You can learn to manage money better, save money toward identified goals, improve your standard of living, and have money for emergencies.

- How long can you leave your money invested? If you have some money you will not need for several years, you might consider investment options such as stocks, bonds, or mutual funds. On the other hand, if you think you might need access to your money right away, it might be best for you to keep it in a savings account where you have immediate access to it.

- How do you feel about risking your money? As we have seen, if you are not comfortable with risk and cannot afford to lose the money, you might consider depositing your money in an insured financial institution. You will need to shop around for the account that best meets your needs.

Chapter 8

Preparing A Budget

Why Budget?

A good way to start taking control of your financial situation is to develop a budget or personal spending plan. A budget is a step-by-step plan for meeting expenses in a given period of time.

Preparing A Budget

Knowing what your income and expenses are every month will help you take control of your financial situation. Then you'll be able to meet some financial goals you might set for yourself. There are four steps to preparing a budget. They are as follows:

1. Keep track of your daily spending.

2. Determine what your monthly income and expenses are the month before they are due.

3. Find ways to decrease spending.

4. Find ways to increase income.

About This Chapter: Excerpted from "Module 3: Setting Financial Goals," *Money Smart for Young Adults*, a CD-based curriculum developed by the Federal Deposit Insurance Corporation (FDIC), March 2008.

Step 1: Keep Track Of Your Daily Spending

Do you know where your money goes each month?

Setting financial goals helps you plan a budget. If you know what you want to do with your money in the future, it will help you spend wisely now and save where you can.

Consider your goals when planning a budget. If you want to save for a car, consider reducing your cell phone bill and using the extra to put in savings. If you want to buy a new outfit for the prom, you might be able to work an extra hour or two at your job.

No matter what goals you have for your money, they should have these characteristics:

> **☞ Remember!!**
> Budgeting is about choices—choosing how to use your money.

- **Be Realistic:** If you work part-time, you probably won't be able to afford a new car every couple of years.

- **Be Specific:** "I plan/want to save $5,000 for a down payment to buy a new Honda Civic."

- **Have A Time Frame:** "I plan/want to pay off my credit card within the next 12 months."

- **Say What You Want To Do:** "I plan/want to start an automatic deposit savings account with monthly withdrawals from my checking account."

- **Have Milestones:** For example, "My goal is to purchase a bicycle that costs $800 by paying for it without having to borrow money. To do so, I have set up with my employer an automatic transfer of $50 into a savings account for that purpose. Every quarter, I plan to check to see how much money I have."

Step 2: Determine Income And Expenses

The next step to perform in preparing a personal spending plan is to determine your monthly income and expenses. Income is money that comes to you from sources such as these:

- Various jobs or work, like cutting grass or babysitting wages

- Allowances

- Odd jobs

- Interest and dividends

- Other sources, such as tips

Expenses are the items you spend money on each month. Here are some examples:

- Cell phone bill

- Car payment

- Movies, CDs or music downloads, or other entertainment

- Clothes

- Eating out

- Personal items (makeup, cologne, etc.)

- Savings for college or other future purchases

Gross Income Vs. Net Income: When planning a budget, remember that your employer has to subtract certain taxes from your paycheck. The time it takes to meet goals for saving may increase.

✎ What's It Mean?

Gross Income: Gross income is your total income without deductions.

Net Income: Net income is gross income minus deductions such as Social Security and other taxes.

Gross Income – Deductions = Net Income

Deductions usually include federal and state taxes. Social Security taxes are also deducted. But why is so much money taken out for Social Security?

Social Security: Social Security is like an insurance plan. On some pay stubs, it is called FICA, which stands for Federal Insurance Contributions Act. Social Security benefits include retirement—paid every month to eligible retired workers, as early as age 62, and disability—paid every month to eligible workers of all ages who have a severe disability.

If you are 25 or older and are not already receiving Social Security benefits, you will receive a Social Security statement just before your birthday every year. This tells how much you've earned and the Social Security taxes you have paid during your working years. The statement provides estimates of the monthly Social Security retirement, disability, and survivors' benefits you and your family could be eligible to receive.

Expenses: Expenses include everything you pay for in a time period. If you're on your own, they might include housing and car payments, gas, food and utilities, or other things like daycare or insurance.

Expenses could include a car payment, car insurance, and a credit card bill. We will consider these fixed expenses. Savings should also be listed as an expense. This is because you should get into the habit of paying yourself first. You can do this by setting aside some money each month from your paycheck for savings. Set a savings goal that is appropriate for you and save toward it.

> **✎ What's It Mean?**
>
> Fixed Expenses: Expanses that do not change from month to month are fixed.
>
> Flexible Expenses: Expenses might change from month to month, like a heating bill that is lower in May than in December, are flexible.

We have to estimate the amount of flexible expenses we pay each month because we are not always sure what the exact amount will be.

Add up your expenses. Compare the income and expenses totals. Is there enough money to pay bills each month? How would you modify expenses to meet your personal needs?

Step 3: Decrease Spending

Hopefully, your income is greater than your expenses. Remember, if you spend less, you have more money left at the end of the month. This is also called "increasing you cash flow."

What are some ways you can reduce your spending?

Step 4: Find Ways To Increase Income

✔ **Quick Tip**

You should complete a monthly income and expense worksheet. It will help you determine how much money you have coming in, how much is going out, and whether or not you have enough income to pay your bills and expenses each month.

Other than finding a job that pays more, there are other ways to increase your income. You can get a second job—or become a successful entrepreneur. As you enter adulthood and start working, there are also federal tax credits that can bring you additional income.

What are some ways you could increase your income?

Budgeting Tools

Listed are some budgeting tools. They will help you keep spending and savings records that will make it easier for you to carry out your budget. These budgeting tools include the following:

- The monthly payment schedule
- The computer system
- The budged box system
- The spending diary
- The monthly payment calendar

The Monthly Payment Schedule

The monthly payment schedule helps you plan in advance when you will pay your bills and lets you record in advance when you will receive income to pay those bills.

The Computer

Another way to track your budget is the computer.

If you don't want to use paper or you pay bills in cash instead of with a checking account, you can use a computer to keep track of expenses.

On a personal computer, you can create your own spreadsheet to track your income and expenses.

You may also want to purchase a personal finance program. They are available for less than $75. Using one of these programs to manage your finances is relatively simple. Once you set it up, updating information is quick and easy. You should enter transactions frequently so that you always have a good grasp on your financial position.

There are many different ways to track your budget. You can find one that works for you.

Budget Box System

- The budget box is a small box with dividers for each day of the month, with one divider for each day of the month.

- When you receive a bill, check the due date and place it behind the divider that represents the bill's due date.

- As you receive income, pay all bills that are due.

Expense Envelope System

- This tool is useful if you pay your bills in cash each month.

- Make an envelope for each expense category, such as rent, gas, electricity, and food.

- Label the envelope with the name of the category, the amount, and the due date.

- When you receive income, divide it into the amounts to cover the expenses listed on the envelope.

• Pay bills right away so you will not be tempted to spend the money on something else.

Sample Daily Spending Diary Worksheet

Use this budgeting tool to track where your money is going (see Figure 8.1). You are far more likely to save your money when you see how much small, miscellaneous purchases, such as coffee and soda, can add up.

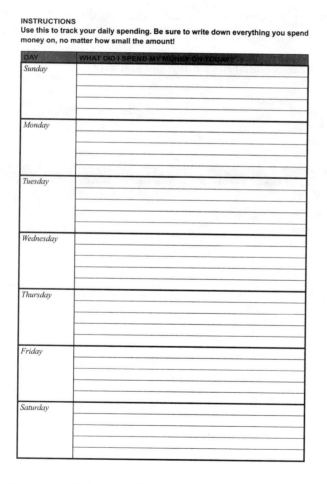

INSTRUCTIONS
Use this to track your daily spending. **Be sure to write down everything you spend money on, no matter how small the amount!**

DAY	WHAT DID I SPEND MY MONEY ON TODAY?
Sunday	
Monday	
Tuesday	
Wednesday	
Thursday	
Friday	
Saturday	

Figure 8.1. Daily Spending Diary. Use this to track your daily spending. Be sure to write down everything you spend money on, no matter now small the amount.

Sample Monthly Payment Calendar

The Monthly Payment Calendar is another way to help you keep a record of your bill payments and due dates (see the sample calendar in Figure 8.2). This tool—in particular—can help you anticipate and plan for expenses and savings. Here's how to use this budgeting tool:

1. Transfer your income sources and amounts from your Income and Expenses Worksheet to the dates income is paid on the Monthly Payment Calendar worksheet.

2. Transfer your expenses to the dates they are due on the Monthly Payment Calendar worksheet.

3. Use different colored ink for income and expenses.

4. Check off each bill as it is paid.

MONTH:

SUN	MON	TUES	WED	THURS	FRI	SAT
1	2 $400 paycheck $25 savings $150 car $25 personal $30 insurance	3 $60 gas/car maintenance	4	5 $25 interest (income)	6 $30 cell phone	7
8	9	10	11	12	13	14
15	16	17	18	19	20 $10 credit card/ loan	21
22	23	24	25	26	27	28 $40 entertainment
29	30	31				

Figure 8.2. Sample Monthly Payment Calendar.

Chapter 9

Banking Basics

What Do Banks Do?

A bank is a business that offers you a safe place to keep your money and uses your deposits to make loans. This business is also called a financial institution. Banks offer many financial services.

Why Keep Money In A Bank?

Many people keep their money in banks. Let's take a look at some reasons.

Safety: Money is safe from theft, loss, and fire.

Convenience: You can get money quickly and easily. Using direct deposit, for example, saves you time and allows you quicker access to your money. Funds that are electronically deposited in your account are available sooner than if you deposited a check.

Cost: Using a bank is probably cheaper than using other businesses to cash your check (check cashing services, for example) or pay bills.

Security: The Federal Deposit Insurance Corporation (FDIC) insures deposits up to the maximum amount allowed by law. This means that if for

About This Chapter: Excerpted from "Module 1: Bank On It," *Money Smart for Young Adults*, a CD-based curriculum developed by the Federal Deposit Insurance Corporation (FDIC), March 2008.

some reason a bank closes and cannot give its customers the money they had in the bank, the FDIC will return the money to the customers.

Financial Future: Building a relationship with a bank establishes a record of paying bills, can help you save money, and is necessary for getting a loan.

♣ **It's A Fact!!**

What Are Banks?

Banks are private, for-profit businesses that offer a variety of services to the public. They provide a place to safely store your money in checking and savings accounts insured by the Federal Deposit Insurance Corporation (FDIC) until you need to take the money out. Banks enable customers to write checks, pay bills, or send money to other people. They also make loans to people and businesses.

Lending money is one of the ways that a bank earns money. And where does the bank get the money to make loans? Mostly, it uses the money that customers have deposited into checking and savings accounts, while ensuring that those depositors can still get their money back when they want it.

"Savings banks" or "savings and loan associations" (also known as "thrift" institutions) are also FDIC insured; their main business usually involves making home loans. To keep things simple, we've used the word "bank" to refer to all of the various types of FDIC-insured banking institutions.

Most but not all banks and thrifts in the U.S. are insured by the FDIC. One way to check whether an institution is FDIC-insured is to call the FDIC toll-free at 877-275-3342.

In addition, you may have heard about credit unions. These are not-for-profit financial institutions that are owned and operated by their members, who are usually people who have something in common, such as the same employer or occupation. You have to become a member of the credit union to keep your money there. Deposits at credit unions are insured by another federal government agency called the National Credit Union Administration.

Source: "What Do Banks Do?" *FDIC Consumer News*, Federal Deposit Insurance Corporation, Summer 2006.

Types Of Financial Institutions

There are three major types of financial institutions:

Bank: A financial institution that is run under federal and state laws and regulations. Banks make loans, pay checks, accept deposits, and provide other financial services.

Credit Union: A non-profit financial institution owned by people who have something in common. You have to become a member of the credit union to keep your money there.

Thrift: A savings bank or savings and loan association that is similar to a bank. Thrifts were created to promote home ownership and must have a majority of their assets in housing-related loans. Although many banks also make home loans, the main function of a thrift is to make home loans.

Opening A Bank Account

A bank account is any account you open at a bank, including checking or savings.

Terms To Know

When you open an account, the bank representative may use some terms you will need to know. They are as follows:

Deposit: A deposit is money you add to your account. It can be in the form of your paycheck, cash, a personal check you may receive from someone, or a cashier's check from another bank.

Deposit Slip: A deposit slip tells the bank how much money you are adding to your account.

Withdrawal: When you make a withdrawal, you are taking money out of your bank account. You do this by writing a check, giving a teller a withdrawal slip, or using an ATM, or automated teller machine, with your debit card.

Balance: Your balance is the amount of money you have in the bank at any given time. Your balance will change whenever you make a deposit or a

♣ It's A Fact!!

You can tell if the Federal Deposit Insurance Corporation (FDIC) insures a bank by the FDIC logo. Most credit unions are insured by the National Credit Union Administration (NCUA). The deposit insurance rules are the same at NCUA-insured credit unions as they are at FDIC-insured banks.

The FDIC has an online tool called the Electronic Deposit Insurance Estimator (EDIE). It lets you calculate the insurance coverage of your accounts at each FDIC-insured institution. You can find EDIE online at http://www.fdic.gov/EDIE.

Source: FDIC, March 2008.

withdrawal. Remember to record all of those in your check register so that you always know your balance.

Fees: Financial institutions charge you fees for different services. For example, you might be charged a monthly maintenance fee for keeping your account open. You might also be charged a penalty fee if you misuse your account, for example, by bouncing a check or taking out more money than you have in it. When this happens, you have overdrawn your account.

Overdraft: An overdraft occurs when you withdraw more money than you have. For example, if you have $50 in your account and you write a check for $60 to pay a bill, then your balance will be -$10. The bank will charge fees as a penalty, sometimes $30 or more, which are also charged to your bank account. You must deposit money to correct this and keep your balance positive.

How Do I Open And Use An Account?

Opening and maintaining a bank account is not as difficult as you might think. There are four basic things you have to do:

• Open the account and go through account verification

- Make deposits and withdrawals
- Record interest and fees
- Keep track of your balance

Account Verification

The first thing you need to do to open a bank account is go through a process called account verification. The bank wants to make sure that you will be a responsible bank account customer. If you did not handle a bank account you had in the past responsibly, they may not want to risk allowing you to open an account now. The bank also needs to make sure that you are who you say you are.

The bank will request your name, address, date of birth, and Social Security number (SSN) or individual taxpayer identification number (ITIN). It will then verify your identity, such as by requesting your state-issued identification card, driver's license, passport, or perhaps even your student ID card. It may ask to see more than one piece of ID—this is for the protection of both you and the bank. Since practices vary, ask your bank what type of identification you need.

Depositing Money

When you open a bank account, you put money into your account. That is called a deposit. Whenever you add money to your account, you must fill out a deposit slip. A deposit slip tells the bank how much money you are adding to your account.

Depending on what you deposit—cash, a payroll check, or a check drawn on an out-of-state bank—you may not have immediate use of the funds. The bank must first make sure there are funds at the originating bank (the bank of the person who wrote the check) to cover your check.

You may ask the bank when you can use the money you deposited. Also, even though the bank gives you access to the funds you deposited doesn't mean the check cleared the other bank. If the check you deposited bounces, the bank will deduct the money it made available from your account.

Deposit And Non-Deposit Accounts

Bank accounts that allow you to add money to the account are called deposit accounts. Checking and savings accounts are two examples of deposit products.

Checking

The financial institution takes the money from your account and pays it to the person named on the check.

The financial institution makes a monthly record of the deposits and withdrawals made available to you either by mail or online. This is called a bank statement.

> ### ✎ What's It Mean?
>
> Checking Account: A checking account is an account that lets you write checks to pay bills or to buy goods.
>
> Savings Account: A savings account is an account that earns interest. You generally cannot write checks on a savings account.
>
> Source: FDIC, March 2008.

Savings Accounts

You can often open a savings account with a few dollars, but you might pay a monthly fee if the balance is below a certain amount.

The bank will generally help you keep track of your account by sending you a statement.

It is a good idea to compare the rules of the different accounts. For example, banks might require you to have a certain balance to open an account, earn interest, or avoid fees. This is usually called a minimum balance.

ATM And Debit Cards

When you open an account, you will probably be given the option to have an ATM card or a debit card. Both types of cards give you access to your account funds when you need them. You can get cash at an ATM or use them at most retailers. ATM and debit cards are similar, but there is one basic difference.

An ATM card allows you to make deposits to and withdrawals from checking and savings. You can usually also check your account balance, print statements, and transfer funds between accounts. Some ATM cards can be used in stores that accept ATMs in your bank's network. It works just like a debit card, but is not as widely available. When you choose an ATM card to make a purchase, the retailer may ask you to sign a receipt instead of inputting your PIN (personal identification number). Ask your bank if there are additional fees for signing a receipt instead of using a PIN number.

A debit card, also known as a check card, card displays a MasterCard or VISA logo. It has all the functions of an ATM card and also allows you to pay for goods and services at locations that accept MasterCard or VISA credit cards. It looks like a credit card but it isn't. Your purchases are immediately withdrawn from your account.

Additional Banking Services

Banks provide additional services with some deposit accounts. It is important to keep track of the fees charged, if any.

Banks might offer these services:

- Direct deposit
- Money order
- Telephone and online banking
- Automated Teller Machine (ATM)
- Money transfer
- Debit card
- Stored value cards
- Loans

♣ It's A Fact!!
Stored Value Cards

Stored value cards are worth a specific amount. They can be confused with ATM or debit cards. Common examples of stored value cards are gift cards from stores or public transportation cards. Some banks also issue stored value cards that you can use at most retailers. You do not have to have a bank account to use them.

You pay a certain amount of money to give the card value, like a gift card from a store. As you use it, the value declines toward 0. Then you add funds as you need them. Usually you can do this with cash at most banks.

Source: FDIC, March 2008.

Your Information Is Private

Privacy notices explain how the company handles and shares your personal financial information. For example, they explain what information the company collects and how you can possibly limit the company from sharing your information with others.

Privacy notices also explain how your personal financial information is protected. You will receive an initial privacy notice when you open your account and then every year thereafter.

Financial institutions may share your information with other companies to offer you other products and services. Federal privacy laws give you the right to stop or "opt out" of some sharing of your personal financial information.

Federal law requires financial institutions to keep your personal financial information private. The general public does not have access to your personal financial information.

Important Bank Employees

A financial institution has people who can help you with different banking services.

Understanding the jobs of these bank workers will allow you to know who you should talk to when you go to the bank.

The primary people in the bank who you should know are the customer service representative, teller, loan officer; and branch manager.

If you do not know who to talk to, ask for help. Someone will take you to the right person. Always ask questions until you are clear on all the information and do not sign anything you do not understand. Ask for written information to take home to review.

Chapter 10
Electronic Banking

On his way home last Friday night, John Jones realized that he had no cash for the weekend. The bank was closed, but John had his bank debit card and the code to use it. He inserted the card into an automated teller machine outside the front door of the bank; then, using a number keypad, he entered his code and pressed the buttons for a withdrawal of $50. John's cash was dispensed automatically from the machine, and his bank account was electronically debited for the $50 cash withdrawal.

John's debit card is just one way to use electronic fund transfer (EFT) systems that allow payment between parties by substituting an electronic signal for cash or checks.

Are we heading for a checkless society? Probably not. But making a dent in the large number of paper checks in the country's banking system is clearly one advantage to electronic banking.

Electronic Fund Transfers (EFT) In Operation

The national payment mechanism moves money between accounts in a fast, paperless way. These are some examples of EFT systems in operation:

About This Chapter: Text in this chapter is from "Electronic Fund Transfers," Federal Reserve Board (www.federalreserve.gov), August 16, 2007.

Automated Teller Machines (ATMs): Consumers can do their banking without the assistance of a teller, as John Jones did to get cash, or to make deposits, pay bills, or transfer funds from one account to another electronically. These machines are used with a debit or EFT card and a code, which is often called a personal identification number or "PIN."

Point-Of-Sale (POS) Transactions: Some debit or EFT cards (sometimes referred to as check cards) can be used when shopping to allow the transfer of funds from the consumer's account to the merchant's. To pay for a purchase, the consumer presents an EFT card instead of a check or cash. Money is taken out of the consumer's account and put into the merchant's account electronically.

Preauthorized Transfers: This is a method of automatically depositing to or withdrawing funds from an individual's account, when the account holder authorizes the bank or a third party (such as an employer) to do so. For example, consumers can authorize direct electronic deposit of wages, social security, or dividend payments to their accounts. Or they can authorize financial institutions to make regular, ongoing payments of insurance, mortgage, utility, or other bills.

Telephone Transfers: Consumers can transfer funds from one account to another—from savings to checking, for example—or can order payment of specific bills by phone.

The Electronic Fund Transfer Act

The Electronic Fund Transfer Act answers several basic questions consumers have about using EFT services.

A check contains information that authorizes a bank to withdraw a certain amount of money from one person's account and pay that amount to another person. Most consumer questions center on the fact that EFT systems transmit the information without the paper:

- What record will I have of my transactions?
- How do I correct errors?
- What if someone steals money from my account?

- What about mail solicitations for debit cards?

- Do I have to use EFT services?

Here are the answers the EFT Act gives to consumer questions about these systems.

What record will I have of my transactions?

A canceled check is permanent proof that a payment has been made. What proof of payment is available with EFT services?

♣ It's A Fact!!

Today, the cost of moving checks through the banking system is estimated to be about $3.00 per check, including the costs of paper, printing, and mailing. Moreover, checks— except your own check presented at your own bank—take time to cash: time for delivery, endorsement, presentation to another person's bank, and winding through various stations in the check-clearing system. Technology now can lower the costs of the payment mechanism (to about $1.50 per transaction) and make it more efficient and convenient by reducing paperwork.

If you use an ATM to withdraw money or make deposits or a POS terminal to pay for a purchase, you can get a written receipt, much like a sales receipt you get with a cash purchase, showing the amount of the transfer, the date it was made, and other information. This receipt is your record of transfers initiated at an electronic terminal.

Your periodic bank statement must also show electronic transfers to and from your account, including those made with debit cards, by a preauthorized arrangement, or under a telephone transfer plan. The statement will also name the party to whom payment has been made and show any fees for EFT services (or the total amount charged for account maintenance) and your opening and closing balances.

What about loss or theft?

It's important to be aware of the potential risk in using an EFT card, which differs from the risk on a credit card.

On lost or stolen credit cards, your loss is limited to $50 per card. On an EFT card, your liability for an unauthorized withdrawal can vary:

♣ It's A Fact!!

How do I correct errors?

The way to report errors is somewhat different with EFT services than it is with credit cards. But as with credit cards, financial institutions must investigate and promptly correct any EFT errors that you report.

If you believe there has been an error in an electronic fund transfer relating to your account:

1. Write or call your financial institution immediately if possible, but no later than 60 days from the date the first statement that you think shows an error was mailed to you. Give your name and account number and explain why you believe there is an error, what kind of error, and the dollar amount and date in question. If you call, you may be asked to send this information in writing within 10 business days.

2. The financial institution must promptly investigate an error and resolve it within 45 days. For errors involving new accounts (opened in the last 30 days), POS transactions, and foreign transactions, the institution may take up to 90 days to investigate the error. However, if the financial institution takes longer than 10 business days to complete its investigation, generally it must put back into your account the amount in question while it finishes the investigation. For new accounts, the financial institution may take up to 20 business days to credit your account for the amount you think is in error.

3. The financial institution must notify you of the results of its investigation. If there was an error, the institution must correct it promptly, for example, by making a recredit final.

If it finds no error, the financial institution must explain in writing why it believes no error occurred and let you know that it has deducted any amount recredited during the investigation. You may ask for copies of documents relied on in the investigation.

- Your loss is limited to $50 if you notify the financial institution within two business days after learning of loss or theft of your card or code.

- But you could lose as much as $500 if you do not tell the card issuer within two business days after learning of loss or theft.

- If you do not report an unauthorized transfer that appears on your statement within 60 days after the statement is mailed to you, you risk unlimited loss on transfers made after the 60-day period. That means you could lose all the money in your account plus your maximum overdraft line of credit, if any.

Example: On Monday, John's debit card and PIN were stolen. On Tuesday, the thief withdrew $250, all the money John had in his checking account. Five days later, the thief withdrew another $500, triggering John's overdraft line of credit. John did not realize his card was stolen until he received his bank statement, showing withdrawals of $750 he did not make. He called the bank right away. John's liability is $50.

Now suppose that when John got his bank statement he didn't look at it and didn't call the bank. Seventy days after the statement was mailed to John, the thief withdrew another $1,000, reaching the limit on John's line of credit. In this case, John would be liable for $1,050 ($50 for transfers before the end of the 60 days; $1,000 for transfers made more than 60 days after the statement was mailed).

What about mail solicitations for debit cards?

A financial institution may send you an EFT card that is valid for use only if you ask for one, or to replace or renew an expiring card. The financial institution must also give you the following information about your rights and responsibilities:

- A notice of your liability in case the card is lost or stolen

- A telephone number for reporting loss or theft of the card or an unauthorized transfer

- A description of its error resolution procedures

- The kinds of electronic fund transfers you may make and any limits on the frequency or dollar amounts of such transfers

- Any charge by the institution for using EFT services

- Your right to receive records of electronic fund transfers

- How to stop payment of a pre-authorized transfer

- The financial institution's liability to you for any failure to make or to stop transfers

- The conditions under which a financial institution will give information to third parties about your account

Generally, you must also get advance notice of any change in the account that would increase your costs or liability, or would limit transfers. A financial institution may send you a card that you did not request only if the card is not valid for use. An unsolicited card can be validated only at your request and only after the institution makes sure that you are the person whose name is on the card. It must also be sent with instructions on how to dispose of an unwanted card.

Do I have to use EFT?

The EFT Act forbids a creditor from requiring you to repay a loan or other credit by EFT, except in the case of overdraft checking plans. With some exceptions, your employer or a government agency can require you to receive your salary or a government benefit by electronic transfer. However, you have the right to choose the financial institution that will receive your funds.

Special Questions About Preauthorized Plans

How will I know that a preauthorized deposit has been made?

There are various ways in which you may be notified. Notice may be given by your employer (or whoever is sending the funds) that the deposit has been sent to your financial institution. Otherwise, a financial institution may provide notice when it has received the credit or will send you a notice only when it has not received the funds. Financial institutions also have the option of giving you a telephone number you can call to check on a preauthorized deposit.

If the payments I preauthorize vary in amount from month to month, how will I know how much will be transferred out of my account?

You have the right to be notified of all varying payments at least 10 days in advance. Or you may choose to specify a range of amounts and to be told only when a transfer falls outside that range. You may also choose to be told only when a transfer differs by a certain amount from the previous payment to the same company.

Do the EFT Act protections apply to all preauthorized plans?

No. They do not apply to automatic transfers from your account to the institution that holds your account or vice versa. For example, they do not apply to automatic payments made on a mortgage held by the financial institution where you have your EFT account. The EFT Act also does not apply to automatic transfers among your accounts at one financial institution.

♣ It's A Fact!!
How do I stop a preauthorized payment?

You may stop any preauthorized payment by calling or writing the financial institution, but your order must be received at least three business days before the payment date. Written confirmation of a telephone notice to stop payment may be required. You should also contact the merchant or organization you authorized to debit your account.

Chapter 11

Avoiding Costly Banking Mistakes

Here are clues to preventing expensive errors with your checking account, credit card, or other financial services. After all, this isn't play money!

To err is human... and sometimes it can be expensive. That's the case for many consumers who have to pay fees and penalties because of mistakes they've made when using their checking account, credit card, or other banking services.

The Federal Deposit Insurance Corporation (FDIC) *Consumer News* wants to help you make smarter decisions and avoid some of these mistakes. So, compiled here is a list of some of the more common and costly slip-ups. Follow these tips and you can enjoy a more satisfying banking relationship and keep more of your cash.

Not Checking Up On Your Checking Account

Many people write checks and use their debit card without paying attention to their account balance. The results can be costly and may include fees from $20 to $35 for each "bounced" check you write when you don't have enough money in your account. Similar fees can be imposed if you overdraw

About This Chapter: Text in this chapter is from "Avoiding Costly Banking Mistakes: No Trivial Pursuit," *FDIC Consumer News*, Federal Deposit Insurance Corporation, Fall 2006.

your account using your debit card at the ATM. There may also be fees if your checking account goes below a required minimum balance. And, if you fail to spot fraudulent transactions, fixing those can be costly and time consuming.

Your lack of attention could make a bad situation worse if fees are assessed for several days or even months. "Account holders can get very frustrated when they suddenly find out that multiple checks and payments have been returned, and a fee has been assessed for each one," says Eloy Villafranca, a Community Affairs Officer with the FDIC.

Villafranca recalled a situation involving a consumer who "was confident that her bank statements were correct so she didn't open them for six months."

✔ Quick Tip
How To Sidestep A Misstep

Comparison shop for the best deals that fit your needs. Look at different types of accounts offered by your bank and a few competitors, and be sure to factor in the fees you're most likely to incur.

Read all the disclosures, from the highlighted details to the fine print. Before you open the account, know the features, fees, and limitations so you can prevent misunderstandings and costly mistakes.

Monitor your accounts. Promptly review bank statements and other mailings. Consider reviewing your account activity online or by phone instead of waiting for statements to arrive in the mail. Look for what can—or did—trigger fees and penalties, so you can avoid unnecessary costs in the future. Contact your financial institution immediately if there's a problem.

Keep good records. Save copies of account descriptions, contracts, and important receipts, which can come in handy if there's a question or a dispute.

Unfortunately for her, a recurring, electronic payment she thought had been stopped continued to be charged against her account, and her account balance was lower than she thought. "As she wrote checks month after month," Villafranca explains, "she was being hit with charges for insufficient funds."

Be aware that if bounced checks are not repaid in a timely fashion they may become part of your record. That could make it difficult to get a merchant to accept your checks. And if your account is closed by the bank because of repeated problems with insufficient funds that you do not repay, you may have difficulty opening a new account elsewhere.

How You Can Avoid Unnecessary Costs

Keep your check register up to date. Deduct for all withdrawals—not only for checks but also for ATM transactions, bank fees, and debit card purchases. Do not rely on your ATM receipt for balance information because it may not reflect outstanding checks or debit card transactions.

Promptly compare your check register with your bank statement to look for errors or unauthorized transactions. Open and review your monthly statement as soon as it arrives in the mail or check your account information more frequently online or by telephone.

"Once I used my debit card to pay an $11 dry-cleaning bill and I was inadvertently charged $1,100," Villafranca says. "This could have caused a number of problems had I not gone online to check my account activity later in the day to pay a bill and noticed the error. I had the funds credited back to my account the next day." (Note: The federal Electronic Fund Transfer Act protects you against billing errors and unauthorized transactions by debit card and other electronic payment methods, but you must notify your bank within 60 days of the mailing of the account statement on which the transaction appears.)

Take additional precautions to avoid fees for insufficient funds. For instance, make sure you have enough money in your account before you write a big check, use your debit card, or arrange for an automatic payment. Also remember that, under federal rules that allow banking institutions to put a temporary "hold" on certain deposits, you may have to wait from one to five

---

✤ It's A Fact!!
How The FDIC Can Help You Avoid Costly Mistakes

- See consumer information on the FDIC website at http://www.fdic.gov/quicklinks/consumers.html.

- Read their quarterly newsletter *FDIC Consumer News*. Find back issues online at http://www.fdic.gov/consumers/consumer/news and sign up for a free e-mail subscription service at http://www.fdic.gov/about/subscriptions/index.html.

- Get answers to questions by phone (toll-free 877-ASK-FDIC or 877-275-3342) or by e-mail (start at http://www2.fdic.gov/starsmail/index.html).

---

business days (in most situations) before you can withdraw funds deposited into your account, and longer in other circumstances (such as deposits over $5,000 or if your account has been repeatedly overdrawn).

Not Considering Fees When Opening A Bank Account

A high interest rate or annual percentage yield (APY) on a checking account is definitely an attention grabber. But that great rate shouldn't divert your attention from fees that can significantly reduce, if not wipe out, your earnings. Examples include monthly fees for going below a minimum balance, monthly or quarterly "inactivity" fees if you've had no deposits or withdrawals for a certain time period, and annual service charges on individual retirement accounts (IRAs). "For small accounts, these fees can make a big difference in the total return," cautions Howard Herman, an FDIC Consumer Affairs Specialist.

For example, a $2,000 IRA with an APY of five percent and a $20 annual service fee "will earn $100 interest after a year but, after deducting the service fee, your actual return is four percent, not five percent," Herman says. "Under federal law, fees are not factored into APY calculations, so consumers are on their own when it comes to determining whether fees will have a negative impact."

To get the best deal possible, first think about how you plan to use the account and how much you expect to keep on deposit, then compare different accounts at a few different institutions. Do the math as best you can, figuring your interest earnings after a year and then subtract the estimated fees for services or a low balance based on your expected use of the account. Sometimes an account that pays no interest can be a better deal than an interest-bearing account that's heavy with fees you are likely to pay.

Also remember that just because an account is advertised as "free" or "no cost" doesn't mean you'll pay nothing. Under Federal Reserve Board rules, an account may be described as free even if certain fees are charged, such as for ATM withdrawals or overdrafts.

Paying Your Credit Card Bill Late

Don't assume it's okay to be late with your card payment just because the minimum payment due is fairly small. In fact, you can be hit with fees or penalties any time you miss a payment deadline, even if it's only by a day.

You can expect a late-payment fee of about $30 or more. You may also face a major hike in your interest rate—often to between 29 and 35 percent—on this credit card and possibly other cards or loans, especially if your credit record shows other signs of risk. And if you're late paying by about a month or more, you might find your credit score reduced, which can make it harder or more expensive to get a new loan or even a new job or insurance (because prospective employers and insurers can review credit histories when deciding on applications).

What can you do to avoid or minimize late payment penalties—beyond just paying your bill on time? First, closely review your card member agreement so you know what may happen if you pay late. "The wrong time to question the consequences of a late payment is after you've missed the deadline," says Kirk Daniels, an FDIC Supervisory Consumer Affairs Specialist.

Also, if you haven't yet missed the deadline but you can't mail the payment on time, consider either making an online payment at your card issuer's website at least a day or two before the due date, or paying by phone by providing bank account information to authorize an electronic fund transfer from your checking account. "Even though there may be a small service charge for these options, it will likely be less than a late-payment fee," Daniels notes.

✔ **Quick Tip**

Words of advice: If you're short on cash, it's better to pay at least the minimum amount due on your credit card on time, rather than withhold payment entirely. And if you do pay late but it's a first-time or rare occurrence that was caused by unusual circumstances, call your card issuer immediately and ask what, if anything, they may be willing to do as a courtesy to a good customer.

Paying As Little As Possible On Your Credit Card Bill Each Month

It sounds like a good idea to pay your credit card company as little as possible each month so you can keep more money to spend on other things. But the reality is that the long-term costs of this strategy can be staggering.

"If you use a credit card to make a major purchase and each month you pay back only the minimum amount you owe, not only will it take you a very long time to pay off the balance but the total interest and fees can sometimes double the cost of what you purchased," says Janet Kincaid, FDIC Senior Consumer Affairs Officer.

For example, suppose you buy a computer for $1,000 and you only pay back the minimum required, which we'll say is $20 a month. At an Annual Percentage Rate (APR) of 18 percent, that $1,000 computer will cost you $2,931 and take more than 19 years to pay off, which is about 15 years longer than you'll probably own the computer.

To minimize your costs, pay as much as you can on your credit card each month—pay the entire balance, if possible—to avoid interest charges. If you can't pay most or all of your credit card bill, try to pay as much above the minimum as possible. "Finding a way to pay a little more each month can make a noticeable difference in reducing your interest costs," Kincaid says. Using our previous example, raising your monthly payment from $20 to $50 will bring the total cost of a $1,000 purchase (including the finance charges) to $1,198, allowing you to pay off the debt in just two years.

However, if all you can afford to pay back each month is the minimum amount, pay that—and pay it on time—to avoid late fees and a bad mark on your credit record, which in itself can be costly.

Signing Up For A New Credit Card Without Understanding The Costs

You've probably seen or heard of all kinds of incentives to convince people to apply for a new credit card or switch from one card to another. Among them: "zero-percent interest" for a certain amount of time on new purchases or a balance transferred from a competitor's card, "no payments" on purchases until the next year, "earn more points" for free travel, or get a free T-shirt if you apply for a new card. Sounds great, but these freebies could end up being expensive, especially if you don't follow the rules of the new card.

"While there are good deals out there on new credit cards, it pays to shop around for a card that best fits your circumstances," says Kincaid. "Also be sure to read the highlighted disclosures as well as the fine print because an uninformed decision can be costly."

For example, let's say you choose a card with a "grace period" (a certain number of days you have to pay the balance before incurring interest or fees) but, after a few months, you decide not to pay your bill in full. With some cards, the issuer might retroactively charge interest on the balance from the previous month, thus eliminating the earlier grace period.

If you get a new credit card promoting zero-percent interest on new purchases and you don't pay off the entire balance by the due date (typically after six to 18 months), you may be charged interest on all your original purchase amounts—not just on your remaining balance—retroactive to the original purchase date. The resulting costs could be more than if you had used a card without a zero-percent offer.

Or, suppose you agree to your card company's offer to "upgrade" to a new version of your card and you don't take the time to study the new card's restrictions or fees, as sometimes happens when customers quickly say "yes" to an offer from a customer service representative over the phone. You might be giving up a better deal you had with your old card. "Make sure the upgrades are what you need and will use," says Kincaid.

Finally, some people transfer a balance from one credit card company to another to take advantage of a low interest rate (say, 2.9 percent) or even zero-percent interest on the balance transferred, but they may end up paying more in other charges than if they had stayed with their old card.

♣ **It's A Fact!!**

What can be bad about signing up for new cards only to take advantage of an introductory offer or even a free T-shirt? Well, you can reduce your credit score and make it costlier to get a loan because each credit card represents money that you could borrow—even if you intend to rarely use the card. To lenders, too many cards in your wallet may mean you could have problems repaying a loan, and that's a reason to charge you a higher interest rate.

"Repeatedly signing up for new cards—even to keep introductory rates going—can give lenders the impression that you may be desperate for funds," says FDIC's Eloy Villafranca. "Unfortunately, some people only realize that they've lowered their credit score after they apply for a mortgage and are penalized with a higher interest rate."

Not Reviewing Your Credit Report

Many people never or rarely look at their credit report (a history of paying debts and other bills) or their credit scores (numerical ratings of credit reports) until they apply for a loan or they have been denied a loan. By then, it's often too late because inaccurate or missing information in your credit report could raise your borrowing costs or cause delays when you're in a rush to make a major purchase, like a new home.

Example: The home of your dreams just went on the market, so you apply for a mortgage. You're sure your credit record is in great shape so there's no need to worry about getting a good deal on a loan. But then you're quoted a rate on a mortgage loan that is much higher than you expected or, worse yet, you are denied a loan! What went wrong? It could be that your credit report contained incorrect information. By the time you can get your report corrected and your credit score increased, it's possible that your dream house was sold to someone else.

Solve this problem by taking advantage of your right under federal law to obtain one free copy of your credit report each year from each of the three nationwide credit bureaus (Equifax, Experian, and TransUnion). Periodically review your report and correct any omissions or errors, especially before you apply for a home loan or seek some other benefit where your credit report could affect the outcome. Doing so can boost your credit score enough to save you hundreds of dollars each year in interest or other charges.

"Some people who get 'subprime' loans, which cost a lot more than most loans, would qualify for lower-cost prime-rate loans if errors in their credit reports were corrected," says Mira Marshall, an FDIC Senior Policy Analyst on consumer protection issues.

Another benefit of reviewing your credit report is that you'll be better prepared to protect yourself from "predatory" lenders who try to trick cash-strapped consumers into accepting high-cost home loans. "Some people who don't know they have a good credit history can be deceived into believing an expensive loan is their only choice," Marshall explains.

Kincaid added that if you apply for insurance or a job, the insurance company or future employer can review your credit report as part of its consideration of your financial responsibility. "You wouldn't want to lose a good job opportunity or a low premium on an insurance policy because of some erroneous information on your credit report," she adds.

For more information about ordering your free report, go to http://www.annualcreditreport.com or call toll-free 877-322-8228.

Getting A Nontraditional Mortgage Without Understanding The Costs

In addition to "traditional" mortgages, which are typically fixed- or adjustable-rate loans for 15 or 30 years, many lenders now offer other mortgages with new features that may be good options for some borrowers but costly mistakes for others.

Nontraditional mortgages generally enable borrowers to lower their monthly payments in the early years in exchange for larger payments later on. An "interest-only mortgage" lets you pay back only the interest on the loan for several years without paying any principal (the amount of money you borrowed). A "payment-option loan" allows you to decide how much to pay from one month to the next based on choices that range from a full monthly payment (what you'd normally pay in principal and interest with a traditional mortgage) to a minimum payment that may not even cover the interest due. Any shortfall is added to your loan balance. Payment-option mortgages usually have adjustable interest rates.

What are the biggest concerns with these types of loans? "Borrowers may experience payment shock if they aren't prepared for increased payments after an initial or promotional period," says Marshall.

For example, let's say a family borrows $200,000 using a 30-year, payment-option mortgage, with a five-year promotional period. For the first five years, they pay only the minimum amount due of $650 a month. That payment isn't enough to cover the interest actually being charged. The unpaid interest during those five years—figure about $16,000—is added to the loan balance. "At the end of the five years, the borrower will be paying the loan at a higher interest rate and on a larger loan amount," Marshall says. In this example, starting in the sixth year, the family's minimum monthly payment will surge to about $1,600, more than double what they were paying before.

To protect yourself from unexpected costs with a nontraditional loan, be sure to ask the lender these two questions before agreeing to anything:

- What will my monthly payments be at different times during the life of the loan? Find out when your payments will or could change, and how much higher the payments would be under different scenarios, such as if you only send in the minimum amount due in the early years or if interest rates go up dramatically. Think carefully about getting a nontraditional loan if you have doubts about your ability to pay more than the minimum payments in the future.

- Does the mortgage have a prepayment penalty? If you pay off some mortgages early (say, within the first three years) by refinancing or selling your home, you may be charged a penalty that can amount to several thousand dollars. Some lenders offer loans with a prepayment penalty at lower interest rates than similar loans without the penalty. These can be a good deal if you don't expect to move within the penalty period, but triggering the penalty can make it more expensive to refinance the loan and can reduce your proceeds if you sell the house.

Also think twice before applying for another nontraditional mortgage that involves little or no documentation of income or assets. While these loans can save you time and are attractive if your source of income is unpredictable, the lender generally charges a higher interest rate. "If you have income that's easy to document, such as regular statements from your employer or a monthly Social Security payment, it's probably not worth paying extra over the long term of the loan just to save a few days during the application period," Marshall says.

Chapter 12

Managing Your Savings Account

Why Start A Savings Account

So, if you haven't had a savings account before, why should you start one? Here are a few reasons:

- Save to pay for the college tuition bill.

- Saving for a major purchase, such as a car, home, or vacation.

- To have an emergency fund when unexpected expenses arise or to help pay expenses if you're unable to work.

- Overdraft protection for a checking account.

- Opportunity to earn interest.

- Planning for the future, such as retirement.

Your reasons for starting a savings account might be completely different. But, no matter why you decide to save your money, choosing to open a savings account is a much better, and safer, option than just putting your money in a shoe box under your bed.

About This Chapter: Reprinted with permission from "Managing Your Savings Account," © 2008 ultimatemoneyskills.com, sponsored by Bank of America and powered by Making It Count.

Types Of Savings Accounts

While many banks might offer a variety of different savings options, most will offer three basic kinds. As you are deciding which kind of account you want, ask yourself how much money you want to save and how often you want access to that money. Then do some comparison shopping, paying special attention to the fees and interest rates associated with each account.

> ♣ **It's A Fact!!**
> Savings accounts are one of the most common bank accounts, and for many people, their first bank account is a savings account.
>
> Source: © 2008 ultimatemoneyskills.com, sponsored by Bank of America and powered by Making It Count.

Basic Savings Accounts

This is probably the most common type of savings account, and the simplest to use. You can usually open a basic or regular savings account, sometimes referred to as a "passbook account," with a small amount of money.

DATE	DESCRIPTION	DEPOSIT(+)	WITHDRAWAL(-)	INT. CREDITED	$ BALANCE	
4/29	Starting Balance				400	00
5/2	Deposit: Pay Check	50 00			400	00
					+50	00
5/16	Deposit: Pay Check	25 00			450	00
					+25	00
5/26	Transfer to Checking		100 00		475	00
					-100	00
5/30	Deposit: Pay Check	25 00			375	00
					+25	00
6/1	Interest Credited			80	400	00
					+80	
					400	80

Figure 12.1. Sample Savings Register (Source: © 2008 ultimatemoneyskills.com, sponsored by Bank of America and powered by Making It Count.)

They will typically have no minimum balance requirement, or a low one, and they will provide you with easy access to your money, though you might be limited to how many withdrawals you can make per month without being charged a fee. This type of savings account often offers a low interest rate, so if you're looking for a higher return on your money, you might want to investigate another type of savings account or look into investing.

♣ It's A Fact!!

It's Amazing:
How A Small Savings Account Can Get Big Over Time

People who put even a small amount of money into a savings account as often as they can and leave it untouched for years may be amazed at how big the account grows. The reason? A combination of saving as much as possible on a regular basis and the impact of interest payments (what the financial world calls "the miracle of compounding").

Here's how you can slowly build a large savings account and experience the miracle of compounding. Let's say you put money into a savings account that pays you interest every month. After the first month, the interest payment will be calculated based on the money you put in. But the next time the bank pays you interest, it will calculate the amount based on your original deposit plus the interest you received the previous month. Later, that larger, combined amount will earn more interest, and after many years it becomes a much larger sum of money. The earnings are called compound interest. You can earn even more in compound interest if you make deposits regularly and stretch to put in as much as you can and leave it untouched. An example would be a savings account started with $50 and earning interest at a rate of 3.5 percent each month. If you add just $10 each month, the account can grow nicely to $714 after five years. If you instead put in a slightly higher amount—$15 each month—you'd have a balance of $1,042 after five years. But if you had increased your deposits to $50 a month, those extra dollars plus the compounding of interest would give you a balance of $3,333 after five years.

Source: From "It's Amazing: How a Small Savings Account Can Get Big Over Time," *FDIC Consumer News*, Federal Deposit Insurance Corporation (FDIC), Summer 2006.

☞ Remember!!

Remember that the more money you deposit, and the longer you keep it in your account, the more you'll earn from interest.

Source: © 2008 ultimatemoneyskills.com, sponsored by Bank of America and powered by Making It Count.

Money Market Accounts

With a money market account, you will receive a higher interest rate than you would with a basic savings account, but you will also have to keep a higher minimum balance (the amount differs from bank to bank). You will still have easy access to the funds in your account, though the number of withdrawals you can make will probably be limited. In addition, you may have the ability to write checks, but the number you are allowed to write will also probably be limited.

CDs (Certificates Of Deposit)

This type of savings account is a little different because you have to leave your money in the account for a specific amount of time, which varies by bank and type of CD, before you can have access to it. If you take money out of a CD before its maturity date, you will likely have to pay a penalty. CDs will also offer a higher interest rate, which will be higher than other types of savings accounts, and will often be fixed. Because of this, CDs are also considered a simple and straightforward form of investing.

Interest Rates

One of the most important factors you'll want to consider when opening a savings account is the interest rate you'll receive and how that interest is paid. Interest rates can vary greatly, depending on the bank and type of account, so research rates at several banks before making your final decision.

Interest on savings accounts is typically compounded, which means the interest is added to the account periodically (monthly, for example), so you earn interest on the interest.

So, how does this work? Let's say you open a savings account that has a 2% interest rate with $500, and you deposit $50 each month. After six months, you'll have earned $6.75 in interest. After a year, you'll have earned $16.50, and after a year and a half, you'll have earned $29.25.

Accessing Funds In Your Account

There are a few ways you can make deposits to and/or withdrawals from your savings account. Keep in mind that, unlike with checking accounts, it's in your best interest to make as few withdrawals as possible so that you can earn more interest and avoid fees your bank might charge.

Deposit/Withdrawal Slip

Usually when you open a savings account, no matter the kind, the bank will give you a book of deposit/withdrawal slips. These forms can be used to move money in and out of your account and will most often be used when you're doing in-person banking at your local branch. Depending on your bank, the slips may look different.

If you're making a withdrawal, the form you use may look a lot like a check.

Figure 12.2. Sample Withdrawal Slip (Source: © 2008 ultimatemoneyskills.com, sponsored by Bank of America and powered by Making It Count.)

ATM/Debit Card

An ATM card allows you to deposit and remove money from your account through an ATM machine. Unlike the debit card you might receive with a checking account, which can be used like a credit card, ATM cards usually don't give you the ability to make store purchases directly. Most banks will offer you a free ATM card with a basic savings account. Just ask yourself whether you'll be tempted to take money out of the account needlessly if it's too convenient to get it.

If you open a money market account, you might also receive a debit card. Debit cards look like credit cards (they will have a Visa or MasterCard logo on them), and they are accepted anywhere credit cards are accepted. You can use debit cards to withdraw money or make purchases without accumulating interest because the money comes directly from your account.

Because of the convenience of using your ATM or Debit card, it's very important that you keep track of how much money you deposit to and withdraw from your account.

Automatic Deposit And Transferring Funds

This is a great way to make sure that you're regularly depositing money into your savings account. There are a couple of ways you might want to have money automatically deposited into your account. One way is to have your paycheck directly deposited into your savings account each month. If you'd rather not deposit your entire paycheck, many banks will allow you to have part of your paycheck deposited into your checking account and part of it deposited into your savings account. Many people find that using direct deposit is the easiest way to handle their paychecks. Direct deposit is usually set up through your employer and will require you to fill out a form and supply them with a voided check or deposit slip so that direct deposit can be set up. Once it's active, your paycheck, or a portion of it, will go directly into your specified account(s) each pay period.

You can also choose to have funds from one account, like your checking account, transferred into your savings account. Of course, the accounts all need to be at the same bank. This is also helpful if you choose to use your savings account as a form of overdraft protection for your checking account, which means money from your savings account will automatically transfer to your checking account if you are overdrawn.

Checks

Checks are basically documents that tell a bank to use money from your account to pay a designated business or person. If you open a money market account, you will be able to write a limited number of checks each month. Many banks will provide you with a free book of checks when you open your account, and some will even give you free checks for the life of your account.

When you write a check, you'll want to make sure to write down the check number, the amount, and who you wrote the check to so you can keep track of how much you've spent.

Maintaining Your Account

It's very important to keep track of your deposits, withdrawals, and transfers so you can avoid any service fees your bank might charge, like a minimum balance fee or a per-withdrawal fee.

When you open your savings account, the bank will give you a register, which you will use to write your beginning balance and your future deposits and withdrawals.

Every month, your bank will either send you a statement in the mail or provide you with your statement online. Some banks will even allow you to combine your savings account statement with your checking account statement. Your statement

> **✔ Quick Tip**
> In order to ensure that you are continually building up the funds in your savings account, you may want to have a portion of your paycheck automatically deposited into your savings account. By "paying yourself first" through automatic deposit, you are less likely to spend that money in other ways allowing it to grow and earn more interest over time.
>
> Source: © 2008 ultimatemoneyskills.com, sponsored by Bank of America and powered by Making It Count.

will list every transaction, along with any fees charged to your account and interest your money has earned. Make sure you compare the entries in your register with your bank statement to ensure you didn't forget to write down any deposits or withdrawals and to make sure the bank didn't make any mistakes.

Chapter 13

What You Should Know About Checking Accounts

Benefits Of Checking Accounts

Do you currently have a checking account? Do your parents have a checking account?

Whether you have a checking account now, or in the future, a checking account is most useful when you are on your own. A checking account allows you to write checks and/or use a debit card to pay bills and buy goods.

With a checking account, the account holder—for example, Todd—deposits money into his bank account. Todd can then write checks. The person who receives the account holder's check—for example, Grace—usually deposits the check into her own checking account. The bank then takes the money from Todd's account and puts it into Grace's account, because she deposited the check.

What are some benefits of a checking account? There are four key benefits of a checking account:

About This Chapter: Excerpted from "Module 2: Check It Out," *Money Smart for Young Adults*, a CD-based curriculum developed by the Federal Deposit Insurance Corporation (FDIC), March 2008.

- Convenience

- Cost

- Better money management

- Safety

Convenience: Checking accounts are convenient because they provide you with quick and easy access to your money. Using checks and debit cards can take the place of carrying cash. Also, having a checking account allows you to direct-deposit money that comes to you from a job, the government, or other source of income. You have immediate access to money that is direct-deposited.

> **♣ It's A Fact!!**
>
> Keeping a checking account can help you build a relationship with the bank. How well you manage your checking account may be a factor the bank considers when deciding whether to grant you a loan. Having a checking account also helps prove you pay your bills on time.

Cost: Using a checking account is usually less expensive than using other services to cash checks or buy money orders. If you have a checking account, you can usually cash a check for free. Check cashing services charge a fee.

Better Money Management: Using a checking account can also help you manage your money. When you write a check, deposit or withdraw money, use your debit card, or have checks direct-deposited into your account, the bank calls this a "transaction." You record every transaction you or the bank makes in your "check register." The check register shows how you are spending your money and how much money is currently in your account.

Safety: Using a checking account can help you keep your cash safe. It is safer to use checks and debit cards than to carry large amounts of cash because you do not have to worry about your cash being stolen or lost. However, if your checkbook or debit card is lost or stolen, report it as soon as possible to your bank. The bank will protect you so that you are not responsible for any purchases you do not make.

Keeping your money in an insured financial institution means your money is safe up to the insured limit. This means that if for some reason the financial institution closes, you will receive your insured deposits. The Federal Deposit Insurance Corporation (FDIC) is the government agency that insures deposits at banks and thrifts. The FDIC has an online tool called Electronic Deposit Insurance Estimator (EDIE). It lets you calculate the insurance coverage of your accounts at each FDIC-insured institution. You can find EDIE online at http://www.fdic.gov/EDIE.

Types Of Checking Accounts

There are four types of checking accounts:

• Free or low-cost checking

• Electronic/ATM checking

• Regular checking

• Interest-bearing checking

Free/Low-Cost Checking: If you do not plan to write many checks, a free or low-cost checking account might be right for you. However, there may be a limit to the number of checks you can write in a month.

Some banks offer special checking and savings account products for students. These may include a waiver of fees, lower minimum balance requirements, and free checks. When shopping for an account, ask the institution if it offers a student account. If it does, be sure to find out what happens when you turn 18 or are no longer a student—specifically, what kind of account the bank will assign to you.

Electronic/ATM Checking: This account usually requires you to use direct deposit. If you do not plan to use teller services often, an electronic checking account might be right for you. This type of account usually allows you to write an unlimited amount of checks per month without incurring a fee for each check you write. However, you may be charged for in-person teller services.

Regular Checking: With a regular checking account, there is usually a minimum balance required to waive the monthly service fee. This type of account usually offers unlimited check-writing privileges.

Interest-Bearing Checking: There are also different interest-bearing accounts:

- The negotiable order of withdrawal (NOW) account
- The money market deposit account (MMDA)

With these accounts, you usually have to maintain a high minimum balance in order to earn interest and avoid fees. The minimum balance is usually at least $1,000.

Comparing Checking Accounts

Checking accounts often have fees that are charged by the bank or credit union. These aren't always the same. Every bank has a "Fee Schedule" that you can get when asking about their services.

Fee Schedule

Ask for a fee schedule that lists all the fees related to the account. Use the fee schedule to compare the costs of each account.

A fee schedule lists the fees you may be charged for certain activities. Some of the most common fees include the following:

- **Monthly Service Fee:** The monthly service fee is also called a maintenance fee. The bank may charge a fee each month just for having the account. You might also be charged a fee if your balance drops below the required minimum.

- **Minimum Balance Fee:** Some accounts may require that a certain amount of money be in the account. If the account goes below that amount, the bank automatically charges a fee.

- **ATM User Fee:** You will likely be charged fees each time you use an ATM at a bank other than your own. Many ATMs at other locations such as shopping malls, gas stations, or convenience stores also charge a fee unless they are affiliated with your bank.

- **Overdraft Fee:** Overdraft fees are also called non-sufficient funds (NSF) fees. The bank will notify you if a check is returned to the person or company to whom it was issued because there wasn't enough money in your account. Your bank will charge you a processing fee for returned checks. Merchants might also charge a fee if a bounced check is used to purchase goods or services.

- **Stop-Payment Fee:** If you lose a check or need to make sure a check is not paid by the bank for some other reason, you can request a "stop payment." There is a fee for this service, and the bank may not be able to catch the check before it is paid.

✔ Quick Tip
Determine Your Checking Account Needs

When you consider opening a checking account, remember that banks offer different types of checking accounts. To determine what you need, think about how you plan to use your checking account. The following questions will help you determine what you need to look for in a checking account.

Consider Convenience

- How many checks do you think you will write every month?
- Do you want a bank that is close to your home or work?
- What are the bank's hours of operation?
- Will you use the ATM often?
- Does the bank have ATMs close to where you live or work?
- How often do you plan to visit the bank to use teller services?
- What other bank services are important to you?

Determine Costs

- How much money will you keep in your account?
- Will you be charged for writing extra checks?
- Are you willing to pay a monthly fee?
- If so, how much?
- Will you be charged to use your bank's ATM?
- Will you be charged for using other banks' ATMs?
- Will you be charged for using teller services?
- Are there ways to avoid paying fees?

Opening A Checking

What's Needed To Open A Checking Account

To open your checking account, you will generally be asked for the following:

- **Photo Identification (ID)**, usually a state-issued identification card, driver's license, passport, or perhaps even your student ID card: Some banks may accept an alternative form of identification such as a Matri´cula Consular card. You might need more than one picture ID to open your account—this is for the protection of both you and the bank. Since practices vary, ask the bank what type of identification you need. Banks need to be sure you are the person you say you are.

- **Your Social Security Number (SSN):** Some banks may accept an alternative such as an individual taxpayer identification number (ITIN). This is generally used to help identify you and to look up your credit history.

- **The Opening Deposit:** This amount could range from $1 on up, depending on which checking account you choose. Some banks will pay for your first box of checks, while other banks will charge you.

The bank may also offer you an ATM card or debit card. The bank will ask you to sign a document that is traditionally called a "signature card." This document identifies you as the owner of the account.

Account Verification

The bank or credit union performs account verification because it wants to make sure that you will be a responsible bank account customer and that no one is trying to steal your identity to open an account. If you have mishandled a checking account or have not been a good banking customer in the past, the bank may not want to risk accepting you as a customer now. The bank may access a system such as ChexSystems to help assess your risk as a potential customer.

If you are unable to open an account because of credit-related problems, ask your bank or a reputable credit counseling agency if you are eligible for any "second chance" checking programs. These programs may allow you to open a checking account after meeting certain requirements, such as completing a check-writing workshop.

Using A Checking Account

A checking account generally has these components:

- A check register

- A checkbook

- An ATM/debit card

Check Register

You use a check register to keep track of the money you put into and take out of your checking account. Before computers and the internet, the paper check register was the only way an account holder could keep track of the money in the account between monthly statements. Today many banks allow users to see their accounts online, and account information can be downloaded to a financial management software program. To understand how a check register works, we are going to use a paper version for an example.

Your check register is a tool that will help you to know how much money you have in your account at all times. Each time you put money into your account, write a check, or take money out, you should record key pieces of information in your check register. The following numbered descriptions refer to the sample check register shown in Figure 13.1 (on page 128).

1. **Check Number:** If you are writing a check, record the check number in this column. If not, leave it blank.

2. **Date:** Write the date on which you wrote a check, made a deposit, or took money out (made a withdrawal) or were charged a service fee.

3. **Description Of Transaction:** Record items such as to whom you wrote the check, the reason for the deposit, or the location of the withdrawal (for example, ATM or debit card).

4. **Payment/Debit (-):** Record the dollar amount of checks written, ATM withdrawals, or debit card transactions.

5. **Fee:** Record any fees charged, such as a monthly maintenance fee or an ATM fee.

6. **Deposit/Credit (+):** Record any deposits or credits made to your account.

7. **Balance:** Add any deposits or credits and subtract any fees, payments, or other debits to your account to get the new balance.

1	2	3	4	5	6	7
Check Number	Date	Description of Transaction	Payment/ Debit (-)	Fee	Deposit/ Credit (+)	Balance

Figure 13.1. Sample Check Register.

Checkbook

The checkbook contains checks and deposit slips for a particular account. The numbers across the bottom of the check contain the routing number of the bank (the bank's number), the account number, and the number of the check. These numbers are printed so that machines can easily read them.

Steps To Writing A Check

A check is a written contract between you and your bank. When you write a check, you are asking the bank to take money from your account and give it to someone else.

There are three steps you need take write a check:

1. Make sure you have enough money in your account.

2. Complete the blank spaces on the check.

3. Record the transaction in your check register.

Step 1: Make Sure You Have Enough Money In Your Checking Account

It is important to record every deposit and withdrawal you make in your check register. When you do this, you can be sure that the amount in the balance column accurately reflects what you have in your account. Banks can use electronic images to transfer checks. This means that a check you present to pay for a good or service may be immediately withdrawn from your account.

Step 2: Complete the Blank Spaces On Check

To write a check, you must fill in the following information:

1. **Date:** Be sure to write the complete date, including the month, day, and year; for example, February 26, 20XX.

2. **Pay To The Order Of** (who is receiving your money): This is where you write the name of the person or company to whom you will give the check. After writing the name, draw a line from the end of the name to the end of the space. This prevents anyone from adding an additional name on your check.

3. **$:** Write the amount of the check in numbers, such as $19.75.

4. **Dollars:** Write the amount of the check in words, such as nineteen and 75/100. After writing out the amount of the check, draw a line to the end. This prevents anyone from adding an additional amount after what you have written.

5. **Memo Section:** Writing in this area is optional. You can use it to remind yourself of the reason you wrote the check or to record the account number of the bill you are paying.

6. **Signature:** Sign your name here.

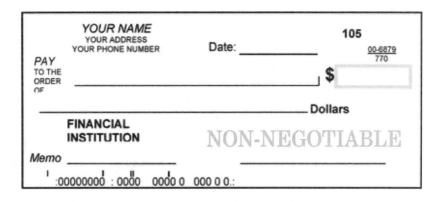

Figure 13.2. Check Example

♣ It's A Fact!!

How To Correct A Mistake On A Check

If you make a small mistake when writing a check, such as starting to write the dollar amount in the "Pay to the Order of" area, cross out the incorrect information and write your initials above what you crossed out. Then write the correct information. Some stores will not accept checks with crossed-out information.

If you make a large mistake, write "VOID" across the check and/or tear it up. A check with VOID across it is no longer usable. Ideally, you should always tear up your check to prevent thieves from stealing your confidential information off the check. Thieves can use the numbers printed along the lower end of the check to steal money from your account.

Regardless of whether you void or destroy a check, record the check as voided in your register so that you have a record that the check was canceled.

Step 3: Record The Transaction In Your Check Register

Record your check in your check register. Fill in the date, description, and amount of the check.

You can also use a check to get cash out of your account at your bank.

♣ It's A Fact!!
How To Write
A Check For Cash

You can also use a check to get cash from your account. This can be done in one of two ways:

1. Write "Cash" in the "Pay to the Order of" blank on your check. Then, enter in the dollar amount you would like to receive.

   Remember: Be careful with a check you write out to cash because anyone can endorse the back of the check and receive the money.

2. Write your name (first and last) in the "Pay to the Order of" blank on your check. Then, enter in the dollar amount you would like to receive.

Using Electronic Banking

Using your ATM card to deposit money into and withdraw money from your account is known as electronic banking. Electronic banking uses computers to move money into and from your account instead of using checks and other paper transactions.

Electronic banking includes ATM transactions, debit card transactions, and electronic bill pay.

ATM Cards And Transactions

ATM stands for automatic (or automated) teller machine. An ATM is a computer terminal that can give you money from your account. You can also deposit money into your account at many ATMs.

In order to use an ATM, you need either an ATM card or a debit card. You generally are offered an ATM card or a debit card at the time you open your bank account. Let's look at how these two cards differ.

An ATM card allows you to use an ATM machine for transactions. In addition, some ATM cards can be used for point-of-sale (POS) transactions at merchants participating in the same network as your card. With a POS transaction, you input your personal identification number (PIN) into a terminal at the time of purchase and funds are immediately withdrawn from your account.

Debit Card Transactions

A debit card, also known as a Checkcard or Mastermoney card, resembles an ATM card, except the debit card displays a MasterCard or VISA logo. A debit card performs all of the same functions as an ATM card (for example you can deposit or withdraw money from your account at an ATM). In addition, the debit card also allows you to pay for goods and services at locations that accept MasterCard or VISA, such as grocery stores, gas stations, or restaurants. This means you can simply sign for your transactions, although you may also have the option to input your PIN.

Personal Identification Number (PIN): The PIN is a code that only you know that allows you to use your card at ATMs or to purchase goods or services in some instances. It is usually mailed to you a few days before or after you receive your card. Your bank may allow you to select your own PIN, or may allow you to change it after you receive the card.

ATM Services: Most people use ATMs to get cash. Other popular uses include checking your account balance and transferring money between your savings and checking account.

You will be charged a fee to use an ATM machine that is not operated by your bank. (Look for the name of your bank on the ATM for an indication whether it is your bank's ATM.) If you must use another ATM, you

✔ **Quick Tip**

Here are a few tips for protecting your money by protecting the PIN:

- Do not tell anyone what your PIN is.

- Do not write it on your card or carry it with you in your wallet or purse.

- Keep a record of your PIN in a location that only you know.

- When using your PIN, make sure no one is trying to watch what number you input.

should look for a sign on the ATM machine or on the screen before you approve the transaction that discloses the fee charged by the ATM's owner. Remember, your bank may also charge an additional fee for using the ATM as well.

Printed Receipts: It is important to get receipts for your records and also to record all ATM and debit card transactions in your check register.

When you withdraw money from your account through the ATM machine, the money is immediately deducted from your account. If you lose track of what you've taken out of your account, you can overdraw your account and the bank will charge you the overdraft fee. This can be expensive and wasteful. If it results in checks "bouncing," you can ruin your reputation and relationships with the people to whom you wrote the checks.

The ATM will ask you if you want a receipt. Be sure to answer "Yes," and then retain the receipt until you reconcile your monthly account statement.

Printed receipts usually include the following information:

• The amount of the transaction

• Any extra fees charged

• The date of the transaction

• The type of transaction, for example, a deposit or withdrawal

• An identification number or code for your account or ATM card

• The ATM location or an identification number or code for the terminal you used

Shopping: When using your debit card while shopping, you may be given the choice of either signing your name or using your personal identification number (PIN). You should ask your financial institution whether it charges any fees or offers special incentives if you sign for transactions rather than input your PIN.

Unlike credit cards, which allow you to make purchases now and pay for them later, debit cards deduct the amount from your checking account as soon as you make the purchase.

You should always expect your purchases to be immediately withdrawn from your account, so always ensure there is enough money in your account to cover the purchase.

Protection From Someone Else Using Your Card: If someone uses your card without your permission, federal law protects you. But the protection differs depending on whether you used your debit or credit card.

- If you used your credit card, you do not have to pay the disputed transaction while the company that issued the credit card is investigating the matter. Your liability for unauthorized transactions is generally capped at $50, although sometimes the credit card company may waive your liability.

- With a debit card, the disputed transaction will have already been withdrawn from your account. The financial institution will re-credit the amount in dispute (less $50) to your account if it is unable to resolve the matter within 10 business days of your filing the complaint. If you do not notify your bank within two days of discovering the loss or other problem, you could potentially be responsible for more than $50 of the unauthorized purchases.

- It is absolutely critical that you let your financial institution know immediately if someone has used your ATM card, debit card, or credit card without your permission.

Electronic Bill Pay

Electronic bill pay is a service that automatically takes money from your account each month to pay your bills. For example, if you have a monthly car insurance payment, you can sign up to have it deducted each month. You can also use bill pay to make payments to businesses to which you owe money, just as if you were writing a check.

Some benefits of electronic bill pay are you do not have to pay for postage and for automatic payments, you also do not have to worry about late payments.

However, you should make sure you have enough money in your account to cover these bills, and make sure you record the payments in your check register.

Adding Money To Your Checking Account

There are four ways to add money to your checking account:

- A cash or check deposit using a teller

- An ATM deposit

- A deposit by mail

- A direct deposit

Deposit With A Slip

To add money to your account, you need to make a deposit. When making a deposit, you fill out a deposit slip to let the teller know how much you are depositing. Deposit slips are included in your checkbook and have your account number printed on them. They are found at the back after the checks.

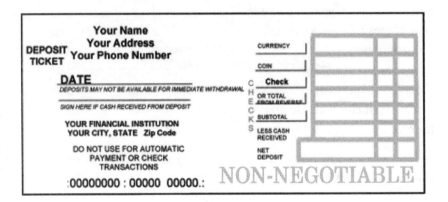

Figure 13.3. Sample Deposit Slip.

Cash: When making a cash deposit with a deposit slip, here are the steps you need to follow:

- Make sure the deposit slip has your correct account and address information

- Write in the transaction date

- Add up the total of paper money and write the amount in the box marked "Cash" or "Currency"

- Add up the coins you wish to deposit and write the amount in the box marked "Coin"

- Add up the "Cash" and "Coin" boxes to get the "Net Deposit"

You then give the teller your deposit slip and your cash. The teller will also count the money before depositing it into your account.

If you run out of deposit slips, you can get blank ones at your bank. Make sure to write your name and account number on the slip so your money does not go into someone else's account.

Checks: The first thing you need to do to deposit your check is sign the back of it.

If you want to deposit the entire check into your account, write "For Deposit Only," your account number, and your signature. By writing "For Deposit Only," you prevent others from cashing your check. It also prevents you from receiving cash back when you make the deposit.

What's It Mean?
Endorsement: When you sign the back of a check, you are "endorsing" it. This means that the check can be cashed.

You will need to fill out a deposit slip when depositing checks into your checking account.

- If you deposit more than one check, make sure to correctly endorse each one and write the amount of each check on your deposit slip. Use a separate line on the deposit slip to list the amount of each check.

- If you have more than a few checks, you can use the back of the deposit slip to list them. You need to add up the amounts of the checks on the back of the deposit slip and transfer this total to the front.

- Enter this amount in the box labeled "Or Total From Reverse."

- When you deposit your check(s), you can also receive cash back if there is enough money in your account to cover the check(s).

- Net deposit is the amount that will go into your account after you subtract any cash that you are receiving.

Please note that the bank may not always allow you to immediately withdraw all the money from a check that you deposited. Ask the bank when the deposited funds will be available for withdrawal.

Every deposit should be recorded in your check register. When you deposit a check and receive cash back, you can record it one of two ways. You can enter it as two entries or as one entry.

For instance, the following shows how the information can be entered as two entries:

- Date: March 23, 20XX
- Deposit/Credit (+): $50.00
- New Balance: $215.00

and

- Date: March 23, 20XX
- Payment/Debit (-): $25.00
- New $190.00

Or you can do it as one entry:

- Date: March 23, 20XX
- Deposit/Credit (+): $50.00
- Payment/(-): $25.00
- New $190.00

Keep in mind that when you deposit a check, it might take a few days before you can use your money. This is because it takes a few days to process the check.

When you make a check deposit, ask the teller when your money will be available.

Be careful not to take out cash or write checks until the money you deposited is available.

ATM Deposits

The second way to make a deposit is to use your bank's ATM. Making an ATM deposit is similar to making an ATM withdrawal. The ATM will prompt you through the steps needed to deposit money into your checking account.

✦ It's A Fact!!

How To Get Cash Back From Your Deposit

You can generally get cash back from any deposit you make, as long as it is less than the deposit amount.

1. Write the amount of cash you want back in the box marked "Less Cash Received" on your deposit slip.

2. Sign on the line: "sign here if cash received from deposit."

3. Then, write the total of your deposit in the "Net Deposit" box. ("Net Deposit" means the amount that is going into your account. To get this amount, subtract the cash you want back from the total amount of the check.

4. Record your deposit in your check register.

ATMs have special envelopes that you use to make deposits. The envelopes are found on or near the ATM.

You do not always have to use a deposit slip when making ATM deposits. But you need to fill in the information listed on the envelope if your bank requests it. This information could include the following:

• Your name

• Phone number

• Account number

• Deposit amount

• Type of account

With some ATM machines, you may not even have to use an envelope, since you enter this information using the machine and then feed your cash or check deposit into the ATM.

Always remember to get a receipt so you have proof that you made the deposit.

Deposit By Mail

You can also make deposits by mail. You can deposit your checks by mailing the checks and a deposit slip to your bank. However, you should never send cash through the mail.

Direct Deposit

The fourth way to add money to your checking account is through direct deposit.

Direct deposit occurs when your employer or a government agency gives you your paycheck or other check electronically.

- You will not receive the check in the mail. In some cases, your payroll or benefits check statement is mailed to your home address.

- The money is immediately available when your bank or credit union opens. Some banks will not charge monthly fees if direct deposit is used.

With direct deposit, the advantages include the following:

- You have one less thing to worry about because it is the safest way for you to receive your money

- You can avoid the inconvenience and/or expense of depositing or cashing a check—you have an easier and more convenient way to access your money

- You take control over your money and your time because it is predictable and dependable

- Signing up is quick and easy—ask your employer for more details

Finally, always remember to record the amount deposited in your check register.

Keeping An Accurate Record Of Your Checking Account

Keeping an accurate record of your checking account activity is very important. It helps you know at all times the exact amount of money you have in your checking account.

To keep an accurate record, you need to take the following steps:

- Record all transactions in your check register
- Record maintenance fees, interest, and other bank charges
- Review the monthly checking account statement
- Reconcile your check register with your monthly checking account statement

Record All Transactions

Be very careful to record deposits and withdrawals in your check register. You should keep all receipts so you can record the transactions.

Record Interest And Maintenance Fees

With an interest-bearing checking account, you find out the interest you receive each month by reviewing the checking account statement the bank sends you. You will need to add this interest to your check register. A good time to do it is when you receive your statement. Record the interest in the "Deposit/Credit (+)" column of the check register.

With a fee-based checking account, you can ask the bank the approximate date it will withdraw the monthly fee from your account. You should record that fee in your check register.

The Monthly Checking Account Statement

The bank will generally prepare a statement for your checking account once a month. The statement lists all of the transactions that occurred during the preceding month. These transactions include the following:

- Checks you wrote that have cleared (been cashed or deposited by the person to whom you wrote the check)

> **✔ Quick Tip**
> Be sure to review your statement as soon as you receive it, particularly to look for errors or transactions you did not make. If you notice something amiss, or have other questions about your statement, be sure to contact your bank's customer service representative immediately.

- All withdrawals and deposits made

- Debit card purchases

- Any fees that the bank charges

The statement is generally mailed to you. Many banks also provide these statements online. You may even be able to ask the bank to forgo sending you a paper statement and just make it available online for you to download.

How To Reconcile Your Checking Account

As you have already seen, balancing means keeping your checkbook register up to date by recording all transactions so you always know how much money is in your account.

When you get your monthly checking account statement, there usually will be a difference between the statement balance and your check register balance.

These differences occur because of events such as the following:

- You did not record fees and interest in your register

- You forgot to record some transactions on the bank statement in your check register

- Some transactions in your check register were made too late to be recorded on the bank statement

Reconciling your checking account helps you find the reasons for the differences. Many people reconcile their accounts using a software application.

See the checking account reconciliation form illustrated in Figure 13.4 (on page 142) and refer to the following steps to reconcile your checking account:

- **Step 1:** On the Checking Account Reconciliation Form, in the area called "Balance shown on this statement," write the amount of the "New Balance."

- **Step 2:** Compare the checks, fees, and other withdrawals you entered in your check register with the checks, fees, and other withdrawals

CHECKS OUTSTANDING - NOT CHARGED TO ACCOUNT		Bank balance shown on this statement	
Check Number	Check Amount		
		Subtract withdrawals outstanding	
		Total	
		Add deposits outstanding	
		Balance	
		This balance should agree with the balance in your check register.	

Figure 13.4. Checking Account Reconciliation Form.

listed on the checking account statement. Make sure everything listed in your check register appears on the checking account statement and that everything on your bank statement is in your register. It is useful to start with the bank statement and check off each item in your register. Then you can quickly see what is not in your register, and what is not on your statement. On the reconciliation form, list any checks or other withdrawals you have made that aren't on your statement, add these up and subtract these from the balance shown on the bank statement.

• **Step 3:** The next step is to add any deposits that were made after the ending date of the checking account statement. These deposits will not appear on the statement.

  • Write these deposits on the area of the Checking Account Reconciliation Form called "Add deposits outstanding." There is space to write each deposit.

  • Now add these deposits to the withdrawals outstanding and put the number in the area of the Checking Account Reconciliation Form called "Balance."

• When the "Balance" number on the Account Reconciliation form equals the number in the check register, you have successfully reconciled your checking account.

How To Report Errors, Change Your Address, And Close Account

If you find errors on your bank statement, contact your bank to have the error corrected. It is a generally a good idea to immediately call or visit the bank to report the error, and then follow up by writing a letter. Keep a copy of the letter for your records. The letter should include the following information:

• Your name

• Your account number

• An explanation and the dollar amount of the error

• The date the error occurred

♣ It's A Fact!!

It is very important it is to keep an accurate balance in your checkbook. If you write a check without enough money in your account to cover the check, it is known as writing a bad check or "bouncing" a check.

Writing bad checks can have very serious consequences for you:

• Each bad check might cost you a fee of as much as $38.

• Checks you write later might not get paid.

• This negative activity can be reported to an account verification company such as ChexSystems or TeleCheck. This can make it difficult in the future to cash or write checks and to open an account.

• Your bank can close your account and send a negative report to the credit bureaus, and the amount of the overdraft and fees might be reported to a collection bureau.

Writing a bad check, when you know it is a bad check, is a crime in every state. Each state has different civil and criminal penalties, such as fines and jail time. For this reason, if you ever do mistakenly write a bad check, you should correct it as soon as possible.

The bank must receive notice of the error no later than 60 days after the date of the statement. But be sure to contact the bank as soon as possible to minimize your potential losses in the event your account information was stolen.

If your address changes, you can complete and return the "change of address" form on the back of your checking account statement or you can call your bank.

If you decide to close your checking account, make sure that all the checks you have written have been cashed before you close it.

Overdraft Protection

Many financial institutions offer "courtesy overdraft protection" or "bounce protection" plans so that your checks do not bounce and you do not overdraw your account. With these plans, you will avoid the merchant's returned check fee, but you still will have to pay the financial institution a fee for each item. These fees can be costly. Also remember that, unlike an overdraft line of credit, with bounce protection there is no guarantee that your bank will cover your checks, ATM withdrawals, and debit card and other electronic transactions that overdraw your account.

You may also be able to have your checking account linked to a credit card or your savings account. When you do not have enough money in your account to cover an item, money is taken from the credit card or savings account to cover it.

The bank may charge a small fee for each transfer from your savings account, but you will not pay interest since you are essentially borrowing from yourself. You can expect to pay a cash advance fee and interest on funds transferred to your checking account from your credit card. Ask your bank's customer service representative for more information.

Chapter 14

Insurance: Protecting Your Assets

Safeguarding Your Money

You know that unexpected things happen and cause you trouble. The dog eats your homework. You spill a quart of milk on the kitchen floor.

But some accidents or unexpected events are more serious and can cost you money. You skid on wet pavement and wreck your bike. You leave your backpack on the bus, and no one turns it in.

These events are called "losses." You no longer have a backpack or a bike. Who replaces these items? What if your parents say that you must replace the lost backpack because you were careless? Do you have enough money saved up?

About Losses

Losses occur in the adult world too, and sometimes losses happen without anyone being careless or making a mistake. A rainstorm floods your basement and ruins everything in it. Your grandmother needs an expensive operation. Someone steals your dad's car.

About This Chapter: This chapter includes "Safeguarding Your Money," "Health Insurance: Protecting Health and Paying for Treatment," "Protecting Property: Replacing and Repairing the Things You Own," "Protecting Autos: The Vehicles and the People in Them," "Life Insurance: Protecting the Family Income," and "Protecting Your Income: When You Cannot Work and Earn," © 2007 Northwestern Mutual Foundation. Reprinted with permission. For additional information, visit www.themint.org.

All these problems cost money. If they all happened at once, they might wipe out the family savings. Adults try to protect themselves by buying insurance, a kind of protection that helps people pay for losses that occur in life.

This chapter explains a few of the different kinds of insurance and how they work.

✎ What's It Mean?

Coverage: An insurance term, coverage means what and how much your insurance pays for.

Premiums: Another word for insurance payments.

Source: "Health Insurance: Protecting Health and Paying for Treatment, © 2007 Northwestern Mutual Foundation.

Protecting Health And Paying For Treatment

Going to the doctor, filling prescriptions, or going to the hospital can be really expensive. Most people buy health insurance to help them pay these bills. Some bills are smaller, like getting a regular checkup or a booster shot. But there are bigger costs, too, like surgeries or hospital stays. These can be huge. So everyone needs health insurance.

As with other kinds of insurance, you can choose from many kinds of help, called insurance coverage. People buy insurance coverage that fits their needs. Let's use two examples to make this point.

Matching Your Needs

Very Healthy Person: If you feel that you are a very healthy young adult, you might choose insurance with lower cost premiums—another word for insurance payments. A less expensive insurance policy may not help you pay for (cover) smaller bills. For example, your insurance may pay for part or most of big costs, like surgery or a hospital stay. But it may not pay for checkups or a test for strep throat.

Person With Health Problems: If you have severe allergies or a weak heart, you may want help paying for more kinds of treatment: doctor visits, everyday medications, and frequent tests.

You Get What You Pay For

Most people buy health insurance through their employer. You are covered by your parent's policy. When you finish school and get your first job, you will then have to buy your own health insurance.

The kind of health coverage you buy depends on two things:

• How much help you want from your insurance in paying medical bills

• How much you are able to spend on premiums (payments for insurance)

The more health insurance you buy, the more your insurance will help you pay for medical care. But the more insurance you buy, the more you also spend on premiums.

♣ It's A Fact!!

Needs change as you grow older. The amount of insurance you buy as a healthy and fit 25-year-old may be very different than the insurance you own as a 50-year-old.

Source: "Health Insurance: Protecting Health and Paying for Treatment, © 2007 Northwestern Mutual Foundation.

As with all insurance, people hope that they will never be given serious reasons to use it. But if people get very sick or need hospital treatment, they will be very glad to have help paying the bills.

Protecting Property: Replacing And Repairing The Things You Own

To help pay for damage to their home, people buy renter's insurance or homeowners insurance. Someday you may have an apartment or a home to protect, so you should know about this insurance.

What Kind Of Damage?

A fire can burn a house to the ground. Nature can damage homes through hurricanes, tornadoes, hail storms, floods, high winds, ice, and sleet.

What else can damage a home? An out-of-control auto could end up on your front porch or in your living room. Kids playing baseball can put a ball through your window. Teenagers can vandalize the outside of your house or drive over your lawn and tear it up. Burglars can break into your home and steal things, like electronics, art, money, or other valuables.

How It Works

If your home caught fire, how would your parents replace the building and all the things in it? The "things" took years to buy. Such a loss would be more than most people could afford. That's why people buy insurance because it will help them pay to repair or rebuild their house or apartment and replace or repair their belongings.

Buy As Much Or As Little As You Want

People who buy homeowners or renters insurance decide how much help they want if a disaster strikes. The more help they want, the more they must pay for their homeowners insurance.

Insurance also costs more if people own very valuable property, like jewels, a rare violin, or a collection of antique clocks.

Most people buy homeowners insurance and then hope they never need to use it. But if something bad does happen, they will have help putting their home back together without losing all of their savings.

Protecting Autos: The Vehicles And The People In Them

You'll learn more about this kind of insurance when you get your driver's license. Most states require that drivers buy auto insurance.

What Auto Insurance Helps You Pay For

Driving is a risky business, and auto insurance can help you pay for:

• Damage that you cause as the driver—whether you hurt other people in an accident or you damage property, like another car or a building.

• Medical treatment you need as a result of the accident.

- Damage caused by any non-insured person involved in the accident. Despite the law, some people drive without insurance. So if your car is damaged by a person without insurance, your insurance will help you pay to get your car repaired.

- Any kind of damage to your car. Your car can be damaged in several ways: an auto accident, a thief who breaks into your car, or a hail storm. Like homeowners/renters insurance, auto insurance protects your vehicle from things like fire, explosions, vandalism, theft, or storms.

About Auto Insurance Payments

Cars are another one of those expensive items in life. The cost of auto insurance payments, called premiums, depends on how expensive your car is, where you live, your driving record—and with teens, your grade point average. High grades mean lower premiums.

When you get your driver's license, you can be added to your parents' auto insurance. Your parents may even ask you to help pay for your part of the insurance as well as the gas you use when you drive. When you are no longer a student, you will have to buy your own auto insurance.

Just as with other kinds of insurance, you can buy lots of insurance (that will pay for lots of damage or medical bills) or less insurance. If you buy less insurance and you get into an accident, you will have to use more of your own money to pay for damage or medical bills.

♣ **It's A Fact!!**
Auto insurance payments for teens are high because as inexperienced drivers, teens get into many more accidents than most adults.

Source: "Protecting Autos: The Vehicles And The People In Them," © 2007 Northwestern Mutual Foundation.

Driving can be dangerous, and the damage can be serious and costly. That's why many people buy as much insurance as they can afford.

Life Insurance: Protecting The Family Income

Many people live long lives, but some don't. Besides the fact that we feel very sad when someone in our family dies, that death may affect the earning power of the family. To protect the family income and the future of the family, people buy life insurance.

Paying The Bills

For example, let's say that your dad is a firefighter and loses his life in a burning building. Your dad's income is no longer there to help the family pay monthly bills. Yet the bills pretty much stay the same. Will your mom's paycheck be able to pay those bills, now that the family has lost a salary?

Different Circumstances

Think about this. How the family is financially affected by the death of a parent depends on when a parent dies.

If a parent dies with three children in elementary school, the living parent must face years of expenses for these children: clothes, tuition, braces, music lessons, sports, and college. There are lots of bills to be paid.

If a parent dies after the family's children are adults, the living parent may be the only person left at home. The many bills that a family pays while children are growing up probably have been taken care of.

Yet the living parent may still need money for daily life: staying in the same house and buying food, clothes, a new car, etc. Without life insurance, the remaining parent might not be able to afford his or her old way of life.

Can you see how parents think about life insurance? Parents hope they will not need to use life insurance anytime soon. But they buy it just in case—if a parent dies, the family will have enough money to go on living the way they always have.

As with all insurance, there are many kinds of life insurance. People can choose how much to buy, depending on their circumstances and their financial needs.

Protecting Your Income: When You Cannot Work And Earn

Like life insurance, disability insurance protects income. If you become too sick from an illness or too injured in an accident to go to work and earn money, disability insurance will help provide an income for you. The accident or the illness has dis-abled you: you are no longer "able" to earn your paycheck.

What if you are a professional football player who has injured his leg? A brain surgeon who has developed arthritis and can no longer use her hands? What if you are a construction worker who injured your back? What if you got in an auto accident and became paralyzed? No matter what the job, people still need an income to live.

People buy disability insurance because it helps replace their lost paycheck—either while they recover from a short or long illness—or for the rest of their life. Because this is a work-related kind of insurance, many people buy this insurance through their employer.

Chapter 15

Another Good Use Of Your Money: Helping Others

Hurricane Katrina. The tsunami in South Asia. 9/11. Your community's local food bank. Your college, the local firefighters' fund, your church, your synagogue, or your mosque. All of these organizations and efforts have one thing in common: they need individuals to donate their goods, services, time and money to fulfill their missions.

Every year millions of people support nonprofit organizations to care for people in their communities, strengthen causes they feel strongly about, and reach out to people affected by disasters. Giving is a noble and generous act of caring and service. But what are some things to consider when thinking about supporting a charitable organization?

It is possible to give from your heart while still using your head. Before committing to volunteer time or donate goods or services to a local charity, or responding to pleas for financial support in the wake of a disaster, consider the following questions:

About This Chapter: "More About... Giving Wisely," © 2008 Securities Industry and Financial Markets Association Foundation for Investor Education (www.sifma.org). Reprinted with permission.

What type of causes do you want to support or what groups of people do you want to care for?

Do you have a particular concern for people with disabilities or children with cancer? Do you want to help victims of domestic violence or disadvantaged youth? Are you passionate about the environment or animals or education and the arts? Knowing what causes you want to help can make it easier to identify which organizations you may choose to support. Creating a plan to give to charities in advance of being solicited can help eliminate a lot of on-the-spot decision-making.

It can also help you determine which agencies or organizations you would like to support in response to immediate demands created by disasters like Hurricane Katrina, 9/11 or the tsunami in South Asia.

Do you have a relationship with any charitable organizations?

Knowing people who work for, or volunteer with,

✔ Quick Tip
How can you get more involved sharing your time and money with others?

Here are some possibilities:

- Donate part of your allowance or gift money to a charity you admire.

- Ask friends and family to donate to a charity instead of giving you birthday or holiday gifts.

- Join or start an organization at school or in your community that helps others.

- Coordinate with friends and parents on a lemonade sale, car wash, a toy or food collection, or some other event for a local charity.

- Volunteer to mow the lawn, rake leaves or handle another chore for an ill or elderly neighbor.

- Help your parents when they volunteer for a good cause or donate items to a charity.

- Participate in a walk or run that raises money for a charity.

Need more ideas or direction? Start by talking to your parents and other family members. Also, your city or county government may have websites that list local charities and volunteer opportunities.

Source: Excerpted from "Another Good Use of Your Money: Helping the Less Fortunate," *FDIC Consumer News*, Federal Deposit Insurance Corporation (FDIC), Summer 2006.

a charitable organization can give you a personal connection to the organization and may help you feel more confident about where your money is going and how it is being used. Ask friends or family members who donate time or money about the charities they support and see if you think it would be a good match for your giving interests. You can also ask at schools or in your workplace, and your public library can provide you with information on charitable organizations, including through your local Foundation Center (https://fndcenter.org) collection. Personal references and a little research can help you get a feel for the activities that an organization undertakes, what results they have achieved to date, and what they commit to do with the resources given by donors such as yourself.

Research potential organizations and carefully evaluate requests for giving.

Before you donate items, volunteer time, send a check or make an online gift, use the internet to research potential charities. Websites such as Guidestar.org, and Give.org (the Better Business Bureau Wise Giving Alliance) offer a wealth of information on nonprofit organizations and things to consider before giving. As you review potential charities take note of:

- The organization's mission statement. Is it in line with your vision for how you want your money to make a difference to the causes that you care about?

- Is the organization a certified 501(c)(3) nonprofit organization? If you're not sure, you can call or e-mail the organization and ask for a copy of their IRS Letter of Determination. According to the IRS, organizations receiving 501(c)(3) status are those considered "charitable, educational, religious, scientific, or literary; those that prevent cruelty to animals: and those that foster national or international amateur sports competitions." The tax-exempt 501(c)(3) status is granted only to organizations that provide detailed financial and organizational information proving it is organized and operated for charitable purposes as outlined by the IRS.

- Does the organization disclose financial information? For example, do they have an audited annual report? Do they make their IRS Form 990 available to donors? Does the organization disclose what percentage of funds is used for direct programs and services versus overhead expenses, operating costs, and fundraising expenses? You might consider requesting a copy of the organization's annual report and latest financial statements to see the activities of the organization and what percentage of funds are used for programs versus fundraising and administrative expenses.

• Is this nonprofit organization accredited by or affiliated with any organizations? Nonprofits can demonstrate their credibility by working with other reputable nonprofit and even for-profit organizations, as well as by voluntarily meeting standards of accrediting bodies like the Better Business Bureau.

• How will your donations be used? If you are donating goods or services, will they be used directly or will they be re-sold to raise funds for the organization? If you are donating money, will it be pooled in a general fund for operating programs and services? Or will your money be directed to a specific project?

• If the organization is international and working to help in other countries, how is money I am donating here being used? Most international nonprofit organizations have U.S. and/or other country based "affiliates" that comply with requirements for charitable giving so that donors can give money responsibly here to help victims in other countries.

• What percentage of your donation will be used for overhead, administrative or fundraising costs versus going directly to meet the organization's stated project needs?

• Who benefits from the work of the organization? If, for example, the organization serves youth, how many kids benefit, how do they benefit and is this a one time event or do the kids participate regularly? What you're looking for is results that the organization has produced with donations to date.

• Who governs the organization? Do they have an independent Board of Directors? Do the members of the Board serve voluntarily or are they compensated for their service? It is best for Boards to be comprised primarily of independent, non-related members (that is, no husband-wife or children of Board members) who are not employed by the organization. Preferably members of the Board will not be compensated for their service.

You should feel comfortable when talking to a representative of a nonprofit organization that they are not pressuring you to give: goods or services, your money, or personal information they can use in the future. If you are uncomfortable about the conversation, feel free to ask that they mail you information (such as a brochure and their most recent annual report) before deciding to give, or politely say "no."

✔ **Quick Tip**

For more tips on what to look for in an organization before giving, read the Better Business Bureau's Wise Giving Alliance Standards for Charity Accountability (available online at http://www.give.org/standards/newcbbbstds.asp).

Source: © 2008 Securities Industry and Financial Markets Association Foundation for Investor Education.

How To Think About Supporting A Charity

While you may receive requests primarily to support charities with financial donations, there are several ways you can be a part of a nonprofit's mission. For example:

- You can donate needed goods (that is, clothes, furniture, non-perishable food, etc.) or services (that is, beauty services, legal services, writing, graphic design, medical care, volunteer time to make and serve meals, etc.) If the organization you choose to support is classified as a 501(c)(3), your donation may be tax-deductible, meaning that you can deduct a percentage of the donation's value from your federal income tax. Make sure that you receive a receipt so that you can itemize this charitable deduction on your tax return.

- Donate benefits you may have accumulated such as frequent flyer miles, rebates or discounts.

- Consider using a credit card that makes a donation to a specified charity for every purchase or transaction. You can research credit card options at Cardweb.com.

- Contact your employer's human relations department to see if there's a company "matching program" to match employees' charitable donations.

- For a special occasion such as a wedding, baby shower, birthday or holiday, consider asking friends and family members to donate to your favorite charity in lieu of giving gifts.

If you choose to give a financial donation, there are several ways to do that. You can:

- Make a donation online through the organization's website using your credit card or registering for monthly automatic deductions from the bank account or credit card of your choice,

- Use an online portal (i.e. Network for Good [http://www.networkforgood.org], America's Charities [http://www.charities.org], Charitable Choices [http://www.charitablechoices.org]) and use a credit card to make your donation,

- Write a check directly to the organization (never to an individual working for the organization), or

- Transfer stock or mutual fund shares.

"Planned giving" is another way to financially support a charity. With planned giving you create a plan to make charitable contributions both while you are alive and after your death. There is a wide array of ways to do planned giving, including charitable trusts, family living trusts, and annuities. It's always a good idea to work with a financial advisor before making such financial plans or commitments or planning to transfer stock or mutual fund shares.

Even though many people give cash, it is better to keep a record of your donations and proof that you gave to a particular organization, such as a canceled check, e-mail, or credit card receipt. Keep your own record of the name of the organization you donated to, the amount of the donation, and the date of the contribution. You should also receive a receipt from the charitable organization if the donation is over $250. The IRS does not require receipts for cash donations under $250.

How To Identify (And Avoid!) Charity Scams And Fraud

Unfortunately there are unscrupulous people and organizations that will attempt to raise funds fraudulently from you. And when a disaster strikes that affects a lot of people, it's especially important to make sure you know exactly to whom you're giving and what they are doing with your funds. Here are a few tips to identify and avoid fundraising scams and fraud:

- If you get a phone solicitation for funds, ask for the exact name of the organization, the caller's title and/or relationship to the organization, and contact information where you can learn more about the organization (that is, a website address, office address, name of other staff, etc.) before you make any donation. If the person is aggressive or obnoxious, thank them politely and hang up. Do not be rushed into making a donation before you are ready. Beware of any organization that offers to send a "runner" to collect your contribution.

♣ **It's A Fact!!**

Don't be fooled into feeling like you have to pay for unsolicited items sent to you in the mail such as keychains, address labels, or notecards. Likewise you should make sure you're not being asked to "pay" for unsolicited appeals disguised as bills or invoices.

Source: © 2008 Securities Industry and Financial Markets Association Foundation for Investor Education.

- Verify the exact name of the charity; following disasters, a number of fraudulent organizations may pop up with names similar to large, credible organizations. For example, during the aftermath of Hurricane Katrina, some websites were set up with the name Katrina in them, or imitated the name and look of more well-known and reputable relief organizations with the name in the title, but had nothing to do with aiding the victims. Also, some e-mail messages may ask you to make a contribution but link you to a website that is actually entirely false, with the purpose of getting you to share personal information such as a credit card number, social security number, etc.

- Most legitimate nonprofit organizations do not ever send out mass e-mails requesting funds. Beware if you receive an e-mail of this sort. Check out the e-mail address at the top of the message. Is it the exact address of the organization? It's better to go into your internet browser and directly type the name of the organization in the address bar to get to the site on your own rather than replying by using a linked address in an e-mail.

- If you are being asked to contribute for disaster relief, make sure the organization soliciting you has experience in disaster relief. Ask the organization to provide you with information that shows you how they deliver assistance to victims in need.

- Do not give personal information or credit card number to an e-mail solicitation nor to a telephone solicitor. Request that information be sent to you in writing on the mission, programs and finances of the organization before you make a donation.

- If you're giving online, first make sure that the internet address of the site exactly matches the organization's name (you can go to an internet search engine like google.com or yahoo.com to verify) and then make sure that the portion where you are entering personal information is encrypted/secure. If it's not, consider giving through a secure online portal instead such as Networkforgood.org or Justgive.org.

- Don't respond to forwarded e-mail requests or chain letters for donations. In fact, such e-mails may contain viruses that can hack into your computer so it's best to delete them.

- Request written confirmation of the gift both by e-mail (if donating online) and by regular mail.

- If you get solicitations through the mail, read them carefully. In addition to getting details and information on the charity (that is, its name, address, mission, leadership, etc.) be sure you know what they're asking for.

- To reduce the number of phone solicitations you get at home, register your phone number on the national do not call list (http://www.donot call.gov).

- If you do not want to receive solicitations from a particular nonprofit organization, ask the caller to remove your name and phone number from their data base and/or write the organization and request they remove your name from their mailing list.

☞ Remember!!

Giving to charitable organizations is an act of caring and kindness. By doing a little bit of homework and giving from your heart while using your head, you can enjoy knowing that your resources are supporting proven, trusted charities that are working hard to advance the causes you believe in and care for people in need.

Source: © 2008 Securities Industry and Financial Markets Association Foundation for Investor Education.

Part Three

Being A Savvy Consumer

Chapter 16

Shopping And Impulse Buying

Buy It Or Not?

We live in a world where the pressure to spend money is constant. You are surrounded by ads. And advertisers are now placing products in movies and inserting messages on TV. They're even in online blogs and message boards.

Resist impulse buying. Advertisers study buyers and buying habits all the time. So these people have got some pretty clever ways to convince you that you must have something. Advertisers don't want you to think about what you're doing. They want you to buy right now—if you stop to think, you might not buy.

How do you hang on to your cash so you don't just buy impulsively? Ask yourself these questions:

- Do I really need this item?
- If I don't need it, why do I really want it?
- Am I sure that I'll use it? Wear it?
- If I buy it now, will I have enough money for other things I might need later on—this week, this month, next month?

About This Chapter: This chapter includes "Buy It Or Not?" "What's It Worth?" and "Smart Shopping," © 2007 Northwestern Mutual Foundation. Reprinted with permission. For additional information, visit www.themint.org.

- Will this purchase take money away from paying off any debts I owe?

- Is there any risk in delaying this purchase in order to think about it longer?

- What are the chances this item might go on sale soon?

- Could I find this item somewhere else cheaper?

- Could I find an item like this, but without a brand name? It will probably cost less.

If you answer HONESTLY, you may not buy it. Well, why can't you just dip into savings—just this once—to make the purchase? Don't even think about it. Once you start spending your savings on things you don't really need, it'll be gone before you know it.

> ✔ **Quick Tip**
> Keep a money diary that tracks what you save and spend. It will tell you about when, why, and how you use money.
>
> Source: © 2007 Northwestern Mutual Foundation.

What's It Worth ?

It's only $79.99! How many times have you heard those words on a commercial or read them in a newspaper ad? The word "only" is supposed to make you think that this is a great price for the product.

But think about this: How long does it take you to earn $79.99? What do you have to do to get that money? Let's say you stock shelves at a discount store, and you're making $7.00 an hour. The little item that's only $79.99 is worth almost 12 hours of your work! And if you are making less than this, how long will it take to earn that much money?

So as you stand in a store, telling yourself you have to buy an item, think of how long you must work to earn the money to pay for it. Is that $85 designer shirt really worth the time and effort it takes you to earn $85? You could probably find a similar shirt at another store for under $35, right?

Even if your parents are still buying your clothes, there's only so much money to go around. If you spend money on one item, you don't have it to spend on anything else. So if you spend the $85 on those jeans, what other opportunities might you be missing out on? You cannot put it in savings. You cannot go snowboarding or to the movies with friends—you won't have the money to go. That is what is called opportunity cost.

Smart Shopping

There are ways of getting what you want without paying top dollar. Here are some of them:

- Don't shop as entertainment. When you hang out at the mall on a Saturday afternoon, you see things you don't need. But because you see them, you want them.

- Shop the sales. If you shop the big sales to buy needed items, your shopping stays focused, and you get more for your money. But don't buy just because something is on sale. Do you really need it?

- Wait for the sale. When you see something you like, approach a salesperson to ask if the item will go on sale anytime soon.

- For gifts, shop in advance instead of the last minute. You may be able to get something on sale. Don't wait until the last minute. If you cannot find just the right thing, you may blow your budget on something else out of desperation.

- Shop places other than the mall. There are plenty of them.

Clothing

- Shop outlet stores. They offer good deals on popular designer names.

- Try discount stores. They can help you cut corners on less important wardrobe items, like underwear, belts, socks, etc. Not everything you own has to have a designer logo. Buy the basics here, and shop specialty stores for accessories.

- Look in consignment or second-hand stores. These stores are usually choosy about accepting only clothes in good condition. You can get some real buys.

Entertainment

- Go to matinees and discount theaters. You know that movie you've been dying to see? Sure, you can go to a full-price theater and pay full price. Or you can look in the newspaper for a discount theater and get a couple bucks off the ticket price. Go to a matinee (tickets are always cheaper).

- Don't spend all that money on drinks and popcorn. Without too much trouble, you can spend more on snacks than on the price of admission. Eat before you go to the movie, buy a beverage during the movie, and

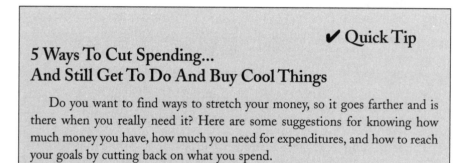

✔ Quick Tip

5 Ways To Cut Spending...
And Still Get To Do And Buy Cool Things

Do you want to find ways to stretch your money, so it goes farther and is there when you really need it? Here are some suggestions for knowing how much money you have, how much you need for expenditures, and how to reach your goals by cutting back on what you spend.

1. Practice Self-Control: To avoid making a quick decision to buy something just because you saw it featured on display or on sale, try these tips:

- Make a shopping list before you leave home and stick to it.

- Before you go shopping, set a spending limit (say, $5 or $10) for "impulse buys"—items you didn't plan to buy but that got your attention anyway. If you are tempted to spend more than your limit, wait a few hours or a few days and think it over.

- Limit the amount of cash you take with you. The less cash you carry, the less you can spend and the less you lose if you misplace your wallet.

2. Research Before You Buy: To be sure you are getting a good value, especially with a big purchase, look into the quality and the reputation of the product or service you're considering. Read "reviews" in magazines or respected websites. Talk to knowledgeable people you trust. Check other stores or go online and compare prices. Look at similar items. This is known as "comparison shopping," and it can lead to tremendous savings and better quality purchases.

then catch a pizza or a burger afterwards. You'll at least be getting more food for your money.

- Don't read the newspaper? Check it out. On Thursdays or Fridays newspapers usually feature ideas of what to do for free this weekend. Some might have it online.

Electronics, Sports Gear, And Big-Ticket Stuff

- Be a smart consumer. Looking for a digital camera? With the internet, you can read people's posted reviews of some products. You can also

And if you're sure you know what you want, take advantage of store coupons and mail-in "rebates."

3. **Keep Track Of Your Spending:** This helps you set and stick to limits—what many people refer to as budgeting. "Maintaining a budget may sound scary or complicated, but it can be as simple as having a notebook and writing down what you buy each month," says Janet Kincaid, Federal Deposit Insurance Corporation (FDIC) Senior Consumer Affairs Officer. "Any system that helps you know how much you are spending each month is a good thing."

Also pay attention to small amounts of money you spend. "A snack here and a magazine there can quickly add up," says Paul Horwitz, an FDIC Community Affairs Specialist. He suggests that, for a few weeks, you write down every purchase in a small notebook. "You'll probably be amazed at how much you spend without even thinking."

4. **Think "Used" Instead Of "New":** Borrow things (from the library or friends) that you don't have to own. Pick up used games, DVDs, and music at second-hand stores around town.

5. **Take Good Care Of What You Buy:** It's expensive to replace things. Think about it: Do you really want to buy the same thing twice?

Source: "5 Ways to Cut Spending... and Still Get to Do and Buy Cool Things," *FDIC Consumer News*, Federal Deposit Insurance Corporation (FDIC), Summer 2006.

learn about brands, models, and features. Not all store clerks really know much about what they sell. The internet can help you compare prices, too, before you visit a store. Getting all this information before you buy helps you find the right camera for your needs. Collecting information makes you a smart shopper—and can save you money.

How Small Savings Add Up

Don't underestimate saving a little here and a little there. Let's take a really common way of saving that everyone is familiar with: grocery shopping. Let's say you buy sale items, clip coupons, and use a preferred-customer card. Your plan pays off. You save $12 a week. Doesn't sound like much, does it? You'd be surprised. At year's end, you will have saved $624. That's a bundle of cash you could probably find a use for!

Chapter 17

It's On Sale, But Is It A Good Deal?

Surfing The Sales

18-HOUR SALE!

BACK-TO-SCHOOL BONANZA!

PRESIDENTS DAY SPECIAL!

Sometimes it seems like life is one big, long sale, doesn't it? It can get really confusing. How do you know you're really getting something for a reduced price? How do you make smart spending choices when there's so much pressure to buy, buy, buy? Here are some important things to think about:

Is It Really Such A Great Bargain?

Before you buy something that's marked down or on sale, think about this: Why is it on sale anyway? Sometimes, stores will lower the price of something because so far, nobody wants to buy it. If you buy a T-shirt on sale that you don't really like that much, or is halfway falling apart, you've just wasted money. A bargain means getting something great at a great price, not getting something so-so at a great price.

About This Chapter: This chapter includes "Spending Smarts: Surfing the Sales" and "Spending Smarts: Ten Super Shopping Tips," reprinted with permission from http://pbskids.org/itsmylife. © 2005 CastleWorks, Inc. All rights reserved.

Are You Really "Saving Money"?

You've probably come across price tags that look something like this: "Full Price: $249.00, Sale Price: $49.99." It looks like if you buy this item, you'll be saving $200.00, doesn't it? Well, not exactly. Usually, that big price was never meant to be the real price of the item, and a store will just put that on the tag to convince you that you're getting an awesome deal (keep a lookout for words like "Suggested Retail Price"). If the item doesn't look like it's worth $250.00, it probably isn't. What matters is the $49.99 that you'd actually be spending; after all, it's not like the $200.00 that was "marked off" the price tag is going to magically appear in your pocket. Ask yourself if this item is really worth the price it is now, and make your decision based on that.

Don't Believe Big Markdowns

It doesn't matter what something used to cost; it only matters what it costs now. If you're tempted to buy a sweater because it's $100.00 less than its original price, try to focus on whether it's a good deal at the CURRENT price, and if you really think you'll wear it. If it's something you like, you have the money, and it's a fair price, that's a good buy.

Relax And Take Your Time

Stores and companies know that when people take the time to really think about the things they buy, they will buy fewer things. They need you to buy NOW, before you have a chance to think about it, so they put a big "SALE" sticker on it.

☞ **Remember!!**

There will always be another sale (some stores seem to have them all year) and there will always be more cool things to buy. Take it easy, take it slow, and always comparison shop.

Source: "Spending Smarts: Surfing the Sales," © 2005 CastleWorks, Inc.

When Sales Are A Good Thing

Okay, so we now know that "sales" are often tricks that stores use to make you buy stuff you wouldn't normally buy. But sales can help you too, and here's how: When you're going to buy something anyway, it's better to get it at a sale price rather than full price.

Say you've been dying for a new bathing suit. The one you wore last year is now a little too small and besides, you want to make a splash with something new! Now that you've got to go shopping, why pay full price? Look for a deal this way:

- Keep an eye on the newspaper ads. Is there a clothing or department store that's having a sale? Check out the suits they offer and see if you spot anything you like that's selling for a good price.

- Ask about sales. If you're in a store and you find something that you think you might want to buy, ask a salesperson if they're having any sales now or in the near future. There may be a sale starting next week, and if you wait, you could get a good discount on that perfect swimsuit.

- Shop in the off-season. The start of the summer is probably the worst time to buy a new bathing suit, because stores know that everyone needs one before the hot weather hits. Prices will be much better in the early spring, when some stores have "pre-season sales," and at the end of summer, when the stores are trying to make room for fall clothes. This kind of shopping takes some planning, but it can really pay off.

Ten Super Shopping Tips

If you can remember these ten big tips and practice them when you're out shopping or having fun, you'll be an official "smart spender."

1. Be Skeptical

- This means that you shouldn't believe everything you see or hear.

- If something is "on sale," take a close look and make sure that the new price is really a good deal.

- If something is promoted as "the best thing ever," don't just blindly buy it—make sure it's something you want or need.

- Don't always trust what you see in ads, and don't believe everyone who says something is "rare" or "collectible."

✔ Quick Tip

Taking The "Bait" Out Of Rebates

Rebate offers can be irresistible to consumers, slashing the price of consumer goods at the time of purchase or promising partial or full reimbursements after the purchase.

Some manufacturers and retailers entice shoppers with instant cash rebates that can be redeemed immediately at the checkout counter. But most rebates are of the mail-in variety. They require consumers to pay the full cost of an item at the time purchase, then to send documentation to the manufacturer or retailer to receive a rebate by mail.

The documentation required generally includes the original sales receipt, UPC code, rebate slip, and the customer's name, address and telephone number. In most cases, this paperwork must be sent to the manufacturer or retailer within 30 days of the purchase. Consumers generally receive their rebates up to 12 weeks later.

But the Federal Trade Commission cautions consumers against being "baited" by rebates that never arrive or arrive far later than promised. By law, companies are required to send rebates within the time frame promised, or if no time is specified, within a "reasonable" time. "Reasonable" in this case often is interpreted as within 30 days.

When purchasing a product that offers a rebate, the FTC encourages consumers to take these steps:

- Follow the instructions on the rebate form and enclose all required documentation in the envelope when filing for a rebate.

- Make a copy of all paperwork to be mailed when applying for a rebate. It's the only record a consumer will have of the transaction if anything goes wrong.

- Contact the company if the rebate doesn't arrive within the time promised.

- If the rebate never arrives or arrives late, file a complaint with the Federal Trade Commission, the state Attorney General or the local Better Business Bureau.

Source: Federal Trade Commission (www.ftc.gov), January 2000. Despite the older date of this document, the suggestions are still pertinent to shoppers planning to seek rebates.

2. Be Choosy

- Don't just spend your money on any old stuff! Make sure that you really like it, that you're going to use it a lot, and that it offers good quality for a good price.

- Compare prices of different items in a store, or the same item in different stores.

3. Be Patient

- Don't be the first person to buy into something new, because it might turn out to be a dud.

- Instead of making quick impulse buys, take the time to think about everything you spend money on.

- Wait for prices to come down on the things you want.

4. Be Firm

- Don't let salespeople talk you into buying something you don't want.

- Don't fall for the "upsell," which is when an employee tries to make you buy more than you asked for, especially in restaurants.

5. Be Yourself

- Following the crowd can be expensive. Instead, invent your own style.

- You don't always have to own the same things or the same clothes as everybody else.

6. Be Informed

- Know exactly what you're getting for your money.

- Do some research before you buy any big-ticket items such as electronics.

- Look for "hidden costs," like extra charges or extra things you have to buy in order for something to work.

7. Be Realistic

- Understand that most things you spend your money on—from a new shirt to a bag of candy—cannot make your life magically better.

- Sellers and advertisers try to make you think that all your problems will disappear if you just spend money on their products, but this is not true.

8. Be Resourceful

- Try to have fun without spending a lot of money.

- Borrow a book or movie from a friend or from the library.

✔ **Quick Tip**

Pricing Accuracy Concerns

When you buy something and a cashier passes the Universal Product Code (UPC) symbol over an electronic scanner, a computer decodes the symbol and sends the price to the register.

Electronic scanning is not foolproof. The reasons: human error, pricing difficulties, and management problems. As a result, consumer advocates and regulators are concerned about inconsistencies between advertised or posted prices and prices stored in the computer, inaccurate prices throughout a chain of stores because of an error in the central computer, and problems for shoppers who may not remember posted prices or special promotions when they check out.

Although the UPC symbol has replaced the traditional readable price tag, it's still possible for consumers to spot pricing errors at the register. Here's how:

- Watch the display screen for prices. If you think you're being overcharged, speak up. Ask about the store's policy on pricing errors, and ask the cashier to make the adjustment before you pay. Although some stores simply adjust the price, others deduct an additional amount. Still others offer the mispriced item for free.

- Bring a copy of the store's flyer or newspaper ad to the checkout counter. Some advertised specials—15 percent off an item for two hours, for example, or a two-for-one promotion—may not be in the computer and must be entered manually by the cashier.

- Consider jotting down prices or special sales as you wend your way through the store. In grocery stores, you may want to note the product prices on the packages.

- Try activities that are free, like going to a park or museum.
- Get creative and add your personal touch to clothing and jewelry.

9. Be In Control

- You have the power to say yes or no when it comes to spending money.
- Avoid the temptation to spend everything you have in your pocket or purse.

- Check your receipt before you walk away. If you notice an error, ask the cashier to adjust the total. If you've already left the cashier's lane, see the store or department manager or the customer service department to correct any mistakes.

    If you notice a pattern of electronic scanning errors in a particular store, talk to the customer service department or the store manager. You also may want to write a letter to the company's headquarters. The retailer may not realize a problem exists until it's pointed out.

    You also may report recurring problems to your state Attorney General's office, state or local consumer protection office, or your state or local office of weights and measures.

    Finally, consider filing a complaint with the Federal Trade Commission (FTC). The FTC works for the consumer to prevent fraudulent, deceptive, and unfair business practices in the marketplace and to provide information to help consumers spot, stop, and avoid them. To file a complaint or to get free information on consumer issues, visit www.ftc.gov or call toll-free, 877-FTC-HELP (877-382-4357); TTY: 866-653-4261.

    Source: Excerpted from "Making Sure the Scanned Price Is Right, Federal Trade Commission (www.ftc.gov), December 1998. Despite the older date of this document, the suggestions are still pertinent to today's shoppers. Individual state laws may govern your rights concerning the correction of electronic scanning errors.

♣ It's A Fact!!
Do You Really Need
Those $125 Designer Sneakers?

A "need" is something you cannot live without. A "want" is something that would be nice to have but isn't necessary.

"A need may be a pair of sneakers, but a want is the $125 pair advertised by your favorite athlete," explains Paul Horwitz of the Federal Deposit Insurance Corporation (FDIC).

When you can control your spending on life's wants, you'll have more money available to save for what you need in the future.

Janet Kincaid of the FDIC offers this tip: "Take a day or two to think about any purchase that will cost a significant portion of your savings," she said. "If you really need to buy the item, it will probably still be there for you. If you don't need it but you still want it, perhaps you can buy something similar that's a lot less expensive and save the remaining money for other things."

Source: *FDIC Consumer News*, Federal Deposit Insurance Corporation (FDIC), Summer 2006.

- Try saying no—and then take the money you don't spend and put it in the bank.

- The more you resist the urge to spend on a whim, the more money you'll have for the stuff that's really important to you.

10. Be Active and Happy

- When you're down on yourself, feeling low, or just plain bored, you'll be tempted to go out and spend money for the sake of it. So find what puts you in a good mood—whether it's playing soccer, making music, reading a book, or whatever—and go do it!

Chapter 18

Online Shopping: A Guide For E-Consumers

Listed below are tips to protect yourself from various forms of internet fraud:

Avoiding Internet Auction Fraud

- Understand as much as possible about how the auction works, what your obligations are as a buyer, and what the seller's obligations are before you bid.

- Find out what actions the website/company takes if a problem occurs and consider insuring the transaction and shipment.

- Learn as much as possible about the seller, especially if the only information you have is an e-mail address. If it is a business, check the Better Business Bureau where the seller/business is located.

- Examine the feedback on the seller.

- Determine what method of payment the seller is asking from the buyer and where he/she is asking to send payment.

- If a problem occurs with the auction transaction, it could be much more difficult if the seller is located outside the U.S. because of the difference in laws.

About This Chapter: From "Internet Fraud," Federal Bureau of Investigation (www.fbi.gov), 2008.

- Ask the seller about when delivery can be expected and if there is a problem with the merchandise is it covered by a warranty or can you exchange it.

- Find out if shipping and delivery are included in the auction price or are additional costs so there are no unexpected costs.

- There should be no reason to give out your social security number or drivers license number to the seller.

Avoiding Non-Delivery Of Merchandise

- Make sure you are purchasing merchandise from a reputable source.

- Do your homework on the individual or company to ensure that they are legitimate.

- Try to obtain a physical address rather than merely a post office box and a phone number, call the seller to see if the number is correct and working.

- Send them e-mail to see if they have an active e-mail address and be wary of sellers who use free e-mail services where a credit card wasn't required to open the account.

♣ It's A Fact!!

The Internet Crime Complaint Center, or IC3, a partnership of the Federal Bureau of Investigation (FBI) and the National White Collar Crime Center, in 2007 released its latest annual report on victims' complaints received and referred to law enforcement. Among the results:

- Internet auction fraud was by far the most reported offense, comprising 44.9% of referred complaints. Non-delivered merchandise and/or payment accounted for 19.0% of complaints. Check fraud made up 4.9% of complaints. Credit/debit card fraud, computer fraud, confidence fraud, and financial institutions fraud round out the top seven categories of complaints referred to law enforcement during the year.

Source: FBI, 2008.

- Consider not purchasing from sellers who won't provide you with this type of information.

- Check with the Better Business Bureau from the seller's area.

- Check out other websites regarding this person/company.

- Don't judge a person/company by their website.

- Be cautious when responding to special offers (especially through unsolicited e-mail).

- Be cautious when dealing with individuals/companies from outside your own country.

- Inquire about returns and warranties.

- The safest way to purchase items via the internet is by credit card because you can often dispute the charges if something is wrong.

- Make sure the transaction is secure when you electronically send your credit card numbers.

- Consider utilizing an escrow or alternate payment service.

Avoiding Credit Card Fraud

- Don't give out your credit card number(s) online unless the site is a secure and reputable site. Sometimes a tiny icon of a padlock appears to symbolize a higher level of security to transmit data. This icon is not a guarantee of a secure site, but might provide you some assurance.

- Don't trust a site just because it claims to be secure.

- Before using the site, check out the security/encryption software it uses.

- Make sure the transaction is secure when you electronically send your credit card numbers.

- You should also keep a list of all your credit cards and account information along with the card issuer's contact information. If anything looks suspicious or you lose your credit card(s) you should contact the card issuer immediately.

✔ Quick Tip
A Checklist For Online International Shopping

- Is the business you're buying from "consumer-friendly" for international e-commerce?

- Does its website clearly disclose information about the company:
  - What kind of business it is and what it sells?
  - Where it is located, including the country?
  - How you can contact the business?

- Does its website clearly disclose information about the product or service:
  - What is being sold, with enough details for you to know exactly what you're buying?
  - The cost of the product or service, and the currency used?

- Does its website clearly disclose information about the sale:
  - The costs, in addition to the price of the product or service, if any, like costs for shipping and handling, taxes and duties?
  - Any restrictions or limitations on the sale?
  - Any warranties or guarantees?
  - The availability of convenient and safe payment options?
  - An estimation of when you will receive the order?

- Does its website clearly disclose information about its consumer protections:
  - The opportunity for you to print or save a record of the transaction?
  - Safeguards for protecting your payment information when it is transmitted online?
  - Policies on what personal identifying information is being collected about you, what the company does with it and whom it shares it with?
  - An opportunity for you to "opt out" of having information about yourself collected?
  - Policies on sending unsolicited e-mail, including an option for you to decline these offers?
  - The return policy, including an explanation of how you can return an item, get a refund or credit or make an exchange?
  - Where you should call, write, or e-mail with complaints or problems?

Source: Excerpted from "Going Shipping? Go Global!" Federal Trade Commission (www.ftc.gov), March 2000. Despite the older date of this document, the suggestions are still pertinent to today's internet shoppers.

Chapter 19

Payment Options For Purchases

When you make a purchase... should you use cash, check, a credit card, debit card, your computer or an automatic payment?

Each payment method has advantages and disadvantages. When you buy something, merchants often offer several different ways to pay. Which way is best? To make a good decision, it's important to think about your options.

Cash

Cash is almost always accepted, but consider:

- Do you have enough cash to pay for your purchase as well as any other things you might have to pay for in the near future, such as a quick meal or an unexpected purchase? If not, more cash is available from an automatic teller machine (ATM), but is there a service charge for using an ATM?

- Are you losing an opportunity to earn interest by carrying too much cash? The more cash you carry, the less that can be deposited in a financial institution in an interest bearing account.

About This Chapter: "Purchase Options for Consumers," reprinted with permission from the Federal Reserve Bank of Chicago, www.chicagofed.org; accessed in June 2008.

184 Cash and Credit Information for Teens, Second Edition

- Is there a possibility you'll return the item you're buying? Will you be able to return it and get cash back, or will you be able to get only a store credit? Will you use the store credit?

- Does your purchase need to be delivered? Do you want to pay in cash for something you haven't received yet? What if the item is damaged in transit, and you've already paid for it? How will you get your money back? It is generally more difficult to get a cash refund, even if you have a receipt.

In general, it's wise not to carry large amounts of cash because of the risk of loss or theft. Use cash only for those items that you'll either use immediately or take with you.

Check

Checks are another payment option. A check represents money but is not cash. It's a piece of paper the check writer uses to instruct his or her financial institution to release funds. With proper identification, you can open a checking account at most financial institutions. Checks are reliable and convenient for most transactions. Using them frees you from the risk of carrying large sums of cash. However, you may want to consider the following:

- Checking accounts often have fees, minimum balance requirements, or a limit on how many checks you can write each month. Therefore, you may not want to write checks for small amounts unless you're mailing a payment.

- If mailing a payment, sending a check is acceptable, but mailing cash can be risky. Cash lost in transit can't be replaced, while a lost check can be.

- Paying with a check through the mail provides proof of payment because the recipient must endorse the check to cash it or deposit it.

- Not everyone is willing to accept checks because they're sometimes returned for reasons such as insufficient funds in the checking account. Merchants are sometimes reluctant to accept a check because they can't be sure it will not be returned.

- There is usually only a day or two between when a merchant receives your check and when the funds in the checking account are actually deducted for payment. Funds in your checking account continue to earn interest during this time. Debit cards and other types of electronic payments are deducted immediately.

Credit Cards

Credit cards and charge cards can be a convenient, efficient and reliable payment method. Actually, they allow the buyer to defer payment. Credit cards are more readily acceptable than checks because the merchant's bank guarantees payment to the merchant. Payment is made when you write a check to the card issuer. If you want to use a credit card to make payments and pay bills there are a number of things you should consider:

- You may have to pay an annual fee to use a credit card.

- Credit cards are more readily acceptable than checks. Sometimes they are the only option acceptable.

✔ Quick Tip
Report Unauthorized
Transactions Immediately

Whether you use a credit card, a debit card, a personal computer or Automated Clearing House (ACH), the transaction is electronic and is governed by the Electronic Fund Transfer Act, or Regulation E. The regulation includes procedures for resolving errors and provides limited liability for unauthorized transactions. Send written notices by certified mail, return receipts requested, and keep a copy of your letter for your own files. However, be aware that liability for credit cards is different than electronic debit transactions. Your maximum liability on a credit card is $50. On an electronic debit, unless you contact your financial institution within 60 days of receipt of your statement, there may be no limit to your liability for unauthorized transactions. Additionally, before you receive your next statement, your checks may be returned for nonsufficient funds.

- If you want to return a purchase, credit card issuers frequently have procedures to facilitate the return.

- Since merchants pay a fee for each credit card transaction processed, they may not want to accept payment using a credit card under a certain dollar amount.

- When you pay with a credit card, you're actually receiving a short-term loan to make the purchase. Unless you pay your credit card bill in full a short time after the bill is received, you'll have to pay an interest charge in addition to the cost of your purchase. The period between when you receive your bill and when the payment is due is usually referred to as the "grace period". Grace periods are generally 14–20 days, but can be up to 30 days. Although many card issuers offer a grace period, not all credit card issuers do. Check the terms of your card to be sure.

- With low minimum payments and high interest rates, credit card and interest payments can extend over long periods of time—sometimes over many years.

- Purchases are conveniently summarized in a monthly statement.

- Credit cards can be too convenient to use. Unless you keep track of your charges, you can quickly owe more money than you can afford.

- Some credit cards offer incentives such as cash back, shopping discounts, rental cars, or airline trips based on how much is charged. These benefits should be weighed against other factors, such as the annual fee and the interest rate charged when you don't pay your bill on time or pay only a portion of your bill.

- If your credit card is stolen or used by an unauthorized user your liability should be no more than $50 if you report the unauthorized transactions to your financial institutions.

Debit Cards

A debit card looks like a credit card but functions differently. It's used to take money out of your checking account at the time of sale. The transaction is similar to writing a check or using a credit card, except using a debit card removes funds from your checking account immediately. When using a debit card, consider the following:

- Because your checking account will be automatically debited, you have to make sure you subtract the right amount from your checking account balance.

- Before you use the debit card, consider how much money is in your checking account and what other expenses (rent, mortgage, utilities, other monthly payments, etc.) you have.

- Unlike a credit card, if your debit card is stolen or used by an unauthorized user, you could be held liable for the entire amount of the loss unless you report the unauthorized transactions to your financial institutions within 60 days of receiving your statement. Also, unlike credit cards, the money has already been deducted from your account. Your money is gone and to get it back you must be able to prove that the transactions were unauthorized. Additionally, your checks may be returned for non- sufficient funds before you receive your next statement because all the money in your account was removed by the unauthorized user.

- Unlike a check, you can't stop an electronic debit once it has been authorized because funds are removed immediately from your account. And unlike a check, there is no lag time between when funds are deducted from your account. And unlike a check, there is no lag time between when payment is made and when funds are deducted from your account.

- If you return the item, can you get cash back or will you be able to get only a store credit? As with cash, if only a credit is available for returns you may want to use another means of payment if you don't think you'll be able to use a store credit.

- Debit cards should not be used for pre-authorized, recurring payments such as insurance premiums or health club dues. Doing so can lead to problems later if you want to cancel your authorization. Safer methods of direct payment are available via your financial institution.

✔ **Quick Tip**

- Since debit cards and credit cards look the same, be sure you know which one you're using when making a transaction.

- Consumer liability on a credit card is generally limited to $50. Be sure to report a lost or stolen credit card immediately to prevent its misuse.

- Under certain conditions, consumer liability on a debit card can be unlimited.

- Save your receipts for transactions made with credit cards or debit cards. Review your statement regularly and report discrepancies at once.

- Do not download files sent to you by strangers or click on hyperlinks from people you don't know. Opening a file could expose your system to a computer virus.

Personal Computer

Paying your bills using your personal computer can be fun and easy. More and more financial institutions offer this type of "home banking" over the internet. Using your computer to pay bills usually functions the same way as using any electronic means to make a payment—an electronic debit is made to your account. Using your home computer to pay bills is just like using your debit card because the amount of the payment is deducted directly from your account, and there is no lag time or float between when the payment is made and when funds are deducted. When you pay bills online, it is important that you make sure your transactions are secure, and that your personal information is protected. Here are some precautions you may want to consider when making payments online:

- Keep personal information—address, telephone number, social security number, and account numbers or e-mail address—private. It is not recommended that you provide this information unless you've initiated the transaction. Don't disclose your personal information unless you know who's collecting the information, why they're collecting it, and how they'll use it.

- Give payment information only to businesses you know and trust, and only in appropriate places like order forms.

- Never give your password to anyone online, even your internet service provider.

- Protect your account numbers and personal information by using software that encrypts or scrambles the purchase information you send over the internet.

- Create and keep records of your online transactions just as you do for your credit and debit card transactions. Review your periodic bank and credit card statements for any billing errors or unauthorized purchases. Notify your credit card issuer or bank immediately if you find any discrepancies.

- Read the policies of websites you frequent and especially the disclosures about their security, refund policies, and privacy policy on collecting and using your personal information.

Automated Transactions

Direct Payment is a safe, reliable service that allows you to pay your bills automatically. With Direct Payment, you authorize a company to deduct money from your checking or savings account in order to pay a monthly bill.

Direct Payment transactions are generally prearranged or recurring payments, such as monthly utilities, insurance premiums, and mortgage payments.

Automated transactions can also be credits or deposits to your account. Many people work for companies that use Direct Deposit to automatically deposit pay into their employees' checking or savings accounts instead of distributing checks on payday. Direct Deposit of Social Security benefits, expense reimbursements, and pension benefits are other examples of automated credit transactions.

Direct Payment and Direct Deposit transactions flow through the Automated Clearing House (ACH) payments network. The ACH network is more than 25-years-old and is an established network responsible for transferring billions of dollars each day between financial institutions. You can learn more about Direct Payment or Direct Deposit by visiting the following site: http://www.electronicpayments.org.

Chapter 20

Facts For Consumers: How To Right A Wrong

Most companies want to make you happy so you'll come back and recommend them to your friends. But when you find a company that's not making the grade, how do you resolve the problem?

This chapter explains your rights when it comes to mail and telephone order shopping, unordered merchandise, and door-to-door sales. It also tells you how to write an effective complaint letter and lists some resources for additional help.

Mail And Telephone Order Sales

Shopping by phone or mail can be a convenient alternative to shopping at a store. But if your merchandise arrives late or not at all, you have some rights.

By law, a company should ship your order within the time stated in its ads. If no time is promised, the company should ship your order within 30 days after receiving it.

If the company is unable to ship within the promised time, they must give you an "option notice." This notice gives you the choice of agreeing to the delay or canceling your order and receiving a prompt refund.

About This Chapter: "How to Right a Wrong," *Facts for Consumers*, Federal Trade Commission (www.ftc.gov), September 2003.

There is one exception to the 30-day rule. If a company doesn't promise a shipping time, and you're applying for credit to pay for your purchase, the company has 50 days to ship after receiving your order.

♣ **It's A Fact!!**
Fair Credit Billing Act (FCBA)

You're protected by the FCBA when you use your credit card to pay for purchases.

Source: FTC, 2003.

Billing Errors

If you find an error on your credit or charge card statement, you can dispute the charge and withhold payment on the challenged amount while the charge is in dispute. The error might be a charge for the wrong amount, for something you did not accept, or for an item that was not delivered as agreed. Of course, you still must pay any part of the bill that isn't in dispute, including the finance charges on the undisputed amount.

If you decide to dispute a charge, follow these steps:

- Write to the creditor at the address indicated on the monthly statement for "billing inquiries." Include your name, address, credit card number, and a description of the billing error.

- Send your letter in a timely fashion. It must reach the creditor within 60 days after the first bill containing the error was mailed to you.

- The creditor must acknowledge your complaint in writing within 30 days after receiving it, unless the problem has been resolved. The creditor must resolve the dispute within two billing cycles (but not more than 90 days) after receiving the letter.

Unsatisfactory Goods Or Services

You also may dispute charges for unsatisfactory goods or services. To take advantage of this protection, you must meet these requirements:

- Have made the purchase in your home state or within 100 miles of your current billing address. The charge must be for more than $50; and

- Make a good faith effort first to resolve the dispute with the seller. However, you are not required to use any special procedure to do so.

Note that the dollar and distance limitations don't apply if the seller is the card issuer or if a special business relationship exists between the seller and the card issuer.

Unordered Merchandise

If you receive merchandise you didn't order, federal law says you can consider it a gift. You can't be forced to pay for the item or return it.

If you decide to keep the merchandise, you may want to send the seller a letter stating your intention, even though you're not legally obligated to do so. Your letter may discourage the seller from sending you repeated bills, or it may clear up an error. It's a good idea to send the letter by certified mail and keep the return receipt and a copy of the letter. These records will help you establish later, if necessary, that you didn't order the merchandise.

Two types of merchandise may be sent legally without your consent: free samples that are clearly marked as such; and merchandise mailed by charities asking for contributions. In either case, you may keep the shipments.

Door-To-Door Sales

Shopping at home can be convenient and enjoyable. But there may be times when you change your mind about an in-home purchase.

The Federal Trade Commission (FTC)'s Cooling-Off Rule gives you three days to cancel purchases of $25 or more made at your home, workplace or dormitory, or at facilities rented by the seller on a temporary short-term basis, such as hotel or motel rooms, convention centers, fairgrounds, and restaurants.

Some Exceptions

Some types of sales can't be canceled even if they occur in locations normally covered by the Rule. The Rule does not cover sales that meet these criteria:

- Are under $25

- Are for goods or services not primarily intended for personal, family, or household use. The Rule applies to courses of instruction or training.

- Are made entirely by mail or telephone

✔ Quick Tip

The Federal Trade Commission, the nation's consumer protection agency, suggests that students and grads tap into these 10 tips to make the most of their money:

1. **Keep your personal information to yourself:** In the past five years, millions of Americans have been victims of identity theft, including many students. Protect your passwords, guard your credit card number, shred sensitive paperwork, and don't leave your mail where it might tempt a potential identity thief.

2. **Socialize safely online:** Social networking sites can expose you to people with less than friendly intentions. Consider restricting access to your page. Post only information that you're comfortable with the whole world knowing, because once it's posted, you can't take it back. Don't post your full name, Social Security number, address, phone number, or bank and credit card account numbers. Be cautious about posting the name of your school, sports team, clubs, and where you work or hang out. Trust your gut and report any suspicions to the site and the police.

3. **Consider the National Do Not Call Registry:** As hard as it may be for your parents to believe, there may be times when you don't want to be on the phone—especially when the caller is a stranger trying to sell you something. Visit donotcall.gov and register your phone number with the National Do Not Call Registry.

4. **Stay away from "guarantees" of scholarships:** Reputable groups don't charge for information about scholarships. Steer clear of anyone "guaranteeing" you financial aid for college or vocational school—especially if they insist you pay them for the information first.

5. **Don't buy bogus weight loss products:** Good health isn't about a number on a scale. It's about cultivating a positive attitude, enjoying a variety of foods, and staying fit and active. Take a pass on any product that promises easy or effortless weight loss; instead, focus on healthy habits that will last a lifetime.

6. **Understand credit:** Credit is more than just a plastic card; it's your financial future. Before you sign on the dotted line, make sure you "speak credit."

- Are the result of prior negotiations at the seller's permanent location where the goods are sold regularly

- Are needed to meet an emergency. Suppose insects suddenly invade your home, and you waive your right to cancel the contract.

That "permanent record" your teachers always warned you about? It's called a credit report. Late payments now will come back to haunt you when you try to buy a car, get an apartment, or even land a job. Once you've established credit, get a free copy of your credit report at annualcreditreport.com.

7. **P2P file-sharing can be risky:** Peer-to-peer file-sharing can open the door to unwanted content, spyware, and viruses. If you decide to use file-sharing software, install it carefully. Otherwise, you might give strangers access not just to the files you intended to share, but also to other information on your hard drive, like e-mail and personal documents. Remember that sharing copyrighted music or other entertainment via P2P can land you in legal hot water.

8. **Travel scams turn spring breaks into spring busts:** Who doesn't dream of spending spring relaxing in the sun or snowboarding on some mountain? Be aware that scam artists target students who are looking for low-cost vacations. Before you show up at the airport with your sunscreen, review the tour package carefully and investigate the operator. Check out http://www.ftc.gov/travel for more travel tips.

9. **Phishing scams reel in personal information:** You've gotten e-mails claiming to be from your bank or ISP asking you to "verify" your credit card or checking account number. They're from fraudsters phishing for your information. Never give out your personal information in response to an e-mail. When in doubt, check it out by calling the company directly. Visit http://www.onguardonline.gov to learn more.

10. **Some employment services are scams:** Bona fide job placement services can help launch you in the career of your dreams. But bogus companies can scam you out of your money. Before paying any money to someone offering to help you land a job, check out who you're doing business with.

Source: "How To Be The Class 'Value-Dictorian,'" Federal Trade Commission, June 2006.

- Are made as part of your request for the seller to do repairs or mainte-nance on your personal property (purchases made beyond the mainte-nance or repair request are covered)

Also exempt from the Rule are sales that involve these issues:

- Real estate, insurance, or securities

- Automobiles, vans, trucks, or other motor vehicles sold at temporary locations, provided the seller has at least one permanent place of business

- Arts and crafts sold at fairs or locations such as shopping malls, civic centers, and schools

Under the Rule, the salesperson must tell you about your cancellation rights at the time of sale. The salesperson also must give you two copies of a cancellation form (one to keep and one to send back) and a copy of your contract or receipt. The contract or receipt should be dated, show the name and address of the seller, and explain your right to cancel. The contract or receipt must be in the same language that's used in the sales presentation.

How To Cancel A Door-To-Door Sale

To cancel a sale, sign and date one copy of the cancellation form. You don't have to give a reason for canceling the purchase. Mail it to the address given for cancellations, making sure the envelope is post-marked before mid-night of the third business day after the contract date. (Saturday is consid-ered a business day; Sundays and federal holidays are not.) Because proof of the mailing date and receipt are important, consider sending the cancella-tion form by certified mail so you can get a return receipt. Keep the other copy of the cancellation form for your records. If the seller did not provide cancellation forms, write your own cancellation letter.

If You Cancel

If you cancel your purchase, the seller has 10 days to cancel and return any promissory notes or other negotiable instruments you signed; refund all your money and tell you whether any product left with you will be picked up; and return any trade-in.

Within 20 days, the seller either must pick up the items left with you, or reimburse you for mailing expenses, if you agreed to send back the items. If you received any goods from the seller, you must make them available to the seller in as good condition as when you received them. If you don't make the items available—or if you agree to return the items but don't—you remain obligated under the contract.

Problems

Try to resolve your dispute with the seller first. Make sure you act quickly. Some companies may not accept responsibility if you fail to complain within a certain period of time.

Send a letter of complaint. A letter is important because it puts your complaint on record and lets the company know you are serious about pursuing the dispute. Be sure you keep a copy for your records.

If you can't get satisfaction, consider contacting the following organizations for further information and assistance:

• State and local consumer protection offices

• Your local Better Business Bureau (BBB)

• Action line and consumer reporters. Check with your local newspaper, TV, and radio stations for a contact.

• Postal Inspectors. Call your local U.S. Post Office and ask for the Inspector-in-Charge.

• The Federal Trade Commission. To file a complaint, visit http://www.ftc.gov or call toll-free, 877-FTC-HELP (382-4357); TTY: 866-653-4261. Although the FTC does not intervene in individual disputes, the information you provide may indicate a pattern of possible law violations requiring action by the Commission.

• Mail/telephone orders only: Write: Direct Marketing Association (DMA), 1111 19th Street, NW, Washington, DC 20036.

• Door-to-Door sales only: The Direct Selling Association (DSA) can help you with your complaint if the door-to-door seller is a member.

✔ **Quick Tip**

Sample Complaint Letter

An effective complaint letter may look something like this sample letter.

(Your address)
(Your City, State, Zip Code)

(Date)

(Name of Contact Person)
(Title)
(Company Name)
(Street Address)
(City, State, Zip Code)

Dear (Contact Person):

On (date), I purchased (or had repaired) a (name of the product with the serial or model number or service performed). I made this purchase at (location, date, and other important details of the transaction).

Unfortunately, your product (or service) has not performed well (or the service was inadequate) because (state the problem).

Therefore, to resolve the problem, I would appreciate your (state the specific action you want). Enclosed are copies (copies, NOT originals) of my records (receipts, guarantees, warranties, canceled checks, contracts, model and serial numbers, and any other documents).

I look forward to your reply and a resolution to my problem, and will wait (set a time limit) before seeking third-party assistance. Please contact me at the above address or by phone (home or office numbers with area codes).

Sincerely,

(Your name)
(Your account number)

Source: FTC, 2003.

Write: Direct Selling Association, 1275 Pennsylvania Avenue, NW, Washington, DC 20004.

Dispute Resolution Programs

You also may want to consider dispute resolution programs. A popular way to settle disagreements, a dispute resolution program can be quicker, less expensive, more private, and less stressful than going to court. Many businesses, private organizations, and public agencies offer these programs. Two resolution techniques are mediation and arbitration.

Through mediation, you and the other party try to resolve the dispute with the help of a neutral third party—a mediator. In the course of informal meetings, the mediator tries to help resolve your differences. The mediator doesn't make a decision; it's up to you and the other party to reach an agreement. The mediator is there to help you find a solution.

In arbitration, you present your case before an arbitrator, who makes a decision. Arbitration is less formal than court, though you and the other party may appear at hearings, present evidence, or call and question each other's witnesses. The decision may be binding and legally enforceable in court.

Contact the following organizations for dispute resolution options in your area: local and state consumer protection offices, small claims courts, BBBs, and bar associations.

For More Information

If you're not sure what federal agency has jurisdiction over your inquiry or complaint, contact the Federal Citizen Information Center's (FCIC) National Contact Center at 800-FED-INFO (333-4636) Monday through Friday 8:00 a.m. to 8:00 p.m. eastern time.

The FTC works for the consumer to prevent fraudulent, deceptive, and unfair business practices in the marketplace and to provide information to help consumers spot, stop, and avoid them. To file a complaint or to get free information on consumer issues, visit ftc.gov or call toll-free, 877-FTC-HELP (877-382-4357); TTY: 866-653-4261. The FTC enters internet, telemarketing, identity theft, and other fraud-related complaints into Consumer Sentinel, a secure online database available to hundreds of civil and criminal law enforcement agencies in the U.S. and abroad.

Chapter 21

What You Should Know About Warranties And Service Contracts

Warranties

When you make a major purchase, the manufacturer or seller makes an important promise to stand behind the product. It's called a warranty. Federal law requires that warranties be available for you to read before you buy even when you're shopping by catalog or on the internet. Coverage varies, so you can compare the extent of warranty coverage just as you compare the style, price, and other characteristics of products.

Written Warranties

Although not required by law, written warranties come with most major purchases. When comparing written warranties, keep the following in mind:

- **How long does the warranty last?** Check the warranty to see when it begins and when it expires, as well as any conditions that may void coverage.

- **Who do you contact to get warranty service?** It may be the seller or the manufacturer who provides you with service.

About This Chapter: This chapter includes "Warranties," October 2001, "Service Contracts," October 2001, and "Auto Service Contracts," May 1997, *Facts for Consumers*, Federal Trade Commission (www.ftc.gov). Despite the older dates of these documents, the information is still pertinent to today's consumers.

- **What will the company do if the product fails?** Read to see whether the company will repair the item, replace it, or refund your money.

- **What parts and repair problems are covered?** Check to see if any parts of the product or types of repair problems are excluded from coverage. For example, some warranties require you to pay for labor charges. Also, look for conditions that could prove expensive or inconvenient, such as a requirement that you ship a heavy object to a factory for service, or that you return the item in the original carton.

> ✔ **Quick Tip**
> **Spoken Warranties**
>
> If a salesperson makes a promise orally, such as that the company will provide free repairs, get it in writing. Otherwise, you may not be able to get the service that was promised.
>
> Source: Federal Trade Commission, October 2001.

- **Does the warranty cover "consequential damages?"** Many warranties do not cover damages caused by the product, or your time and expense in getting the damage repaired. For example, if your freezer breaks and the food spoils, the company will not pay for the lost food.

- **Are there any conditions or limitations on the warranty?** Some warranties provide coverage only if you maintain or use the product as directed. For example, a warranty may cover only personal uses—as opposed to business uses—of the product. Make sure the warranty will meet your needs.

Warranty Pieces

When you buy a car, home, or major appliance, you may be offered a service contract. Although often called "extended warranties," service contracts are not warranties. Service contracts, like warranties, provide repair and/or maintenance for a specific time. Warranties, however, are included in the price of the product; service contracts costs extra and are sold separately. To determine whether you need a service contract, consider these issues:

- Whether the warranty already covers the repairs and the time period of coverage that you would get under the service contract

- Whether the product is likely to need repairs and the potential costs of such repairs

- The duration of the service contract

- The reputation of the company offering the service contract

Implied Warranties

Implied warranties are created by state law, and all states have them. Almost every purchase you make is covered by an implied warranty.

The most common type of implied warranty—a "warranty of merchantability," means that the seller promises that the product will do what it is supposed to do. For example, a car will run and a toaster will toast.

Another type of implied warranty is the "warranty of fitness for a particular purpose." This applies when you buy a product on the seller's advice that it is suitable for a particular use. For example, a person who suggests that you buy a certain sleeping bag for zero-degree weather warrants that the sleeping bag will be suitable for zero degrees.

If your purchase does not come with a written warranty, it is still covered by implied warranties unless the product is marked "as is," or the seller otherwise indicates in writing that no warranty is given. Several states, including Kansas, Maine, Maryland, Massachusetts, Mississippi, Vermont, West Virginia, and the District of Columbia, do not permit "as is" sales.

If problems arise that are not covered by the written warranty, you should investigate the protection given by your implied warranty.

Implied warranty coverage can last as long as four years, although the length of the coverage varies from state to state. A lawyer or a state consumer protection office can provide more information about implied warranty coverage in your state.

Preventing Problems

To minimize problems, take these steps:

- Read the warranty before you buy. When online, look for hyperlinks to the full warranty or to an address where you can write to get a free copy. Understand exactly what protection the warranty gives you. If a copy of the warranty is available when shopping online, print it out when you make your purchase and keep it with your records.

- Consider the reputation of the company offering the warranty. Look for an address to write to or a phone number to call if you have questions or problems. If you're not familiar with the company, ask your local or state consumer protection office or Better Business Bureau if they have any complaints against the company. A warranty is only as good as the company that stands behind it.

- Save your receipt and file it with the warranty. You may need it to document the date of your purchase or prove that you're the original owner in the case of a nontransferable warranty.

- Perform required maintenance and inspections.

- Use the product according to the manufacturer's instructions. Abuse or misuse may void your warranty coverage.

Resolving Disputes

If you have problems with a product or with getting warranty service, take these steps:

- Read your product instructions and warranty carefully. Don't expect features or performance that your product wasn't designed for, or assume warranty coverage that was never promised in writing. A warranty doesn't mean that you'll automatically get a refund if the product is defective—the company may be entitled to try to fix it first. On the other hand, if you reported a defect to the company during the warranty period and the product wasn't fixed properly, the company must correct the problem, even if your warranty expires before the product is fixed.

- Try to resolve the problem with the retailer. If you can't, write to the manufacturer. Your warranty should list the company's mailing address. Send all letters by certified mail, return receipt requested, and keep copies.

- Contact your state or local consumer protection office. They can help you if you can't resolve the situation with the seller or manufacturer.

- Research dispute resolution programs that try to informally settle any disagreements between you and the company. Your local consumer protection office can suggest organizations to contact. Also, check your warranty; it may require dispute resolution procedures before going to court.

- Consider small claims court. If your dispute involves less than $750, you can usually file a lawsuit in small claims court. The costs are relatively low, procedures are simple, and lawyers usually aren't needed. The clerk of the small claims court can tell you how to file your lawsuit and your state's dollar limits.

- If all else fails, you may want to consider a lawsuit. You can sue for damages or any other type of relief the court awards, including legal fees. A lawyer can advise you how to proceed.

✤ It's A Fact!!

For More Information

The Federal Trace Commission (FTC) works for the consumer to prevent fraudulent, deceptive, and unfair business practices in the marketplace and to provide information to help consumers spot, stop, and avoid them. To file a complaint or to get free information on consumer issues, visit ftc.gov or call toll-free, 877-FTC-HELP (877-382-4357); TTY: 866-653-4261. The FTC enters internet, telemarketing, identity theft, and other fraud-related complaints into Consumer Sentinel, a secure online database available to hundreds of civil and criminal law enforcement agencies in the U.S. and abroad.

Source: Federal Trade Commission, October 2001.

Service Contracts

If you are buying a car or major appliance, whether in a retail store, by catalog, or online, you may be offered a service contract. To many consumers, buying a service contract is like buying "peace of mind" from repair hassles. An estimated 50% of all new car buyers, and many used-car and major appliance buyers, purchase service contracts. The cost can range from $50 to $500, depending on the length and amount of coverage provided. Some consumers, however, may be paying for more protection than they need.

Before you buy a service contract, consider the following:

What does the service contract offer?

A service contract, like a warranty, provides repair and/or maintenance for a specific time period. Warranties, however, are included in the price of the product, while service contracts cost extra and are sold separately.

What is covered by the service contract?

A service contract may cover only certain parts of the product or specific repairs. When online, look for hyperlinks to the terms of the seller's service contract. Read the contract carefully and, if it does not list something as specifically covered, assume that it is not. Service contracts do not cover repairs resulting from misuse or failure to maintain the product properly. Also, you may be obligated to take certain action, such as notifying the company of problems, to insure the service contract is not voided.

Is the product likely to need repairs?

You may not benefit from a service contract if the product is unlikely to need servicing or if the potential cost of repairs is very low.

What other costs will you have?

You may have other expenses after you buy a service contract. Service contracts, like insurance policies, often have deductible amounts. Or, you may be charged each time the item is serviced. Some expenses are limited or excluded. For example, auto service contracts may not completely cover towing

♣ It's A Fact!!
**What will the service contract
give you that the warranty will not?**
Before considering a service contract, make sure you know
what your warranty coverage is. If these documents are available online, print them out to make it easier for you to read them.
Then, carefully compare the coverage of your warranty to the coverage offered by the service contract to decide if the service contract is worth
the additional expense. For more information about warranties, send for
Warranties, a free brochure from the Federal Trade Commission, by
writing to: Public Reference, Federal Trade Commission, Washington, D.C. 20580. You also may write to this address to
receive a free copy of *Best Sellers*, a listing of all the FTC's
consumer publications.

Source: Federal Trade Commission,
October 2001.

or rental car expenses. In addition, you may have to pay cancellation or transfer
fees if you sell the covered product or wish to end the contract.

Where can you get service?

If the service contract is offered by a local retailer or dealer, you may only
be able to get local service. Consider the possibility that problems may develop while you are traveling or after you move away from the area.

Who is responsible for the contract?

The Federal Trade Commission often gets letters from consumers who
ask what they can do about a service contract company that has gone out of
business and cannot repay claims. Unfortunately, there is little recourse available to these consumers. The best way to avoid this situation is to consider,
before you sign a contract, whether the company is reputable. Look for an
address to write to or a phone number to call if you have questions or problems. Ask your local or state consumer protection office, Better Business

Bureau, or state insurance commission if they have any complaints against the company.

Can you purchase a service contract later?

You may be better able to decide if you need a service contract after you have owned the product for some time. Consider waiting until your warranty period expires to buy a service contract.

Auto Service Contracts

Buying a car? You also may be encouraged to buy an auto service contract to help protect against unexpected, costly repairs. While it may sound like a good idea, don't buy in until you understand both the terms of the contract and who is responsible for providing the coverage.

The Auto Service Contract

A service contract is a promise to perform (or pay for) certain repairs or services. Sometimes called an "extended warranty," a service contract is not a warranty as defined by federal law. A service contract may be arranged at any time and always costs extra; a warranty comes with a new car and is included in the original price.

The separate and additional cost distinguishes a service contract from a warranty.

Before deciding whether to buy an auto service contract, ask these questions:

Does the service contract duplicate any warranty coverage?

Compare service contracts with the manufacturer's warranty before you buy. New cars come with a manufacturer's warranty, which usually offers coverage for at least one year or 12,000 miles, whichever comes first. Even used cars may come with some type of coverage.

You may decide to buy a "demonstrator" model—a car that has never been sold to a retail customer but has been driven for purposes other than test drives. If so, ask when warranty coverage begins and ends. Does it date from when you purchase the car or when the dealer first put the car into service?

Who backs the service contract?

Ask who performs or pays for repairs under the terms of the service contract. It may be the manufacturer, the dealer, or an independent company.

Many service contracts sold by dealers are handled by independent companies called administrators. Administrators act as claims adjusters, authorizing the payment of claims to any dealers under the contract. If you have a dispute over whether a claim should be paid, deal with the administrator.

If the administrator goes out of business, the dealership still may be obligated to perform under the contract. The reverse also may be true. If the dealer goes out of business, the administrator may be required to fulfill the terms of the contract. Whether you have recourse depends on your contract's terms and/or your state's laws.

Learn about the reputation of the dealer and the administrator. Ask for references and check them out. You also can contact your local or state consumer protection office, state Department of Motor Vehicles, local Better Business Bureau, or local automobile dealers association to find out if they have public information on the firms. Look for the phone numbers and addresses in your telephone directory.

Find out how long the dealer or administrator has been in business, and try to determine whether they have the financial resources to meet their contractual obligations. Individual car dealers or dealer associations may set aside funds or buy insurance to cover future claims. Some independent companies are insured against a sudden rush of claims.

Find out if the auto service contract is underwritten by an insurance company. In some states, this is required. If the contract is backed by an insurance company, contact your State Insurance Commission to ask about the solvency of the company and whether any complaints have been filed.

How much does the auto service contract cost?

Usually, the price of the service contract is based on the car make, model, condition (new or used), coverage, and length of contract. The upfront cost can range from several hundred dollars to more than $1,000.

Used Cars: Warranty Protection

✤ It's A Fact!!

When shopping for a used car, look for a Buyer's Guide sticker posted on the car's side window. This sticker is required by the Federal Trade Commission (FTC) on all used cars sold by dealers. It tells whether a service contract is available. It also indicates whether the vehicle is being sold with a warranty, with implied warranties only, or "as is."

- **Warranty:** If the manufacturer's warranty is still in effect on the used car, you may have to pay a fee to obtain coverage, making it a service contract. However, if the dealer absorbs the cost of the manufacturer's fee, the coverage is considered a warranty.

- **Implied Warranties Only:** There are two common types of implied warranties. Both are unspoken and unwritten and based on the principle that the seller stands behind the product. Under a "warranty of merchantability," the seller promises the product will do what it is supposed to do. For example, a toaster will toast, a car will run. If the car doesn't run, implied-warranties law says that the dealer must fix it (unless it was sold "as is") so that the buyer gets a working car. A "warranty of fitness for a particular purpose" applies when you buy a vehicle on a dealer's advice that it is suitable for a certain use, like hauling a trailer. Used cars usually are covered by implied warranties under state law.

- **As Is—No Warranty:** If you buy a car "as is," you must pay for all repairs, even if the car breaks down on the way home from the dealership. However, if you buy a dealer-service contract within 90 days of buying the used car, state law "implied warranties" may give you additional rights.

Some states prohibit "as is" sales on most or all used cars. Other states require the use of specific words to disclaim implied warranties. In addition, some states have used car "lemon laws" under which a consumer can receive a refund or replacement if the vehicle is seriously defective. To find out about your state laws, check with your local or state consumer protection office or attorney general.

Source: Federal Trade Commission, May 1997.

In addition to the initial charge, you may need to pay a deductible each time your car is serviced or repaired. Under some service contracts, you pay one charge per visit for repairs—no matter how many. Other contracts require a deductible for each unrelated repair.

You also may need to pay transfer or cancellation fees if you sell your car or end the contract. Often, contracts limit the amount paid for towing or related rental car expenses.

What is covered and not covered?

Few auto service contracts cover all repairs. Indeed, common repairs for parts like brakes and clutches generally are not included in service contracts. If an item isn't listed, assume it's not covered.

Watch out for absolute exclusions that deny coverage for any reason. Here are some examples:

- If a covered part is damaged by a non-covered component, the claim may be denied.

- If the contract specifies that only "mechanical breakdowns" will be covered, problems caused by "normal wear and tear" may be excluded.

- If the engine must be taken apart to diagnose a problem and it is discovered that non-covered parts need to be repaired or replaced, you may have to pay for the labor involved in the tear-down and re-assembling of the engine.

You may not have full protection even for parts that are covered in the contract. Some companies use a "depreciation factor" in calculating coverage: the company may pay only partial repair or replacement costs if they consider your car's mileage.

How are claims handled?

When your car needs to be repaired or serviced, you may be able to choose among several service dealers or authorized repair centers. Or, you may be required to return the vehicle to the selling dealer for service. That could be inconvenient if you bought the car from a dealership in another town.

Find out if your car will be covered if it breaks down while you're using it on a trip or if you take it when you move out of town. Some auto service contract companies and dealers offer service only in specific geographical areas.

Find out if you need prior authorization from the contract provider for any repair work or towing services. Be sure to ask about these issues:

• How long it takes to get authorization

• Whether you can get authorization outside of normal business hours

• Whether the company has a toll-free number for authorization. Test the toll-free number before you buy the contract to see if you can get through easily.

You may have to pay for covered repairs and then wait for the service company to reimburse you. If the auto service contract doesn't specify how long reimbursement usually takes, ask. Find out who settles claims in case you have a dispute with the service contract provider and need to use a dispute resolution program.

✔ Quick Tip
Complaints

To report contract problems with a service provider, contact your local and state consumer protection agencies, including the state insurance commissioner and state attorney general.

If you need help resolving a dispute, contact the Better Business Bureau, the state attorney general, or the consumer protection office in your area. Also, contact law schools in your area and ask if they have dispute resolution programs.

Source: Federal Trade Commission, May 1997.

Are new or reconditioned ("like") parts authorized for use in covered repairs?

If this concerns you, ask. Some consumers are disappointed when they find out "reconditioned" engines are being used as replacement parts under some service contracts. Also ask whether the authorized repair facility maintains an adequate stock of parts. Repair delays may occur if authorized parts are not readily available and must be ordered.

What are your responsibilities?

Under the contract, you may have to follow all the manufacturer's recommendations for routine maintenance, such as oil and spark plug changes. Failure to do so could void the contract. To prove you have maintained the car properly, keep detailed records, including receipts.

Find out if the contract prohibits you from taking the car to an independent station for routine maintenance or performing the work yourself. The contract may specify that the selling dealer is the only authorized facility for servicing the car.

What is the length of the service contract?

If the service contract lasts longer than you expect to own the car, find out if it can be transferred when you sell the car, whether there's a fee, or if a shorter contract is available.

Other Tips

If you're told you must purchase an auto service contract to qualify for financing, contact the lender yourself to find out if this is true. Some consumers have had trouble canceling their service contract after discovering the lender didn't require one.

If you decide to buy a service contract through a car dealership—and the contract is backed by an administrator and/or a third party—make sure the dealer forwards your payment and gives you written confirmation. Some consumers have discovered too late that the dealer failed to forward their payment, leaving them with no coverage months after they signed a contract.

Contact your local or state consumer protection office if you have reason to believe that your contract wasn't put into effect as agreed.

In some states, service contract providers are subject to insurance regulations. Find out if this is true in your state. Insurance regulations generally require companies to meet these requirements:

- Maintain an adequate financial reserve to pay claims

- Base their contract fees on expected claims. Some service providers have been known to make huge profits because the cost of their contracts far exceeds the cost of repairs or services they provide.

- Seek approval from the state insurance office for premiums or contract fees.

Chapter 22

Shopping For A Cell Phone Plan

More and more people are buying wireless telephone service. With a cell phone, you can keep in touch with family, friends, and work, even when you're on the go. Companies' plans change constantly. Whether you already have wireless service or you're just getting started, it's a good idea to shop around, read each company's offers carefully, and to ask questions, such as these:

- How will I use my cell phone? Only for emergencies or more frequently?

- When will I make most of my calls? During the day, at night, or on the weekends?

- Where will I be making and receiving calls? Close to home or far away?

- How much does my monthly budget allow for telephone service, including wireless?

How Will You Use Your Phone?

Wireless plans commonly offer "buckets" of minutes. You pay for a specific number of minutes each month, whether you use them all or not.

About This Chapter: "Going Wireless," © 2002 National Consumers League (www.nclnet.org). Reprinted with permission.

- If you use more than your monthly allotment, you pay a much higher charge for the extra minutes.

- Unused minutes may not carry over to the next month.

- Most wireless plans count the minutes for both calls you make and receive.

- Charges are usually rounded up. For example, a call that takes one minute and three seconds may be charged as a two-minute call.

- Unlike traditional phone service, most wireless providers start the clock when you press the "talk" or "send" button, not when the person at the other end of the line picks up.

- You use minutes when you call toll-free numbers.

- Some services allow you to check by telephone or online to find out how many minutes you have left in your billing cycle. Depending on how often that information is updated, it may not be absolutely current.

Some service providers offer prepaid plans. Instead of getting a monthly bill, you pay in advance for a certain number of minutes. When you use them up, you can add more. Prepaid plans may be more expensive per minute than the monthly calling plans, but they can be very useful for people who don't use the service much, have limited budgets, or want to control their children's cell phone use. They may also be a good choice for people who are trying to rebuild their credit.

Another alternative is a plan with a preset spending limit; when you reach the limit, you have to pay your bill before you can continue to use the service.

Where Will You Use Your Phone?

Wireless phone service uses radio waves, much like radios and televisions. As with those devices, your cell phone might have static, drop calls, get busy signals, or not work at all depending on where you are, the weather, and other factors. Your location may also determine how much it costs to make calls. Some wireless plans are based on "home areas." Others offer nationwide service.

- It's important to select a service that works in your neighborhood and other places where you plan to use it.

- If you use your phone outside of your home area, you are connecting to the network through another company. Some wireless plans charge a "roaming" fee, on top of the minutes you use, for those calls.

- Even within your "home area," some calls may be long-distance. Some plans include long-distance calls for the same rate, while others charge more (on top of the minutes you use).

You could pay roaming charges, long-distance charges, and have your minutes assessed, all for the same call, depending on your wireless plan and your location. When comparing plans, consider where and how you'll be using your phone.

♣ It's A Fact!!
Wireless Internet Service And Messaging

Many wireless companies provide internet access, including e-mail and web browsing. As wireless technology advances, internet services are becoming faster and more varied.

- Some plans charge by the minute. Ask whether internet use counts against the number of minutes in your plan or if you have a separate "bucket" of minutes for it.

- If the charges are by the kilobyte, consider how many you are likely to use. The average 100-word e-mail without attachments or graphics is one kilobyte, but things like graphics and music files are much larger and take up many more kilobytes (1,024 kilobytes equal one megabyte).

Some plans provide unlimited internet service. Another popular service is text-messaging, which enables you to send small notes to other wireless users. Ask the provider what the per-message charge is and whether you can send messages to people who use other companies' services.

Read The Fine Print

It may be hard to catch all the details in advertisements for wireless service, so be sure you understand the terms before you sign up. Wireless plans often require signing a contract for a year or longer, so be sure you know:

- Whether your minutes can be used any time, including "peak times" (usually weekdays), or if there is a certain number of minutes that are restricted to "off-peak times" (nights and weekends), and what the cutoff times are;

- How much it costs if you use more than your allotted number of minutes;

- The charges, if any, for roaming and/ or long-distance;

- The cancellation policy. Many carriers charge more than $100 to end your contract early;

- Whether you can increase or decrease the number of minutes or make other changes to your contract after you've activated your phone and started using it, and what the terms would be;

> **✔ Quick Tip**
>
> "Cramming," unauthorized charges for services you never agreed to, can occur on wireless as well as landline telephone bills. You should also be aware that downloading games, custom ring-tones, or other products or services may result in charges. Read your bills carefully as soon as you receive them and contact your wireless provider promptly about any questionable charges.

- If features such as voicemail and Caller ID are included, or if they are extra;

- The cost for 800-number or directory assistance calls; and,

- What happens when your contract ends—do the terms of service and charges change?

Get all promises in writing. Ask if there is a grace period within which you can cancel for no or a small charge if the service doesn't meet your expectations. Try it out as soon as possible to see how it works in the places you would normally use it.

Choosing The Phone That's Right For You

Wireless providers sell a variety of phones that work with their service; sometimes they offer free or discounted phones as part of their promotions. When choosing a cell phone, consider:

- The size that you want;

- Whether you can use the keypad easily; and,

- Whether it can handle features you might want such as Caller ID and internet services.

Some cell phones work with older analog networks. Most sold today work with newer digital networks, and some (called dual-band) work with both. If the phone only works with digital networks, you may not be able to "roam"—make or receive calls outside your home area.

To accommodate people with special needs, some phones can operate with voice-activated commands. Many have raised numbers on the keypads. All providers must offer at least one phone that works with TTY devices. People who use hearing aids should ask if the phones are compatible with them.

It's also important to know that if you switch your wireless provider, you may have to get another phone, and you won't be able to keep the same number (consumers will be able to retain their cell phone numbers when they switch providers under federal rules that took effect in late 2003).

Going Completely Wireless

More and more people are using wireless phones for all of their calls and abandoning "landlines" entirely. For some consumers, just going wireless could be a better deal than keeping their landline phone service, too. Be aware that:

- You might not get good (or any) reception inside your house or apartment building.

- Weak or dead batteries can also prevent your cell phone from working when you need to make a call. If that happens in an emergency situation, you would be unable able to dial 911.

Families with children, people who work at home, people who are homebound, and other people who depend on phone service may want the security of having a landline as well as a wireless phone.

Avoid Wireless Fraud

If your phone is stolen or someone uses the electronic serial number to "clone" your phone, calls could be made against your account. To prevent unauthorized charges and protect sensitive information such as your account number:

- Keep your bills and service agreements locked away.

- Store your phone out of sight in a secure place.

Wireless Resources On The Web

For more information, check out:

- National Consumers League (www.nclnet.org/phonesand utilities)

- Federal Communications Commission (www.fcc.gov/ cgb/cellular.htm)

- Telecommunications Research and Action Center (www.trac.org/tips/wireless .html)

✔ **Quick Tip**
Cell Phone Safety
And Etiquette

Use your wireless phone in a responsible and considerate manner. You should know that:

- It's safest to drive with both hands on the wheel. Taking your hand off the wheel to dial or talk on your wireless phone can be dangerous; in some places it's illegal.

- Many wireless providers offer hands-free kits and voice-dialing features to improve safety. However, talking on the phone while driving can still be distracting. If you need to make or receive a call, the best thing to do is to pull over safely.

- You may be unable to use your phone in an emergency if coverage is poor in your location. As long as the service works, you can make 911 calls at no charge even if your phone has been disconnected or you haven't activated the service yet.

- When you're in a meeting, a concert, a movie, a restaurant, or any place where a ringing phone might disturb others, turn your phone off.

- If you're talking on your cell phone in a public place, speak softly to avoid bothering other people and keep your conversation private.

Chapter 23

Buying A Computer

Tips For Buying A Computer

What Do I Buy?

Computer technology is in a constant state of evolution. If you are in the market for a new PC, you may quickly become confused by the cryptic terminology and frustrated with the number of options from which to choose. Several factors influence speed and power. Making an educated choice will require that you become familiar with some basic concepts and answer some basic consumer questions.

- How complex are my tasks? Surfing the internet requires less computing power than running a multimedia program. If you know the types of programs you will be using, check out their requirements. Most programs state optimum computing capacity on the box labeling.

- Do you require portability? A "notebook" computer may be preferable to a "desktop" computer. Today's notebooks are generally just as fast and powerful as a desktop but have physical size limitations. As notebooks

About This Chapter: This chapter begins with "Tips for Buying a Computer," by Vince Ory, Baton Rouge General Medical Center, Medical Library, Baton Rouge, LA, for the National Network of Libraries of Medicine, South Central Region, July 2006. Additional text is from "Big Print. Little Print. What's the Deal?" Federal Trade Commission (www.ftc.gov), 2007.

are frequently utilized without external power sources, "on board battery capacity" is an important factor in notebook selection.

• Do you prefer to buy your unit locally or mail order? This is an important choice, for it often dictates what kind of product support you will receive. Do you prefer to take your unit to a local dealer for service or are you comfortable with telephone technical support? Most large manufacturers offer factory direct orders. This allows you to choose from a variety of component specifications rather than settle for what a local vendor happens to have in stock.

• How much can I afford? If your computing needs outstrip your resources, be aware many large manufacturers offer late model factory refurbished machines or closed product lines with variable warranties. Factor in the cost of any extended warranty you may desire. Again, the operational requirements will influence power and options you need. Most systems easily accept memory, video, sound, modem, and storage space upgrades. A quality electrical surge protector is a must.

Deciphering The Language

The computer utilizes many complex components. Unless you build a machine from scratch, you have little choice over some specifications. While a discussion on each component could fill a chapter, this chapter covers basic component selections you are likely to encounter. Let's take a look at specifications from a typical advertisement and break it down.

"Computer package includes: Pentium 4 processor at 2.40 GHz with 533 mhz system bus and 512K L2 Cache, 256 MB RDRAM, 16x Max. DVD-ROM drive, 40 GB Ultra ATA Hard Drive (7200 RPM), 128 Mb DDR graphics card, 17" (16.0" v.i.s.) dot pitch 0.26 mm monitor, 4 PCI Slots, 1 AGP Slot, 4 USB ports, Front audio jack. 56k modem."

Pentium 4 Processor At 2.4 GHz With 533 Mhz System Bus And 512K L2 Cache: Processor (AKA: central processing unit, CPU, microchip, microprocessor, or chipset). The CPU handles the computer's complex computations. CPU speed (clock speed) is measured in the number of cycles per second executed measured in "hertz" (megahertz/millions or gigahertz/billions). Some processors have performance improving temporary storage areas located within them, known as "Level 1 Cache" (L1) and "Level 2 Cache" (L2). Economy priced processors often lack the L2 cache. Currently 512 kilobytes of Level 2 (L2) Cache is common. The most common processors are the: Pentium II, Pentium III, Pentium IV, Celeron, Duron, and Athlon. At 1.0 to 3.0 GHz. Components inside the computer transmit data to each other via circuit paths (bus) on the main circuit board (motherboard) The width of the data path and the speed at which data moves along these paths dictates the systems BUS Speed. The faster the system bus speed the faster the computer will finish a task.

256 MB RDRAM: Random access memory (AKA: RAM, memory, memory chips, or temporary memory). Random access memory functions as a temporary data storage area for use by the CPU. RAM memory is housed in series microchips and generally speaking more RAM memory means faster computing. RAM memory is measured in units called bytes. (Megabytes/ millions or gigabytes/billions). Most systems allow you to easily upgrade RAM memory. Currently 128 to 512 megabyte offerings are common in SD RAM or the faster more expensive RD RAM.

40 GB Ultra ATA Hard Drive (7200 RPM): Hard drive (AKA memory). the hard drive is a magnetically sensitive disc(s) that serves as a permanent storage area for data and programs. Like RAM memory hard drive storage capacity is measured in bytes. Be aware of the size of the programs you will be using and estimate your base hard drive requirements. Most system easily allow for adding or upgrading the hard drive (20 to 70 gb).

17" (16.0" v.i.s.) Dot Pitch 0.26 mm Monitor: As with a television, screen size and picture quality enhances viewing pleasure and reduces eyestrain. Values for diagonal distance from corner to corner of the glass is the viewable image size (V.I.S). V.I.S is generally smaller than stated size of the monitor as in our example advertisement. "Notebooks tend toward smaller screens but 15" and 17" are common. Screens up 21" are now available with 17" the most popular for desktops. Flat-panel (FP) monitors, standard on notebooks, are now available for desktops. FP monitors have a much thinner front to back profile and thus require less space. Additionally, FP monitors make use of eye-saving liquid crystal display (LCD). FP monitors are much more expensive than older technology, cathode ray tube (CRT) monitors but typically last longer. If you opt for the CRT monitor you may want to consider a model with an eye saving flat glass screen. Picture quality is a function of several factors but typically higher resolution screens have smaller "dot pitch" values. Dot pitch ranges from 0.18 mm to 0.39 mm (the smaller the better) with 0.28 mm being the largest value for a CRT monitor without undue eyestrain.

128 Mb DDR Graphics Card: The video graphics card is a separate circuit board plugged into you computers main circuit board expansion slots. The video card has its own processing chip (coprocessor) and RAM memory that handles video information to relieve the CPU of that duty. Most late model computers come with a video card or easily accept installation and upgrades.

16x Max. DVD-ROM Drive: Various types of disc drives are available. They offer the ability to upload and download data, record and play music, and play movies. Drive ability is measured in multiples of a base standard of 150 kilobytes per second (KBS) data transfer rate. A 16X disc drive operates at a 16 X 150 KBS (2400 kbs) transfer rate. CD ROM drives will read text and play music but not record. A CD RW drive will play music and allow you to record music or text onto recordable discs. DVD ROM and DVD RW share a similar relationship. A disc drive is a good means of backing up you computer hard drive information in case of failure.

4 PCI Slots, 1 AGP Slot: The computers main circuit board (motherboard) has sockets (expansion slots) for adding additional circuit boards. Currently, several peripheral component interconnect (PCI) slots and one video dedicated advanced graphics port (AGP) slot are common offerings. PCI slots allow quick installation of new circuit devices without extensive software reconfiguring (Plug and Play). AGP allows installation and efficient use of the video card.

4 USB Ports: Serial ports and parallel ports are standard equipment but an important item not to overlook is the universal service bus (USB) port. USB offers high speed data exchange and allows several devices to be plugged into a single hub in a process know as "daisy chaining" greatly expanding the number of devices you can attach to one USB port. USB also allows devices to be disconnected and reconnected without shutting down the computer's main power.

Front Audio Jack: Audio jacks allow quick access for audio appliances. Often they indicate the presence of an audio card (also known as, sound cards). Audio cards allow the computer to process sound incoming and outgoing from equipment like microphones and external speakers and graphical and game devices like joysticks. The sound card enables the computer to function much like a stereo system.

Modems: Modems allow you to connect your computer to the internet. Modems can be part of the internal or external circuitry of your computer. dial-up modems utilizing standard telephone lines are the most prevalent with a 56K (56,000 bits per second) the minimum desirable. Most "off the shelf" computers come with 56k modem standard. Digital subscriber line (DSL) modems utilize high-speed digital connections via standard phone lines. DSL access is much faster than a standard 56k connection but more expensive. Additionally, DSL can remain continuously connected to the internet so the dial-up process is eliminated. Cable modems allow very high-speed internet access over the same types of lines cable television utilizes. The cable modem can be bought or leased from cable companies. If you select cable access you computer will need an Ethernet card installed. For possible DSL or cable internet access check with you local phone company or cable company for availability and terms before you invest in the hardware.

Other Stuff: There is an expanding number of devices to make you computer more useful: printers, cameras, speakers, scanners, joysticks, networking options, and dedicated backup devices.

Big Print. Little Print. What's The Deal?
How To Disclose The Details

Some advertisements for "low cost" computers omit important restrictions or conditions about the "deal," or bury them in fine print or obscure locations. This information should be disclosed clearly and conspicuously in the advertising so that consumers can evaluate the merits of an offer and make an informed purchasing decision.

Rebated Computers And Internet Service

Many rebate promotions use big print to tout the after-rebate price of the computer. But often, the total price the consumer must pay up-front is buried in the fine print, if it's included at all. Advertisements should prominently state the before-rebate cost of the computer, as well as the amounts of

---

♣ It's A Fact!!

Disclosures In Internet Advertising

Information affecting the actual cost of an offer should be disclosed close to the advertised price—that is, on the same electronic page and next to the price. Advertisers should not use pop-up windows or hyperlinks to other electronic pages to display key cost information. Hyperlinks may be useful to tell consumers about less critical terms and conditions of an offer, especially when the information may be extensive. For example, in rebate offers that require the purchase of internet service, the cost of the internet service should be disclosed on the same page as the advertised price of the computer. But hyperlinks may be used to direct the consumer to the cancellation terms and additional internet connection costs of many internet rebate offers.

When using a hyperlinked disclosure, advertisers should clearly label the hyperlink so it shows the importance, nature, and relevance of the information to which it links (for example, "Early cancellation of internet service may result in substantial penalties. Click here."). The hyperlink should be prominent, near the claim it is qualifying, easily noticeable, and lead directly to the qualifying information. Vague labels like "Terms and Conditions" are not enough to direct consumers to important restrictions or qualifications.

In addition, information that is significant to the advertised offer should not be buried at the end of a long web page that requires consumers to scroll past unrelated information. Consumers should not have to wander through an electronic maze to discover important conditions or limitations of an offer.

Source: Federal Trade Commission, 2007.

the rebates. Only then will consumers know their actual out-of-pocket cost and have the information they need to comparison shop.

In addition, advertisers should prominently disclose whether the consumer is required to purchase internet service to qualify for the "low cost" deal. The ad should state the key terms of the purchase requirements, including the cost and duration of the consumer's commitment to the internet service.

Rebate promotions should clearly detail any additional terms and conditions that consumers need to know, like the following:

• Penalties or fees for canceling the internet service contract early. Some rebate offers require consumers to pay back all or a portion of the rebate; others tack on an additional fee.

• Additional connection charges to access the internet service. For example, consumers should be told that to access the internet they may have to pay long distance phone charges, or expensive hourly surcharges for use of an 800, 888 or 877 phone number. This charge is in addition to the basic monthly internet service fee. Consumers also should be told how to find out if local internet access is available.

• How long before they will receive the rebate.

Advertisers should tell consumers what components are included in the offer. For example, if a monitor is pictured in the ad but is not part of the deal, the ad must state this fact clearly and prominently. The ad also should include the cost of the monitor if it's sold as an add-on.

Don't Bury The Details

Ads should clearly and conspicuously disclose all the information about an offer that is likely to affect a consumer's purchasing decision. Disclose the most important information—like the terms affecting the basic cost of the offer—near the advertised price.

Print advertisers should not attempt to hide the real cost or the critical terms or conditions by putting them in obscure locations, such as the border area on a print ad; burying them in numerous, densely packed lines of fine print; or including them in small-type footnotes.

Television advertisers should not hide key information in a fast moving "crawl"; superscripts or subscripts using small print sizes or a color that fades into the background; type that disappears from the screen too fast for consumers to read and comprehend; or the middle of a long statement that scrolls vertically on the screen within a short period of time.

Chapter 24

Buying Jewelry

Buying jewelry can be fun, exciting, and confusing. Whether you're considering a gift of jewelry for someone special or as a treat for yourself, take some time to learn the terms used in the industry. Here's some information to help you get the best quality jewelry for your money, whether you're shopping in a traditional brick and mortar store, by catalog, or online.

Gold

The word gold, used by itself, means all gold or 24 karat (24K) gold. Because 24K gold is soft, it's usually mixed with other metals to increase its hardness and durability. If a piece of jewelry is not 24 karat gold, the karat quality should accompany any claim that the item is gold.

The karat quality marking tells you what proportion of gold is mixed with the other metals. Fourteen karat (14K) jewelry contains 14 parts of gold, mixed in throughout with 10 parts of base metal. The higher the karat rating, the higher the proportion of gold in the piece of jewelry.

Most jewelry is marked with its karat quality, although marking is not required by law. Near the karat quality mark, you should see the name or the

About This Chapter: "All That Glitters... How to Buy Jewelry," *Facts for Consumers*, Federal Trade Commission (www.ftc.gov), March 2008.

U.S. registered trademark of the company that will stand behind the mark. The trademark may be in the form of a name, symbol, or initials. If you don't see a trademark accompanying a quality mark on a piece of jewelry, look for another piece.

Jewelry can be plated with gold in a variety of ways. Gold plate refers to items that are either mechanically plated, electroplated, or plated by any other means with gold to a base metal. Eventually, gold plating wears away, but how soon will depend on how often the item is worn and how thick the plating is.

♣ **It's A Fact!!**

Solid gold refers to an item made of any karat gold, if the inside of the item is not hollow. The proportion of gold in the piece of jewelry still is determined by the karat mark.

Gold-filled, gold overlay, and rolled gold plate (RGP) are terms used to describe jewelry that has a layer of at least 10 karat gold mechanically bonded to a base metal. If the jewelry is marked with one of these terms, the term or abbreviation should follow the karat quality of the gold used (for example, 14K Gold Overlay or 12K RGP). If the layer of karat gold is less than 1/20th of the total weight of the item, any marking must state the actual percentage of karat gold, such as 1/40 14K Gold Overlay.

Gold electroplate describes jewelry that has a layer (at least .175 microns thick) of a minimum of 10 karat gold deposited on a base metal by an electrolytic process. The terms gold flashed or gold washed describe products that have an extremely thin electroplating of gold (less than .175 microns thick). This will wear away more quickly than gold plate, gold-filled, or gold electroplate.

Platinum, Silver, And Other Metals

Platinum is a precious metal that costs more than gold. It usually is mixed with other similar metals, known as the platinum group metals: iridium, palladium, ruthenium, rhodium, and osmium.

Different markings are used on platinum jewelry as compared with gold jewelry, based on the amount of pure platinum in the piece. The quality markings for platinum are based on parts per thousand. For example, the marking 900 Platinum means that 900 parts out of 1000 are pure platinum, or in other words, the item is 90% platinum and 10% other metals. The abbreviations for platinum—Plat. or Pt.—also can be used in marking jewelry.

Items that contain at least 950 parts per thousand pure platinum can be marked simply platinum. Items that have at least 850 parts per thousand pure platinum can be marked with the amount of pure platinum and the word platinum or an abbreviation (for example, 950 platinum, 900 Plat., or 850 Pt.). Jewelry that contains less than 850 parts per thousand pure platinum, but has a total of 950 parts per thousand of platinum group metals (of which at least 500 parts is pure platinum), may be marked with both the amount of pure platinum and the amount of the other platinum group metals in the piece. For example, the marking 600 Plat. 350 Irid. means that the item has 600 parts per thousand (60%) platinum, and 350 parts per thousand (35%) iridium, totaling 950 parts per thousand of platinum group metals, and 50 parts per thousand (5%) other metals.

The words silver or sterling silver describe a product that contains 92.5% silver. Silver products sometimes may be marked 925 which means that 925 parts per thousand are pure silver. Some jewelry may be described as silverplate: a layer of silver is bonded to a base metal. The mark coin silver is used for compounds that contain 90% silver. According to the law, quality-marked silver also must bear the name or a U.S. registered trademark of the company or person that will stand behind the mark.

Vermeil (ver-may), a special type of gold plated product, consists of a base of sterling silver that is coated or plated with gold.

Pewter items may be described and marked as such if they contain at least 90% tin.

Gemstones

Natural gemstones are found in nature. Laboratory-created stones, as the name implies, are made in a laboratory. These stones, which also are referred to as laboratory-grown, [name of manufacturer]-created, or synthetic, have essentially the same chemical, physical, and visual properties as natural gemstones. Laboratory-created stones do not have the rarity of naturally colored stones and they are less expensive than naturally mined stones. By contrast, imitation stones look like natural stones in appearance only, and may be glass, plastic, or less costly stones. Laboratory-created and imitation stones should be clearly identified as such.

Gemstones may be measured by weight, size, or both. The basic unit for weighing gemstones is the carat, which is equal to one-fifth (1/5th) of a gram. Carats are divided into 100 units, called points. For example, a half-carat gemstone would weigh .50 carats or 50 points. When gemstones are measured by dimensions, the size is expressed in millimeters (for example, 7x5 millimeters).

Gemstone treatments or enhancements refer to the way some gems are treated to improve their appearance or durability, or even change their color. Many gemstones are treated in some way. The effects of some treatments may lessen or change over time and some treated stones may require special care. Some enhancements also affect the value of a stone, when measured against a comparable untreated stone.

♣ **It's A Fact!!**
Jewelers should tell you whether the gemstone you're considering has been treated when: the treatment is not permanent; the treated stone requires special care; or the treatment significantly affects the value of the gemstone.

Some common treatments that you may be told about and their effects include the following:

• Heating can lighten, darken, or change the color of some gems, or improve a gemstone's clarity.

• Irradiation can add more color to colored diamonds, certain other gemstones, and pearls.

• Impregnating some gems with colorless oils, wax, or resins makes a variety of imperfections less visible and can improve the gemstones' clarity and appearance.

- Fracture filling hides cracks or fractures in gems by injecting colorless plastic or glass into the cracks and improves the gemstones' appearance and durability.

- Diffusion treatment adds color to the surface of colorless gems; the center of the stone remains colorless.

- Dyeing adds color and improves color uniformity in some gemstones and pearls.

- Bleaching lightens and whitens some gems, including jade and pearls.

Diamonds

A diamond's value is based on four criteria: color, cut, clarity, and carat. The clarity and color of a diamond usually are graded. However, scales are not uniform: a clarity grade of "slightly included" may represent a different grade on one grading system versus another, depending on the terms used in the scale. Make sure you know how a particular scale and grade represent the color or clarity of the diamond you're considering. A diamond can be described as "flawless" only if it has no visible surface or internal imperfections when viewed under 10-power magnification by a skilled diamond grader.

As with other gems, diamond weight usually is stated in carats. Diamond weight may be described in decimal or fractional parts of a carat. If the weight is given in decimal parts of a carat, the figure should be accurate to the last decimal place. For example, ".30 carat" could represent a diamond that weighs between .295–.304 carat. Some retailers describe diamond weight in fractions and use the fraction to represent a range of weights. For example, a diamond described as 1/2 carat could weigh between .47–.54 carat. If diamond weight is stated as fractional parts of a carat, the retailer should disclose two things: that the weight is not exact, and the reasonable range of weight for each fraction or the weight tolerance being used.

Some diamonds may be treated to improve their appearance in similar ways as other gemstones. Since these treatments improve the clarity of the diamond, some jewelers refer to them as clarity enhancement. One type of treatment—fracture filling—conceals cracks in diamonds by filling them with a foreign substance. This filling may not be permanent and jewelers should tell you if the diamond you're considering has been fracture-filled.

Another treatment—lasering—involves the use of a laser beam to improve the appearance of diamonds that have black inclusions or spots. A laser beam is aimed at the inclusion. Acid is then forced through a tiny tunnel made by the laser beam to remove the inclusion. Lasering is permanent and a laser-drilled stone does not require special care.

While a laser-drilled diamond may appear as beautiful as a comparable untreated stone, it may not be as valuable. That's because an untreated stone of the same quality is rarer and therefore more valuable. Jewelers should tell you whether the diamond you're considering has been laser-drilled.

> ♣ **It's A Fact!!**
>
> Imitation diamonds, such as cubic Zirconia, resemble diamonds in appearance but are much less costly. Certain laboratory-created gemstones, such as lab-created moissanite, also resemble diamonds and may not be adequately detected by the instruments originally used to identify cubic Zirconia. Ask your jeweler if he has the current testing equipment to distinguish between diamonds and other lab-created stones.

Pearls

Natural pearls are made by oysters and other mollusks. Cultured pearls also are grown by mollusks, but with human intervention; that is, an irritant introduced into the shells causes a pearl to grow. Imitation pearls are man-made with glass, plastic, or organic materials.

Because natural pearls are very rare, most pearls used in jewelry are either cultured or imitation pearls. Cultured pearls, because they are made by oysters or mollusks, usually are more expensive than imitation pearls. A cultured pearl's value is largely based on its size, usually stated in millimeters, and the quality of its nacre coating, which gives it luster. Jewelers should tell you if the pearls are cultured or imitation.

Some black, bronze, gold, purple, blue, and orange pearls, whether natural or cultured, occur that way in nature; some, however, are dyed through various processes. Jewelers should tell you whether the colored pearls are naturally colored, dyed, or irradiated.

A Jewelry Shopper's Checklist

When you're in the market for a piece of jewelry for yourself or someone you love, shop around. Compare quality, price, and service. If you're not familiar with any jewelers in your area, ask family members, friends, and co-workers for recommendations. You also should take these steps:

- Ask for the store's refund and return policy before you buy.

- Check for the appropriate markings on metal jewelry.

- Ask whether the pearls are natural, cultured, or imitation.

- Ask whether a gemstone is natural, laboratory-created, or imitation.

- Ask whether the gemstone has been treated. Is the change permanent? Is special care required?

- Make sure the jeweler writes on the sales receipt any information you relied on when making your purchase, such as the gem's weight or size. Some jewelers also may supply a grading report from a gemological laboratory.

In addition, these tips apply when you're shopping for jewelry online:

- Shop with companies you know or do some homework before buying to make sure a company is legitimate before doing business with it.

- Get the details about the product, as well as the merchant's refund and return policies, before you buy.

- Look for an address to write to or a phone number to call if you have a question, a problem or need help.

For More Information

If you have a problem with the jewelry you purchased, first try to resolve it with the jeweler. If you are dissatisfied with the response, contact your local Better Business Bureau or local consumer protection agency. You also may contact the Jewelers Vigilance Committee's Alternative Dispute Resolution Service. This program assists consumers and businesses in resolving disputes about jewelry. The Jewelers Vigilance Committee (JVC) is an independent, non-profit organization formed to advance ethical practices in the jewelry industry. You may contact the JVC by mail: 25 West 45th Street, Suite 400, New York, NY 10036-4902, or by phone: 212-997-2002.

The Federal Trade Commission (FTC) works for the consumer to prevent fraudulent, deceptive, and unfair business practices in the marketplace and to provide information to help consumers spot, stop, and avoid them. To file a complaint or to get free information on consumer issues, visit http://www.ftc.gov or call toll-free, 877-FTC-HELP (877-382-4357); TTY: 866-653-4261. The FTC enters internet, telemarketing, identity theft, and other fraud-related complaints into Consumer Sentinel, a secure online database available to hundreds of civil and criminal law enforcement agencies in the U.S. and abroad.

Chapter 25

Buying Your First Car

Buying A Used Car

"I can't wait to get my own car."

Sound familiar? Before you start shopping for a used car, do some homework. It may save you serious money. Consider driving habits, what the car will be used for, and your budget. Research models, options, costs, repair records, safety tests, and mileage through libraries, book stores, and websites.

Cash Or Credit?

Once you've settled on a particular car, you have two payment options: paying in full or financing over time. Financing increases the total cost of the car because you're also paying for the cost of credit, including interest and other loan costs. You also must consider how much money you can put down, the monthly payment, the loan term, and the annual percentage rate (APR). Rates usually are higher and loan periods shorter on used cars than on new ones. Dealers and lenders offer a variety of loan terms. Shop around and negotiate the best possible deal. Be cautious about financing offers for first-time

About This Chapter: This chapter includes text from the following documents produced by the Federal Trade Commission (FTC): "Buying A Used Car," April 1998; "Car Ads: Reading Between the Lines," March 1997, and "Auction Guides: Not So Hot Properties," June 2000. Despite the older dates of these documents, the advice is still pertinent to car-buyers.

buyers. They can require a big down payment and a high APR. To get a lower rate, you may need to have your parents cosign the loan. If money is tight, you might consider paying cash for a less expensive car than you first had in mind.

Dealer Or Private Sale?

The Federal Trade Commission's Used Car Rule requires dealers to post a Buyers Guide in every used car they offer for sale. The Buyers Guide gives a great deal of information, including the following:

- Whether the vehicle is being sold "as is" or with a warranty

- What percentage of the repair costs a dealer will pay under the warranty

- The fact that spoken promises are difficult to enforce

- The major mechanical and electrical systems on the car, including some of the major problems you should look out for

The Buyers Guide also tells you to take the following steps:

- Get all promises in writing

- Keep the Buyers Guide for reference after the sale

♣ It's A Fact!!
Other Costs To Consider

There's more to buying a car than just paying for it. Other items to budget for include insurance, gas, maintenance, and repairs. Here are some tips to help you save money:

- Compare coverage and premiums with several insurance companies. Buy from a low-price, licensed insurer or see if you can be added to your parents' policy. Some companies offer discounts to students with good grades. It also pays to drive safely and observe speed limits. Traffic violations can cost money in tickets and higher insurance premiums.

- Pump your own gas and use the octane level your owner's manual specifies.

- Keep your car in safe driving condition. Following the vehicle's maintenance schedule can help forestall costly repairs.

- Look for a mechanic who is certified, well established, and communicates well about realistic repair options and costs. Find one who has done good work for someone you know.

Source: FTC, April 1998.

- Ask to have the car inspected by an independent mechanic before the purchase

Buying a car from a private individual is different from buying from a dealer. That's because private sales generally aren't covered by the Used Car Rule or by "implied warranties" of state law. A private sale probably will be "as is"—you'll have to pay for anything that goes wrong after the sale.

Before You Buy

Whether you buy a used car from a dealer or an individual, take these precautions:

- Examine the car using an inspection checklist. You can find checklists in magazines and books and on internet sites that deal with used cars.

- Test drive the car under varied road conditions—on hills, highways, and in stop-and-go-traffic.

- Ask for the car's maintenance record from the owner, dealer, or repair shop.

- Hire a mechanic to inspect the car.

New Car Ads: Reading Between The Lines

Many new car dealers advertise unusually low interest rates and other special promotions. Ads promising high trade-in allowances and free or low-cost options may help you shop, but finding the best deal requires careful comparisons.

Many factors determine whether a special offer provides genuine savings. The interest rate, for example, is only part of the car dealer's financing package. Terms like the size of the down payment also affect the total financing cost.

Questions About Low Interest Loans

A call or visit to a dealer should help clarify details about low interest loans. Consider asking these questions:

- Will you be charged a higher price for the car to qualify for the low-rate financing? Would the price be lower if you paid cash, or supplied your own financing from your bank or credit union?

- Does the financing require a larger-than-usual down payment? Perhaps 25 or 30 percent?

- Are there limits on the length of the loan? Are you required to repay the loan in a condensed period of time, say 24 or 36 months?

- Is there a significant balloon payment—possibly several thousand dollars—due at the end of the loan?

- Do you have to buy special or extra merchandise or services such as rustproofing, an extended warranty, or a service contract to qualify for a low-interest loan?

- Is the financing available for a limited time only? Some merchants limit special deals to a few days or require that you take delivery by a certain date.

- Does the low rate apply to all cars in stock or only to certain models?

- Are you required to give the dealer the manufacturer's rebate to qualify for financing?

Questions About Other Promotions

Other special promotions include high trade-in allowances and free or low-cost options. Some dealers promise to sell the car for a stated amount over the dealer's invoice. Asking questions like these can help you determine whether special promotions offer genuine value.

- Does the advertised trade-in allowance apply to all cars, regardless of their condition? Are there any deductions for high mileage, dents, or rust?

- Does the larger trade-in allowance make the cost of the new car higher than it would be without the trade-in? You might be giving back the big trade-in allowance by paying more for the new car.

- Is the dealer who offers a high trade-in allowance and free or low-cost options giving you a better price on the car than another dealer who doesn't offer promotions?

- Does the "dealer's invoice" reflect the actual amount that the dealer pays the manufacturer? You can consult consumer or automotive publications for information about what the dealer pays.

- Does the "dealer's invoice" include the cost of options, such as rustproofing or waterproofing, that already have been added to the car? Is one dealer charging more for these options than others?

- Does the dealer have cars in stock that have no expensive options? If not, will the dealer order one for you?

- Are the special offers available if you order a car instead of buying one off the lot?

- Can you take advantage of all special offers simultaneously?

You're not limited to the financing options offered by a particular dealer. Before you commit to a deal, check to see what type of loan you can arrange with your bank or credit union.

Once you decide which dealer offers the car and financing you want, read the invoice and the installment contract carefully. Check to see that all the terms of the contract reflect the agreement you made with the dealer. If they don't, get a written explanation before you sign. Careful shopping will help you decide what car, options, and financing are best for you.

Auction Guides: Not So Hot Properties

SEIZED CARS FROM $500

Ads like these in newspapers and magazines, on television and the internet, and in coupon mailings to your home may sound like the ticket to your dream car. They offer the chance to buy a big ticket item at auction—for well below its market value. What deals! Just call the toll-free number for more information.

Is there a catch? You bet!

Don't Be Mis-Guided

If you respond, you're likely to hear pitches for guides to cars being sold in your area at great prices. But the guides aren't always what they're promised to be. And if you buy one, you may end up spending more than you planned.

You'll be charged about $50 for each guide, either to your credit card or through a withdrawal from your checking account. You may even be billed for a guide you didn't order.

Here's how it happens: When you place an order, the salesperson might offer to include another guide as well. What you won't be told is that you'll be charged for the second guide, even though you never agreed to buy it.

In many cases, the businesses bill your credit card or debit your checking account even if you never agreed to buy anything. They get your bank account or credit card information under false pretenses, sometimes claiming that they need the account number to verify your credit history or to "hold" your order.

♣ **It's A Fact!!**

Despite what you might hear about auction guides or see in the ads, cars at auction typically sell for their fair market value. These auctions attract a variety of buyers, including used car dealers, so the bidding can get competitive. At many government sales, the items are appraised before the sale and won't be sold if the bidding runs too low. Indeed, it's rare to find high-end or late model vehicles for sale, especially at "bargain basement" prices. And the truth be told, the cars that sell for $500 or less usually are damaged or junk vehicles purchased for scrap.

Source: FTC, June 2000.

And when auction guides arrive in the mail, chances are that they contain far less information than you expected. Actually, it's information that is readily available elsewhere for free.

The bottom line: While it's possible to buy cars at auction, you won't find the "deals" advertised in auction guides sold by fraudulent promoters.

Auto Auctions

Despite claims to the contrary, the auto auction guides these companies sell don't contain specific information about dates and locations of auto auctions or lists of available cars. Rather, they contain general information about auto auctions and addresses and phone numbers—all of which are available in your phone book. You'll still need to call for details about upcoming auctions.

Chapter 26

CD, Book, And Video Buying Clubs

Prenotification Negative Option Plans

You see the ads on TV, in magazine and newspaper inserts, and on the internet: "5 Books for $1," "10 CDs for FREE," or "4 Videos for 49¢ each." By joining some of the clubs that are offering these deals, you may become a member of a "prenotification negative option plan." That means you are agreeing to receive merchandise automatically unless you tell the club not to send it.

How Prenotification Plans Work

Often, you can join a plan simply by accepting an introductory offer of some merchandise, often at a discounted price. Then, you pay full price for additional merchandise.

Joining a plan means you agree to the plan's sales method as long as you're a member. As a plan member, you will receive periodic announcements describing merchandise that you can buy. These announcements are important because the merchandise is sent to you automatically unless you return the form rejecting the offer within the specified time.

About This Chapter: This chapter includes text from the following documents produced by the Federal Trade Commission (www.ftc.gov): "Prenotification Negative Option Plans," May 2001; and "Continuity Plans: Coming to You Like Clockwork," June 2002. Despite the older dates of these documents, the information is still pertinent to today's consumers.

Each time you receive an announcement, you have two choices:

- **A.** If you want the merchandise, do nothing. It will be sent automatically. Some plans require you to pay for the merchandise when you get it. Other plans send the merchandise "on approval," which means you can try it for a specified period. If you return the merchandise, you don't have to pay for it.

OR

- **B.** If you don't want the merchandise, you must say so and return the rejection form included with the announcement within a specified time, usually 10 days. Make sure you follow the instructions on the form. Some plans also let you use the rejection form to order other merchandise.

The Prenotification Negative Option Rule

The Federal Trade Commission enforces the Prenotification Negative Option Rule. The Rule requires companies to give you information about their plans, clearly and conspicuously, in any promotional materials that consumers can use to enroll. If the sales presentation for a plan is made orally, say on the phone, the terms and conditions still must be disclosed clearly and conspicuously during the presentation. For example, companies must tell you the following facts:

- Whether there's a minimum purchase obligation
- How and when you can cancel your membership
- How many announcements and rejection forms you'll receive each year, and how often you'll receive them
- How to reject merchandise
- The deadline for returning the rejection form to avoid shipment of the merchandise
- Whether billing charges include postage and handling.

Minimum Purchase Obligations And Canceling Memberships

Some plans require that you buy a certain amount of merchandise at the club's regular prices. If that's the case, the minimum purchase obligation must be disclosed clearly and conspicuously. Once you've satisfied the minimum purchase requirements, you can cancel your membership. If the club has no minimum purchase obligation, you can cancel your membership any time.

If you want to cancel your membership, send your request in writing. The company must cancel your membership promptly. If the company sends additional merchandise after receiving your written cancellation notice, you need to return the first item that is sent. You may consider any additional shipments as unordered merchandise and keep them as a gift.

However, to avoid dunning notices, it's best to tell the company that you're no longer a member each and every time you receive unordered merchandise. You can do that by sending the company a copy of your cancellation letter.

Announcements And Rejection Forms

The company must tell you how often and how many announcements and rejection forms you'll receive each year and how often you will receive them. The company also must tell you whether billing charges for each item include postage and handling.

The rejection form comes with, or is a part of, the announcement. In some plans, the rejection form can be used to decline merchandise and to choose a different item. The announcement must give you at least 10 days to decide if you want the merchandise and mail back the form. The form includes a "return date"—the date the form must be received by the company, or a "mailing date"—the date you must mail the form to the company. No matter which date the company uses, you have at least 10 days to respond.

If you don't get at least 10 days, and you receive an unwanted shipment, you can return the merchandise to the company for a full credit to your account. The company must pay for the return postage.

Bonus Merchandise

To attract new members, some companies advertise special introductory offers, like "5 Books for $1." By law, a company must ship the merchandise within 30 days of receiving your order. If the merchandise can't be shipped within that time, the company may offer you an equivalent alternative. If you don't want the

✔ Quick Tip

Is a negative option plan right for you?

A negative option plan is included in most book, video, and CD/audio club offers. Consider the following information before subscribing to a negative option plan.

Signing Up: After you sign and return the club's written offer you will receive their products and mailings. They will usually offer free or inexpensive merchandise to entice consumers into joining their club. Check the availability of the club's internet accessibility and options.

Buying Other Products At The Regular Price: After receiving the free or reduced priced items consumers usually have to purchase several other products at the club's regular price.

Returning The Form: You will receive frequent mailings of the club's latest offers. If you are not interested in the selection return the enclosed form, otherwise the selection will be automatically sent. The club must inform the consumer of at least two methods by which he or she can cancel the goods or services, one of which has to be expense-free to the consumer.

Canceling Membership: Remember, you must fulfill all the requirements of the agreement before you may cancel your membership with the club.

A negative option plan may seem like a great savings because of the "free" or "discounted" products you will receive. You need to consider the overall cost of the plan, including the requirements to purchase regular priced items. You may want to compare the regular priced items of several different clubs. If you do subscribe keep dated copies of all forms you receive as well as copies of any "negative option" forms you return to the seller. This information will prove valuable if a problem arises.

Source: "Negative Option Plans," © 2008 Office of the Attorney General - State of Idaho. Reprinted with permission. The Consumer Protection Division enforces Idaho's consumer protection laws, provides information to the public on a wide variety of consumer issues, and offers an informal mediation process for individual consumer complaints. If you have a consumer problem or question, please call (208) 334-2424 or, in-state toll-free, 800-432-3545. TDD access is available.

alternative, you can cancel your membership. The company must honor your cancellation request, as long as you return the introductory merchandise.

Protect Yourself

Before you agree to any prenotification plan, take these steps:

- Read the terms and conditions of the plan carefully so you understand the obligations of membership before you join.

- Compare costs. The introductory merchandise may be substantially discounted but you may be required to buy additional merchandise at the club's regular prices and to pay shipping and handling on those purchases. Do the math to compare the club's prices and the shipping charges against those of other sellers.

- Keep copies of plan documentation that explain the terms and conditions of the plan and the rejection forms you return to the seller. It's also a good idea to keep documentation of the date you mailed the rejection forms.

- Check out the seller. Contact your local consumer protection agency or the Better Business Bureau to find out if they have any complaints on file. A record of complaints may indicate questionable practices, but a lack of complaints doesn't necessarily mean that the seller is without problems. Unscrupulous businesses or business people often change names and locations to hide complaint histories.

Continuity Plans: Coming To You Like Clockwork

They're on TV, in print, and on the internet: Ads for "clubs" that automatically send you a product or service—like flowers, books, movies, or software. If you join one of these "continuity" plans, you're agreeing to receive merchandise or services automatically at regular intervals (often monthly), without advance notice, until you cancel.

How Continuity Plans Work

Often, you can join a plan simply by accepting an introductory offer of merchandise or services. Continuity plans may offer an introductory "free trial period" to let you check out the merchandise or service and decide whether to join the plan. If you keep the merchandise beyond the free trial period or fail to cancel the service within the free trial period, not only must you pay, you automatically become a plan member.

Joining a continuity plan means you agree to the plan's sales method as long as you're a member. You'll automatically get periodic shipments of merchandise or delivery of services. You won't get any announcements or rejection forms before each shipment or service period. The shipments or services continue until you cancel your membership.

Some continuity plans give you an "approval" period. That way, you can check out the merchandise and decide whether to keep it and pay for it. Many programs selling collectibles, like stamps, or coins, work this way. Other continuity plans require you to pay for merchandise when you receive it.

Terms And Conditions

Sellers must give you information about the plan's terms and conditions, clearly and conspicuously, in their promotional materials. These terms may include the following:

- That you become a member if you accept the introductory merchandise or initial round of services—unless you cancel

- That periodic delivery of merchandise or services will occur—with no further action on your part

- A description of the merchandise or services you agree to buy

- Whether there's a minimum purchase

- How often you'll receive the products or services

- An explanation of the plan's billing procedure for each shipment or period of service

- How much time you have to review "on approval" merchandise before you have to pay

- The terms of the plan's refund or return policy

- How and when you can cancel your membership

- The price of the goods or services if you fail to cancel, including shipping and handling, if applicable

Usually a plan will use the same billing method for future shipments that it used for the introductory merchandise or service period. For example, if the plan sent you a bill for the introductory merchandise, you will likely get bills each time you get another shipment. If you used a credit or debit card to buy the introductory merchandise, however, the plan may seek your consent, at the time you enroll, to charge that card automatically for all future shipments.

✔ **Quick Tip**
Where To Complain

If you have a problem with your plan, try to resolve it with the seller first. If you're dissatisfied with the response, contact your local Better Business Bureau or local consumer protection agency.

You also may file a complaint with the FTC. The FTC works for the consumer to prevent fraudulent, deceptive, and unfair business practices in the marketplace and to provide information to help consumers spot, stop, and avoid them. To file a complaint or to get free information on consumer issues, visit ftc.gov or call toll-free, 877-FTC-HELP (877-382-4357); TTY: 866-653-4261.

Source: FTC (www.ftc.gov).

Protect Yourself

Continuity plans are promoted in newspapers, magazines, TV and radio commercials, direct mail, and over the telephone and the internet. Before you agree to any plan, take these steps:

- Read the terms and conditions of the plan carefully so you understand the obligations of membership before you join.

- Keep copies of plan documentation that explain the terms and conditions of the plan. Some plans may send you this information with the introductory shipment.

- If an offer is made over the phone, listen carefully and, if you don't understand the terms, ask the seller to repeat them. Write down important information, such as the customer service telephone number or address. Don't give in to high-pressure sales tactics; if you don't want the offer, feel comfortable hanging up.

- Check out the seller. Contact your local consumer protection agency or the Better Business Bureau to find out if they have any complaints on file. A record of complaints may indicate questionable practices, but a lack of complaints doesn't necessarily mean that the seller doesn't have problems. Unscrupulous businesses or business people often change names and locations to hide complaint histories.

Part Four

Using Credit And Credit Cards

Chapter 27

What You Need To Know About Credit

Getting Credit

The decisions you make now about how you manage your finances and borrow money will affect you in the future—for better or worse.

Did you know that there are companies that keep track of whether you pay your debts and if you make payments on time? Then these companies make this information available in the form of a credit report and score.

A bad credit history can haunt you for a long time—seven years or more. That's why the best thing to do is learn how to maintain good credit before there's a problem. While this might seem complicated at first, it gets easier once you understand the basics of credit and how it works.

Credit is more than just a plastic card you use to buy things—it is your financial trustworthiness. Good credit means that your history of payments, employment and salary make you a good candidate for a loan, and creditors—those who lend money or services—will be more willing to work with you. Having good credit usually translates into lower payments and more ease in borrowing money. Bad credit, however, can be a big problem. It usually

About This Chapter: This chapter includes excerpts from "Getting Credit: What You Need to Know about Credit," Federal Trade Commission (FTC), July 2003; and "Your Access to Free Credit Reports," FTC, March 2008.

results from making payments late or borrowing too much money, and it means that you might have trouble getting a car loan, a credit card, a place to live and, sometimes, a job.

Your Credit

Most creditors use credit scoring to evaluate your credit record. This involves using your credit application and report to get information about you, such as your annual income, outstanding debt, bill-paying history, and the number and types of accounts you have and how long you have had them. Potential lenders use your credit score to help predict whether you are a good risk to repay a loan and make payments on time.

Many people just starting out have no credit history and may find it tough to get a loan or credit card, but establishing a good credit history is not as difficult as it seems.

• You might apply for a credit card issued by a local store, because local businesses are more willing to extend credit to someone with no credit history. Once you establish a pattern of making your payments on time, major credit card issuers might be more willing to extend credit to you.

✎ What's It Mean?

Charge Card: If you use a charge card, you must pay your balance in full when you get your regular statement.

Credit Card: You can use a credit card to buy things and pay for them over time. But remember, buying with credit is a loan—you have to pay the money back. What's more, if the credit card company sends you a check, it's not a gift. It's a loan you have to pay back. In addition to the cost of what you bought, you will owe a percentage of what you spent (interest) and sometimes an annual fee.

Debit Card: This card allows you to access the money in your checking or savings account electronically to make purchases.

Source: Federal Trade Commission (FTC), July 2003.

- You might apply for a secured credit card. Basically, this card requires you to put up the money first and then lets you borrow 50 to 100 percent of your account balance.

- You might ask other people who have an established credit history to co-sign on an account. By co-signing, the person is agreeing to pay back the loan if you don't.

The Fine Print

When applying for credit cards, it's important to shop around. Fees, charges, interest rates, and benefits can vary drastically among credit card issuers. And, in some cases, credit cards might seem like great deals until you read the fine print and disclosures. When you're trying to find the credit card that's right for you, look at the following:

Annual Percentage Rate (APR): The APR is a measure of the cost of credit, expressed as a yearly interest rate. Usually, the lower the APR, the better for you. Be sure to check the fine print to see if your offer has a time limit. Your APR could be much higher after the initial limited offer.

Grace Period: This is the time between the date of the credit card purchase and the date the company starts charging you interest.

Annual Fees: Many credit card issuers charge an annual fee for giving you credit, typically $15 to $55.

Transaction Fees And Other Charges: Most creditors charge a fee if you don't make a payment on time. Other common credit card fees include those for cash advances and going beyond the credit limit. Some credit cards charge a flat fee every month, whether you use your card or not.

Customer Service: Customer service is something most people don't consider, or appreciate, until there's a problem. Look for a 24-hour toll-free telephone number.

Other Options: Creditors may offer other options for a price, including discounts, rebates and special merchandise offers. If your card is lost or stolen, federal law protects you from owing more than $50 per card—but only if

♣ **It's A Fact!!**
Credit Scores

It has become very common for lenders to make decisions on the basis of a credit "score."

A credit score is a number that helps creditors determine how likely you are to pay your credit card bill when it is due. It is calculated based on information in your credit report.

Credit card companies may use one or more credit scores. Credit scores may either be calculated by the creditor itself; or the creditor may use a score purchased from another firm.

Two of the scores that creditors may purchase from other firms include the Fair Isaac (FICO) score and the VantageScore.

FICO Scores: Your FICO score is the main factor lenders consider when deciding whether to grant you credit.

- A FICO score is calculated using a computer model that compares the information in your credit report to what is on the credit reports of countless other customers. FICO scores range from about 300 to 900.

- Generally, the higher the score, the lower the credit risk.

Vantage Score: In 2006, the three credit reporting agencies announced that they had agreed on a new credit scoring system, called VantageScore.

Because all three credit reporting agencies will be using the same scoring system, you should have the same VantageScore from each agency.

The new VantageScore ranges from 501 to 990. It also groups scores into letter categories covering an approximately 100-point range, just like grades you receive on a report card. For example, if you had 501 to 600 points, your credit grade would be "F." If you had 901 points or more, your credit grade would be "A."

Source: Excerpted from *Money Smart for Young Adults: A Financial Education Program*, a CD produced by the Federal Deposit Insurance Corporation (FDIC), March 2008.

you report that it was lost or stolen within two days of discovering the loss or theft. Paying for additional protection may not be a good value.

Your Personal Financial Information

Banks and other financial companies may share your personal financial information with their subsidiaries and other companies. But you can limit some of that sharing if you want to. "Opting out" can help keep much of your financial information private and reduce unsolicited offers that come in the mail. But it also means you may not see offers that could interest you. Your financial institutions will send you a privacy notice once a year in your statement or as a separate mailing. Be sure to read these notices carefully. Get answers to your questions from these companies. If you decide you want to opt out, follow the company's instructions—you may need to call them, return a form, or go online. You can shop around for a financial institution with the privacy policy you want.

Do The Math

Keep in mind that credit card interest rates and minimum monthly payments affect how long it will take to pay off your debt and how much you'll pay for your purchase over time.

Suppose when you're 22, you charge $1,000 worth of clothes and CDs on a credit card with a 19 percent interest rate. If you pay $20 every month, you'll be over 30 by the time you pay off the debt. You'll have paid an extra $1,000 in interest. And that's if you never charge anything else on that card!

Keep Your Credit Record Clean

Good credit is important, now and in the future. In most cases, it takes seven years for accurate, negative information to be deleted from a credit report. Bankruptcy information takes even longer to be deleted—10 years.

Know What Creditors Look For On Credit Reports: Understanding what types of information most creditors evaluate is important. Your credit report is a key part of your credit score, but it is not the only factor. You get points for other things like the following:

- Your bill-paying history

- How many accounts you have and what kind

- Late payments

- Longevity of accounts

- The unused portions of lines of credit

- Collections actions

- Outstanding debt

Keep Credit Cards Under Control

Whether you shop online, by telephone, or by mail, a credit card can make buying many things much easier; but when you use a credit card, it's important to keep track of your spending. Incidental and impulse purchases add up, and each one you make with a credit card is a separate loan. When the bill comes, you have to pay what you owe. Owing more than you can afford to repay can damage your credit rating.

Keeping good records can prevent a lot of headaches, especially if there are inaccuracies on your monthly statement. If you notice a problem, promptly report it to the company that issued the card. Usually the instructions for disputing a charge are on your monthly statement. If you order by mail, by telephone, or online, keep copies and printouts with details about the transaction.

These details should include the company's name, address, and telephone number; the date of your order; a copy of the order form you sent to the company or a list of the stock codes of the items ordered; the order confirmation code; the ad or catalog from which you ordered (if applicable); any applicable warranties; and the return and refund policies.

Finally, if you have a credit card, take the following precautions:

- Never lend it to anyone.

- Never sign a blank charge slip. Draw lines through blank spaces on charge slips above the total so the amount can't be changed.

- Never put your account number on the outside of an envelope or on a postcard.

- Always be cautious about disclosing your account number on the telephone unless you know the person you're dealing with represents a reputable company.

- Always carry only the cards you anticipate using to prevent the possible loss or theft of all your cards or identification.

- Always report lost or stolen ATM and credit cards to the card issuers as soon as possible. Follow up with a letter that includes your account number, when you noticed the card was missing, and when you first reported the loss.

Protect Your Identity

Identity theft involves someone else using your personal information to create fraudulent accounts, charge items to another person's existing accounts, or even get a job. You can minimize the risks by managing your personal information wisely and cautiously. Here are some ways to protect yourself from identity theft:

- Before you reveal any personally identifying information, find out how it will be used and whether it will be shared.

- Pay attention to your billing cycles. Follow up with creditors if your bills don't arrive on time.

- Guard your mail from theft. Deposit outgoing mail in post office collection boxes or at your local post office. Promptly remove mail from your mailbox after it has been delivered. If you're planning

✔ **Quick Tip**
What To Do If You're A Victim Of Identity Theft

If your cards, bills or identification have been misused to open new accounts in your name, file a complaint with the Federal Trade Commission. Call toll-free 877-ID-THEFT (877-438-4338); TDD: 202-326-2502, or visit http://www.consumer.gov/idtheft.

Source: Federal Trade Commission (FTC), July 2003.

✔ Quick Tip
When To Contact Creditors

If you're having trouble paying your bills, contact your creditors immediately. Tell them why it's difficult for you, and try to work out a modified plan that reduces your payments to a more manageable level. Don't wait until your accounts have been turned over to a debt collector. Take action immediately and keep a detailed record of your conversations and correspondence.

Source: Federal Trade Commission (FTC), July 2003.

to be away from home and can't pick up your mail, call the U.S. Postal Service toll-free at 800-275-8777, or visit http://www.usps.gov to request a vacation hold.

- When possible, put passwords on your credit card, bank, and phone accounts. Avoid using easily available information like your mother's maiden name, your birth date, the last four digits of your Social Security number or telephone number, or a series of consecutive numbers. It's a good idea to keep a list of your credit card issuers and their telephone numbers.

- Don't give out personal information on the telephone, through the mail, or over the internet unless you've initiated the contact or you know whom you're dealing with.

- Protect personal information in your home. For example, tear or shred documents like charge receipts, copies of credit offers and applications, insurance forms, physician's statements, discarded bank checks and statements, and expired credit cards before you throw them away. Be cautious about leaving personal information in plain view, especially if you have roommates, employ outside help, or are having service work done.

- Find out who has access to your personal information at work and verify that the records are kept in a secure location.

- Never carry your Social Security card; leave it in a secure place at home. Give out your Social Security number only when absolutely necessary.

- Order your credit report from each of the three major credit reporting agencies every year to make sure it is accurate and includes only those activities you've authorized.

- Carry only the identification that you actually need.

Improve Your Credit Record

A lot of people spend more than they can afford and pay less toward their debts than they should. To get control over your finances and to manage your debt, try:

Budgeting: In many cases, people design and then stick to a budget to get their debt under control. A budget is a plan for how much money you have and how much money you spend. Sticking to a realistic budget allows you to pay off your debts and save for the proverbial rainy day.

Credit Counseling: Many universities, military bases, credit unions, and housing authorities operate nonprofit financial counseling programs. Some charge a fee for their services. Creditors may be willing to accept reduced

✔ **Quick Tip**
Buyer Beware!
Ads Promising "Debt Relief"
Actually May Be Offering Bankruptcy

As you try to take control of your debt, be on the lookout for advertisements that offer quick fixes. While ads pitch the promise of debt relief, they rarely mention that this relief comes in the form of bankruptcy. Because bankruptcy stays on your credit report for 10 years and hinders your ability to get credit, it's important to ask for details before agreeing to any debt-relief services.

Source: Federal Trade Commission (FTC), July 2003.

payments if you're working with a reputable program to create a debt repayment plan. When you choose a credit counselor, be sure to ask about fees you will have to pay and what kind of counseling you'll receive. A credit counseling organization isn't necessarily legitimate just because it says it's nonprofit. You may want to check with the Better Business Bureau for any complaints

✔ Quick Tip
What To Do If Your Request For Credit Is Denied

If your request for credit is denied, you will receive a denial notice, sometimes called an adverse action notice.

It lists the reasons for denying your application. If you do not receive this notice or the notice does not explain why the credit was denied, ask the credit card company.

You have the right to have the credit card company give you the reasons that the credit was denied. While each creditor has its own reasons for denying credit, some reasons for denial might include the following:

• You have a bad credit history

• You have not been at your current address or job long enough

• Your income does not meet the credit card company's criteria

If you are denied credit because of information in your credit report, federal law requires the credit card company to give you the name, address, and telephone number of the credit bureau that supplied the information. If you contact the credit bureau within 60 days of receiving the denial, you are entitled to a free copy of your credit report.

You have a right to dispute, or argue, any incorrect information in your credit report with the credit reporting agency, and also with the company that gave the information to the credit reporting agency. It is important to review your credit report from all three agencies to ensure that they have correct information.

Source: Excerpted from *Money Smart for Young Adults: A Financial Education Program*, a CD produced by the Federal Deposit Insurance Corporation (FDIC), March 2008.

against a counselor or counseling organization. Visit http://www.bbbonline.org/ for your local Better Business Bureau's telephone number.

Bankruptcy: Bankruptcy is considered the credit solution of last resort. Unlike negative credit information that stays on a credit report for seven years, bankruptcies stay on a credit report for 10 years. Bankruptcy can make it difficult to rent an apartment, buy a house or a condo, get some types of insurance, get additional credit, and, sometimes, get a job. In some cases, bankruptcy may not be an easily available option.

Use Caution When Seeking Help With Debt

Turning to a business that offers help in solving debt problems may seem like a reasonable solution when your bills become unmanageable. Be cautious. Before you do business with any company, check it out with your local consumer protection agency or the Better Business Bureau in the company's location. One rule to remember is that if a credit repair offer seems too easy or just too good to be true, it probably is too good to be true. And knowing your rights can help you steer clear of rip-offs. For example, according to state and federal laws, companies that help people improve their credit rating cannot do the following:

• Make false claims about their services

• Charge you until the services are completed

• Perform services until the waiting period has passed. After you sign the written contract, you have three days to change your mind and cancel the services.

Avoid Advance Fee Loan Scams

Offers that guarantee you a credit card for a fee—before you even apply—are against the law. These scams often target consumers with credit problems. If someone calls you making that kind of promise, tell the caller not to call you anymore and hang up.

If you've had a problem, the Federal Trade Commission (FTC) works for the consumer to prevent fraudulent, deceptive and unfair business practices in the marketplace and to provide information to help consumers spot, stop, and avoid them. To file a complaint or to get free information on consumer issues, call toll-free, 877-FTC-HELP (877-382-4357), or visit http://www.ftc.gov/ftc/consumer.htm. The FTC enters internet, telemarketing, identity theft, and other fraud-related complaints into Consumer Sentinel, a secure, online database available to hundreds of civil and criminal law enforcement agencies in the United States and abroad.

It's a good idea to contact your local consumer protection agency, state attorney general, or Better Business Bureau, too. Many attorneys general have toll-free consumer hotlines. To find the number for your state's attorney general, check with your local directory assistance.

Don't Be Lost

A lost or stolen wallet or purse is a gold mine of information for identity thieves. If your wallet or purse is lost or stolen, follow these steps:

- File a report with the police immediately and keep a copy.

- Cancel your credit cards. Call the issuer(s) immediately. Many companies have 24-hour toll-free numbers to deal with such emergencies. The number is on your monthly statement.

- Get new cards with new account numbers.

- Call the fraud departments of the major credit reporting agencies, and ask each agency to put a "fraud alert" on your account: Equifax (800-525-6285); Experian (888-397-3742); TransUnion (800-680-7289)

> ### ♣ It's A Fact!!
> ### About Lost Or
> ### Stolen Credit Cards
>
> If your card is lost or stolen, federal law protects you from owing more than $50 per card—but only if you report that the card was lost or stolen within two days of discovering the loss or theft. If you suspect any fraudulent purchases, you may be asked to sign a statement under oath that you did not make the purchase(s) in question. It's important to ask for details before agreeing to any debt-relief services.
>
> Source: Federal Trade Commission (FTC), July 2003.

- Report the loss to the fraud department of the bank where you have your checking and savings accounts. Ask about the next steps regarding your accounts, including your ATM or debit card.

- Review your credit reports regularly and have them corrected when necessary.

- Report a missing driver's license to your state department of motor vehicles.

- Change your home and car locks, if your keys were taken.

Your Access To Free Credit Reports

The Fair Credit Reporting Act (FCRA) requires each of the nationwide consumer reporting companies—Equifax, Experian, and TransUnion—to provide you with a free copy of your credit report, at your request, once every 12 months. The FCRA promotes the accuracy and privacy of information in the files of the nation's consumer reporting companies. The Federal Trade Commission (FTC), the nation's consumer protection agency, enforces the FCRA with respect to consumer reporting companies.

A credit report includes information on where you live, how you pay your bills, and whether you've been sued or arrested, or have filed for bankruptcy. Nationwide consumer reporting companies sell the information in your report to creditors, insurers, employers, and other businesses that use it to evaluate your applications for credit, insurance, employment, or renting a home.

Here are the details about your rights under the FCRA and the Fair and Accurate Credit Transactions (FACT) Act, which established the free annual credit report program.

How do I order my free report?

The three nationwide consumer reporting companies have set up a central website, a toll-free telephone number, and a mailing address through which you can order your free annual report.

To order, visit http://annualcreditreport.com, call 877-322-8228, or complete the Annual Credit Report Request Form and mail it to: Annual Credit

Report Request Service, P.O. Box 105281, Atlanta, GA 30348-5281. The form is available online for you to print at http://www.ftc.gov/credit. Do not contact the three nationwide consumer reporting companies individually. They are providing free annual credit reports only through http://annualcreditreport.com, 877-322-8228, and Annual Credit Report Request Service, P.O. Box 105281, Atlanta, GA 30348-5281.

You may order your reports from each of the three nationwide consumer reporting companies at the same time, or you can order your report from each of the companies one at a time. The law allows you to order one free copy of your report from each of the nationwide consumer reporting companies every 12 months.

✔ Quick Tip
A Warning About "Impostor" Websites

Only one website is authorized to fill orders for the free annual credit report you are entitled to under law—http://annualcreditreport.com. Other websites that claim to offer "free credit reports," "free credit scores," or "free credit monitoring" are not part of the legally mandated free annual credit report program. In some cases, the "free" product comes with strings attached. For example, some sites sign you up for a supposedly "free" service that converts to one you have to pay for after a trial period. If you don't cancel during the trial period, you may be unwittingly agreeing to let the company start charging fees to your credit card.

Some "impostor" sites use terms like "free report" in their names; others have URLs that purposely misspell annualcreditreport.com in the hope that you will mistype the name of the official site. Some of these "impostor" sites direct you to other sites that try to sell you something or collect your personal information.

Annualcreditreport.com and the nationwide consumer reporting companies will not send you an e-mail asking for your personal information. If you get an e-mail, see a pop-up ad, or get a phone call from someone claiming to be from annualcreditreport.com or any of the three nationwide consumer reporting companies, do not reply or click on any link in the message. It's probably a scam. Forward any such e-mail to the FTC at spam@uce.gov.

Source: Federal Trade Commission (FTC), March 2008.

What information do I need to provide to get my free report?

You need to provide your name, address, Social Security number, and date of birth. If you have moved in the last two years, you may have to provide your previous address. To maintain the security of your file, each nationwide consumer reporting company may ask you for some information that only you would know, like the amount of your monthly mortgage payment. Each company may ask you for different information because the information each has in your file may come from different sources.

Why do I want a copy of my credit report?

Your credit report has information that affects whether you can get a loan—and how much you will have to pay to borrow money. You want a copy of your credit report to do the following:

- Make sure the information is accurate, complete, and up-to-date before you apply for a loan for a major purchase like a house or car, buy insurance, or apply for a job.

- Help guard against identity theft. That's when someone uses your personal information—like your name, your Social Security number, or your credit card number—to commit fraud. Identity thieves may use your information to open a new credit card account in your name. Then, when they don't pay the bills, the delinquent account is reported on your credit report. Inaccurate information like that could affect your ability to get credit, insurance, or even a job.

How long does it take to get my report after I order it?

If you request your report online at http://annualcreditreport.com, you should be able to access it immediately. If you order your report by calling toll-free 877-322-8228, your report will be processed and mailed to you within 15 days. If you order your report by mail using the Annual Credit Report Request Form, your request will be processed and mailed to you within 15 days of receipt.

Whether you order your report online, by phone, or by mail, it may take longer to receive your report if the nationwide consumer reporting company needs more information to verify your identity.

There also may be times when the nationwide consumer reporting companies receive a high volume of requests for credit reports. If that happens, you may be asked to re-submit your request. Or, you may be told that your report will be mailed to you sometime after 15 days from your request. If either of these events occurs, the nationwide consumer reporting companies will let you know.

Are there any other situations where I might be eligible for a free report?

Under federal law, you're entitled to a free report if a company takes adverse action against you, such as denying your application for credit, insurance, or employment, and you ask for your report within 60 days of receiving notice of the action. The notice will give you the name, address, and phone number of the consumer reporting company. You're also entitled to one free report a year if you're unemployed and plan to look for a job within 60 days; if you're on welfare; or if your report is inaccurate because of fraud, including identity theft. Otherwise, a consumer reporting company may charge you up to $10.50 for another copy of your report within a 12-month period.

To buy a copy of your report, contact:

- Equifax: 800-685-1111; http://www.equifax.com
- Experian: 888-397-3742; http://www.experian.com
- TransUnion: 800-916-8800; http://www.transunion.com

Under state law, consumers in Colorado, Georgia, Maine, Maryland, Massachusetts, New Jersey, and Vermont already have free access to their credit reports.

Should I order a report from each of the three nationwide consumer reporting companies?

It's up to you. Because nationwide consumer reporting companies get their information from different sources, the information in your report from one company may not reflect all, or the same, information in your reports from the other two companies. That's not to say that the information in any of your reports is necessarily inaccurate; it just may be different.

✔ Quick Tip

Should I order my reports from all three of the nationwide consumer reporting companies at the same time?

You may order one, two, or all three reports at the same time, or you may stagger your requests. It's your choice. Some financial advisors say staggering your requests during a 12-month period may be a good way to keep an eye on the accuracy and completeness of the information in your reports.

Source: Federal Trade Commission (FTC), March 2008.

What if I find errors—either inaccuracies or incomplete information—in my credit report?

Under the FCRA, both the consumer reporting company and the information provider (that is, the person, company, or organization that provides information about you to a consumer reporting company) are responsible for correcting inaccurate or incomplete information in your report. To take full advantage of your rights under this law, contact the consumer reporting company and the information provider.

Tell the consumer reporting company, in writing, what information you think is inaccurate. Consumer reporting companies must investigate the items in question—usually within 30 days—unless they consider your dispute frivolous. They also must forward all the relevant data you provide about the inaccuracy to the organization that provided the information. After the information provider receives notice of a dispute from the consumer reporting company, it must investigate, review the relevant information, and report the results back to the consumer reporting company. If the information provider finds the disputed information is inaccurate, it must notify all three nationwide consumer reporting companies so they can correct the information in your file.

When the investigation is complete, the consumer reporting company must give you the written results and a free copy of your report if the dispute results in a change. (This free report does not count as your annual free report under the FACT Act.) If an item is changed or deleted, the consumer reporting company cannot put the disputed information back in your file unless the information provider verifies that it is accurate and complete. The consumer reporting company also must send you written notice that includes the name, address, and phone number of the information provider.

Tell the creditor or other information provider in writing that you dispute an item. Many providers specify an address for disputes. If the provider reports the item to a consumer reporting company, it must include a notice of your dispute. And if you are correct—that is, if the information is found to be inaccurate—the information provider may not report it again.

What can I do if the consumer reporting company or information provider won't correct the information I dispute?

If an investigation doesn't resolve your dispute with the consumer reporting company, you can ask that a statement of the dispute be included in your file and in future reports. You also can ask the consumer reporting company to provide your statement to anyone who received a copy of your report in the recent past. You can expect to pay a fee for this service.

If you tell the information provider that you dispute an item, a notice of your dispute must be included any time the information provider reports the item to a consumer reporting company.

How long can a consumer reporting company report negative information?

A consumer reporting company can report most accurate negative information for seven years and bankruptcy information for 10 years. There is no time limit on reporting information about criminal convictions; information reported in response to your application for a job that pays more than $75,000 a year; and information reported because you've applied for more than $150,000 worth of credit or life insurance. Information about a lawsuit or an unpaid judgment against you can be reported for seven years or until the statute of limitations runs out, whichever is longer.

Can anyone else get a copy of my credit report?

The FCRA specifies who can access your credit report. Creditors, insurers, employers, and other businesses that use the information in your report to evaluate your applications for credit, insurance, employment, or renting a home are among those that have a legal right to access your report.

Can my employer get my credit report?

Your employer can get a copy of your credit report only if you agree. A consumer reporting company may not provide information about you to your employer, or to a prospective employer, without your written consent.

Chapter 28

Borrowing Basics

Types Of Loans

At some point in your life, you will need to borrow money. If you want to purchase a car or a house, you may need to get a loan. There are three types of loans:

- Credit cards
- Consumer installment loans
- Home loans

Credit Cards

Credit cards give you the ongoing ability to borrow money.

With a credit card, you can buy things without actually having the money right away. However, this can get you into big trouble if you aren't careful. You need to be able to pay your monthly credit card bill.

Consumer Installment Loans

A consumer installment loan is used to buy personal items for you and your family. It is called an "installment loan" because you pay the same amount

About This Chapter: Excerpted from "Module 5: Borrowing Basics," *Money Smart for Young Adults*, a CD-based curriculum developed by the Federal Deposit Insurance Corporation (FDIC), March 2008.

each month in installments. Examples are automobiles and computers. For example, with her birthday money, Grace decides to buy a new laptop. She paid $250 as a down payment and got an installment loan for the rest, the balance. She pays in installment payments of $100 per month for 12 months.

Home Loans

The third type of loan is a home loan. There are three main types of home loans:

- Home purchase loans

- Home refinance loans

- Home equity loans

All three loans are based on the value of the home. If the borrower does not pay back the loan on time, the lender can take possession of the home.

♣ **It's A Fact!!**
Barriers To
Borrowing Money

If a lender finds a history of being irresponsible, that tells the lender immediately that the borrower is a risk. Examples of the sort of past history a lender will be concerned about include the following:

- Consistently making late payments

- Filing for bankruptcy

- Having property repossessed or foreclosed on

- Having a court order requiring a debtor to pay money to the creditor

Source: Federal Deposit Insurance Corporation (FDIC), March 2008.

Home purchase loans are made for the purpose of buying a house. They are usually called mortgages.

Home refinancing is a process by which an existing home loan (or mortgage) is paid off and replaced with a new loan. Reasons homeowners might want to refinance their home loan include the following:

- A lower interest rate

- Money for home repairs or improvements

- Money for other needs

- A way to consolidate debts

Home equity loans can be used for any reason. The amount that a person can borrow depends on the amount of "equity" they have in the house. Sometimes banks will give the borrower a checkbook to use to borrow money. It looks like a normal check, but in fact it is a loan that the borrower has to start paying back right away.

The Cost Of Credit

When you get a loan, there are generally two costs you must pay: fees and interest.

Fees

Fees are charged by financial institutions for activities such as servicing the account and reviewing your loan application. Here are some examples:

- A credit card company might charge you an annual fee of $30.

- A credit card company will probably also charge fees when you get a cash advance or when your balance exceeds your credit limit. (Your credit limit is how much money the credit card issuer agreed to loan to you.)

- A lender might charge a $25 late fee when you do not pay your bill on time.

Interest

Interest is the amount of money a financial institution charges for letting you use its money. The interest rate can be either fixed or variable.

- Fixed rate means the interest rate stays the same throughout the term of the loan.

- Variable rate means the interest rate may change during the loan term. The loan agreement will explain how the rate may change.

Truth In Lending Disclosures

The federal Truth In Lending law requires banks to state charges in a clear and uniform manner so you can easily see the cost of borrowing money. This law allows you to comparison shop between lenders for credit cards and other loans.

What Lenders Must Disclose

- **Amount Financed:** The amount of the loan the lender is letting you borrow.

- **Annual Percentage Rate (APR):** The cost of your loan expressed as a yearly percentage rate. Using an APR of 12 percent as the example. The APR reflects the total cost of lending rather than just the interest charge. It is the primary tool you should use to compare lending options. The law generally requires that the APR appear in 18-point font on most credit card applications so it is easily seen.

- **Finance Charge:** The total dollar amount the loan will cost you. It includes items such as interest, service charges, and loan fees. For example

---

♣ It's A Fact!!
Getting A Loan: A Responsibility To Be Taken Seriously

Borrowing money can be a great way to buy something now and pay for it over time. And yes, there are ways for a teen to borrow money. But there are some important things to remember if you borrow money. One is that borrowing usually involves a cost called "interest," which is the fee to compensate the bank or other lender when you use their money. This is the reverse of what happens when the bank pays you interest to put your money in the bank.

Also, when you borrow money you are promising to repay the loan on a schedule. If you don't keep that promise, the results can be very costly—either in late payments you'll owe or in damage to your reputation, which means you could have a tougher time borrowing money in the future.

Here are some of your options...and important considerations.

- For many teens, their first lenders are their parents. If your parents are willing to lend you money, they probably will set repayment terms (how much to pay back and when). They also may require you to pay more money than you borrowed, as a bank would do when it lends people money and charges interest.

- You may be able to get access to a credit card or bank loan. Under most state laws, for example, you must be at least 18 years old to obtain your own credit card and be held responsible for repaying the debt. If you're under 18, though, you can qualify for a credit card along with a parent or other adult.

for a loan of $5,000 where the interest is 12% APR, the finance charge total is $600.

• **Total Payments:** The amount you will have paid after you have made all payments as scheduled.

Two terms associated with credit card APRs with which you should be aware are "penalty APR" and "universal default."

• **Penalty APR:** The terms of your credit card agreement may provide that the creditor will permanently increase the interest rate on your credit card by a large amount if you do not pay your credit card bill on time or if you exceed your credit limit. For example, the penalty rate

---

• If you and your parents are comfortable with you having access to a credit card, there are cards designed just for teens. One is a credit card with a low credit limit (maximum amount you can borrow), which can keep you from getting deeply in debt.

• An alternative to buying with a credit card is to use a debit card, but this also comes with costs and risks. A debit card allows you to make purchases without paying interest or getting into debt because the money is automatically deducted from an existing savings or checking account. Again, if you're under 18, you may qualify for this card with a parent or other adult.

• One example of a debit card that may be appropriate for teens 13 and older is a pre-paid card that carries a certain value from which purchases are deducted. This kind of debit card isn't linked to your bank account. Instead, just like with a pre-paid telephone plan, there is a limit on how much you may spend. Keep in mind that many debit cards have fees that can add up quickly, so make sure you ask about fees before using a debit card. Also, because a debit card can provide a thief easy access to an account, you need to protect your card and any PINs (personal identification numbers) that go with it.

Source: "Getting a Loan: A Responsibility to Be Taken Seriously," *FDIC Consumer News*, Federal Deposit Insurance Corporation, Summer 2006.

♣ It's A Fact!!
Small Payments Can Mean Big Costs When Borrowing

It's never too early to begin learning how credit (borrowing) works. The main message is this: The longer you take to pay back what you owe on a credit card or loan, the more you'll pay the lender in interest charges. In particular, if you use a credit card to make a major purchase and you only pay back a little of what you owe each month, "it will take you a very long time to pay off the balance, and the interest costs can be shocking," according to Janet Kincaid, Federal Deposit Insurance Corporation (FDIC) Senior Consumer Affairs Officer.

Table 28.1 shows what an expensive purchase will really cost you if you charge it and only pay back the minimum amount due each month, which may be something like $20 or $30. In this example, a $500 stereo would end up costing you about $900 when you figure in the total interest you'd pay, and a $1,000 computer would set you back more than $2,100. Instead, if you pay back as much as you can each month—the entire balance, if possible—you can really limit interest charges.

Table 28.1. How Much Does It Really Cost?

Item	Purchase Price	Years to Pay Off With Minimum Monthly Payments	Total Interest Paid	Total Cost
Stereo	$500	7	$367	$867
Computer	$1,000	13	$1,129	$2,129

Note: Years are rounded to the nearest whole year. These examples assume an interest rate (Annual Percentage Rate) of 18 percent and a minimum monthly payment of the interest due plus one percent of the outstanding balance owed.

Source: "Small Payments Can Mean Big Costs When Borrowing," *FDIC Consumer News*, Federal Deposit Insurance Corporation, Summer 2006.

may apply if you are late on more than two payments in a six-month period. The Truth in Lending disclosures will provide details on whether the creditor has penalty APRs and when they apply.

- **Universal Default:** A related concept is universal default. Some lenders have policies that will raise your credit card interest rate to the highest possible rate if you are late on any other account. Example: If you have five credit cards and you are late on one, the interest rate for the other four cards may be increased by a large amount. The Truth in Lending disclosures will tell you if your lender has such a policy.

Equal Credit Opportunity Act

The Equal Credit Opportunity Act (ECOA) ensures that all people are given an equal chance to obtain credit. This doesn't mean all those who apply for credit get it: factors such as income, expenses, debt, and credit history are legitimate considerations for creditworthiness. Rather, the law prohibits a bank from discriminating against you because of your race, color, marital status, religion, national origin, age, receipt of public assistance, or whether you are male or female when deciding whether to issue you a loan.

How Credit Decisions Are Made

The Four Cs Of Credit Decision Making

When you apply for credit, the lender will review the "Four Cs" to decide whether you are a good credit risk, or in other words, whether you are likely to pay back the loan.

- Capacity refers to your present and future ability to meet your payments.
- Capital refers to the value of your assets and your net worth.
- Character refers to how you have paid your bills or debts in the past.
- Collateral refers to property or assets offered to secure the loan.

Capacity: Capacity refers to your present and future ability to meet your payments. Lenders will ask the following questions:

- Do you have a job? Generally, a lender would like to see that you have a job and have held the same job or same type of job for at least a year.

- How much money do you make each month?

- What are your monthly expenses?

A bank will compare your monthly loan payments, if any, and your other monthly expenses to your monthly income. By doing so, they will determine your debt-to-income ratio. It helps determine how much money you can afford to borrow. Look at the following example:

- Income from a job for one month: $300

- Expenses

  - Cell phone bill for one month: $50

  - Installment loan payment for computer: $100

- Total expenses: $150

Total expenses $150 / Total Income $300 = 50% debt to income ratio. In most cases, lenders like to see a 36% or lower ratio before they loan money.

Capital: Capital refers to the value of your assets and your net worth.

✔ **Quick Tip**
Tips For Managing Your Credit

Once you have decided you want to get a loan and have been approved, you need to keep these tips in mind to use the money you have borrowed wisely.

- For a credit card, if possible, pay off your entire bill each month. If you cannot, try to pay more than the minimum balance due. This will reduce finance charges and total interest paid.

- If you can't pay off your credit card completely, stop using it. Do not allow yourself to get into more debt.

- Pay on time to avoid late fees and to protect your credit history. When the bill arrives, check the due date. It may be very soon. If you cannot pay on time, call your creditor immediately to explain the situation. The creditor may waive the late fees or be willing to make other payment arrangements. Always check your monthly statement to verify that it accurately lists the things you bought. Call your creditor right away if you suspect errors.

- Ignore offers creditors may send you to reduce or skip payments. You will still be charged finance charges during this period.

- Think about the cost difference if you purchase your item with cash versus if you purchase your item with credit.

Source: Federal Deposit Insurance Corporation (FDIC), March 2008.

Lenders want to determine the value of your assets. Assets are things you own that have financial value. Lenders will also compare the difference between the value of your assets and the amount of debt you have. This is called net worth. A positive net worth demonstrates your ability to manage your money. Lenders will ask the following:

- How much money do you have in your checking and savings accounts?

- Do you have investments or other assets (for example, a car)?

Typically an asset is something large like a house, a car, or a piece of large furniture. Smaller items such as household appliances and clothing are not considered assets.

An investment is when you have purchased an item or product that is expected to increase in value over time. Not all investments increase in value over time; you could even lose money.

Character: Character refers to how you have paid your bills or debts in the past. Lenders will ask the following:

- Have you had credit in the past? If you have a good credit history of repaying your other loans, you will have an easier time getting your loan request approved and at the best rate. For instance, you can build a positive credit history by making your student loan payments on time.

- How many credit accounts do you have? If you have never had a credit account, you may have difficulty getting approved for a loan. Having a good credit history shows a lender you can borrow money responsibly. Some lenders let you prove this without a credit history. For example, they might ask for proof that you pay your rent and utility and phone bills on time or that you make regular deposits to a savings account. Other examples of alternative ways to show a creditor that you are a good credit risk may include insurance premium payments, payments for school tuition; and payments of personal loans (documented by a written loan agreement and canceled checks). Ask the lender to consider alternative forms of history. If a lender is not willing to do this, shop around for one who will.

Banks will use credit reports to obtain character information. You can request a copy of your credit report by visiting http://www.annualcredit report.com or calling 877-322-8228.

Collateral: Collateral refers to what you own that you can use to offer the lender in the event that you default on the loan. Lenders will ask: Do you have assets to provide to secure the loan beyond your capacity to pay it off?

Collateral is security you provide the lender. Giving the lender collateral means that you pledge an asset that you own, such as your home, property you own, or other object that has value, to the lender with the agreement that it will be the repayment source in case you cannot repay the loan.

Sometimes a person with no credit history will ask another person to cosign a loan. The cosigner is equally responsible for repaying the loan. If the borrower defaults, the cosigner has to pay.

Chapter 29

Choosing A Credit Card

Shopping around for a credit card can save you money on interest and fees. You'll want to find one with features that match your needs. The information in this chapter can help you understand the features of credit cards, compare credit card features and costs, know your rights when using your credit card, and file a complaint if you have a problem with your credit card.

How will you use your credit card?

The first step in choosing a credit card is thinking about how you will use it.

- If you expect to always pay your monthly bill in full—and other features such as frequent flyer miles don't interest you—your best choice may be a card that has no annual fee and offers a longer grace period.

- If you sometimes carry over a balance from month to month, you may be more interested in a card that carries a lower interest rate (stated as an annual percentage rate, or APR).

- If you expect to use your card to get cash advances, you'll want to look for a card that carries a lower APR and lower fees on cash advances. Some cards charge a higher APR for cash advances than for purchases.

About This Chapter: From "Choosing a Credit Card," Federal Reserve Board, October 19, 2004.

♣ **It's A Fact!!**

Can Teens Get Credit Cards?

Yes, teens can get... or get access to... credit cards and debit cards. Under most state laws, for example, you must be at least 18 years old (a young adult) to obtain your own credit card and be held responsible for repaying the debt. And if you're under 18, you can qualify for a credit card if a parent co-signs, but only the parent can be held accountable for the payments.

Credit and debit cards can be good ways for teens to pay without carrying cash or checks, and they can help teach kids about how to manage money. But teens—and their parents—need to be especially careful to avoid serious debt problems or a bad credit record at a young age.

First, make financial education a priority, especially the lessons about borrowing responsibly. "Teens need to be aware that a bad credit record can affect their ability to rent an apartment or even find employment after graduation," says Lynne Gottesburen, a Federal Deposit Insurance Corporation (FDIC) Consumer Affairs Specialist.

Also, understand the alternatives. There are cards with features sometimes described as "training wheels" for young cardholders. One is a credit card with a low credit limit—say, $300 or $500—which can keep a teen from getting too deeply in debt. Another is a pre-paid, re-loadable payment card that parents can get for teens aged 13 or older and that comes with parental controls, including spending limits. A debit card also enables a teen to make purchases without paying interest or getting into debt because the money is automatically deducted from an existing bank account.

Source: From "Credit and Debit Cards," *FDIC Consumer News*, Federal Deposit Insurance Corporation (FDIC), Fall 2002.

What are the APRs?

The annual percentage rate—APR—is the way of stating the interest rate you will pay if you carry over a balance, take out a cash advance, or transfer a balance from another card. The APR states the interest rate as a yearly rate.

A single credit card may have several APRs:

- **Multiple APRs:** One APR for purchases, another for cash advances, and yet another for balance transfers. The APRs for cash advances and balance transfers often are higher than the APR for purchases (for example, 14% for purchases, 18% for cash advances, and 19% for balance transfers).

- **Tiered APRs:** Different rates are applied to different levels of the outstanding balance (for example, 16% on balances of $1–$500 and 17% on balances above $500).

- **A Penalty APR:** The APR may increase if you are late in making payments. For example, your card agreement may say, "If your payment arrives more than ten days late two times within a six-month period, the penalty rate will apply."

- **An Introductory APR.** A different rate will apply after the introductory rate expires.

- **A Delayed APR:** A different rate will apply in the future. For example, a card may advertise that there is "no interest until next March." Look for the APR that will be in effect after March.

If you carry over a part of your balance from month to month, even a small difference in the APR can make a big difference in how much you will pay over a year.

How long is the grace period?

The grace period is the number of days you have to pay your bill in full without triggering a finance charge. For example, the credit card company may say that you have "25 days from the statement date, provided you paid your previous balance in full by the due date." The statement date is given on the bill.

The grace period usually applies only to new purchases. Most credit cards do not give a grace period for cash advances and balance transfers. Instead, interest charges start right away.

If you carried over any part of your balance from the preceding month, you may not have a grace period for new purchases. Instead, you may be charged interest as soon as you make a purchase (in addition to being charged interest on the earlier balance you have not paid off). Look on the credit card application for information about the "method of computing the balance for purchases" to see if new purchases are included or excluded.

♣ It's A Fact!!
Fixed vs. Variable APR

Some credit cards are "fixed rate"—the APR doesn't change, or at least doesn't change often. Even the APR on a "fixed rate" credit card can change over time. However, the credit card company must tell you before increasing the fixed APR.

Other credit cards are "variable rate"—the APR changes from time to time. The rate is usually tied to another interest rate, such as the prime rate or the Treasury bill rate. If the other rate changes, the rate on your card may change, too. Look for information on the credit card application and in the credit card agreement to see how often your card's APR may change (the agreement is like a contract—it lists the terms and conditions for using your credit card).

Source: Federal Reserve Board, October 19, 2004.

How is the finance charge calculated?

The finance charge is the dollar amount you pay to use credit. The amount depends in part on your outstanding balance and the APR.

Credit card companies use one of several methods to calculate the outstanding balance. The method can make a big difference in the finance charge you'll pay. Your outstanding balance may be calculated over one billing cycle or two; using the adjusted balance, the average daily balance, or the previous balance, and including or excluding new purchases in the balance.

Depending on the balance you carry and the timing of your purchases and payments, you'll usually have a lower finance charge with one-cycle billing and either the average daily balance method excluding new purchases, the adjusted balance method, or the previous balance method.

Minimum Finance Charge: Some credit cards have a minimum finance charge. You'll be charged that minimum even if the calculated amount of your finance charge is less. For example, your finance charge may be calculated to be 35¢—but if the company's minimum finance charge is $1.00, you'll pay $1.00. A minimum finance charge usually applies only when you must pay a finance charge—that is, when you carry over a balance from one billing cycle to the next.

What are the fees?

Most credit cards charge fees under certain circumstances:

- **Annual Fee** (sometimes billed monthly): Charged for having the card.

- **Cash Advance Fee:** Charged when you use the card for a cash advance; may be a flat fee (for example, $3.00) or a percentage of the cash advance (for example, 3%).

- **Balance-Transfer Fee:** Charged when you transfer a balance from another credit card. (Your credit card company may send you "checks" to pay off the other card. The balance is transferred when you use one of these checks to pay the amount due on the other card.)

- **Late-Payment Fee:** Charged if your payment is received after the due date.

- **Over-The-Credit-Limit Fee:** Charged if you go over your credit limit.

- **Credit-Limit-Increase Fee:** Charged if you ask for an increase in your credit limit.

- **Set-Up Fee:** Charged when a new credit card account is opened.

- **Return-Item Fee:** Charged if you pay your bill by check and the check is returned for non-sufficient funds (that is, your check bounces).

- **Other Fees:** Some credit card companies charge a fee if you pay by telephone (that is, if you arrange by phone for payment to be transferred from your bank to the company) or to cover the costs of reporting to credit bureaus, reviewing your account, or providing other customer services. Read the information in your credit card agreement to see if there are other fees and charges.

What are the cash advance features?

Some credit cards let you borrow cash in addition to making purchases on credit. Most credit card companies treat these cash advances and your

---

♣ It's A Fact!!
Credit Card Balance Computation Methods

- **Average Daily Balance:** This is the most common calculation method. It credits your account from the day the issuer receives your payment. To figure the balance due, the issuer totals the beginning balance for each day in the billing period and subtracts any credits made to your account that day. While new purchases may or may not be added to the balance, cash advances typically are included. The resulting daily balances are added for the billing cycle. Then, the total is divided by the number of days in the billing period to get the "average daily balance."

- **Adjusted Balance:** This usually is the most advantageous method for cardholders. The issuer determines your balance by subtracting payments or credits received during the current billing period from the balance at the end of the previous billing period. Purchases made during the billing period aren't included. This method gives you until the end of the billing period to pay a portion of your balance to avoid the interest charges on that amount. Some creditors exclude prior unpaid finance charges from the previous balance.

- **Previous Balance:** This is the amount you owed at the end of the previous billing period. Payments, credits, and purchases made during the current billing period are not included. Some creditors exclude unpaid finance charges.

- **Two-Cycle Or Double-Cycle Balances:** Issuers sometimes calculate your balance using your last two month's account activity. This approach eliminates the interest-free period if you go from paying your balance in full each month to paying only a portion each month of what you owe. For

purchases differently. If you plan to use your card for cash advances, look for information about the following items:

- **Access:** Most credit cards let you use an ATM to get a cash advance. Or the credit card company may send you "checks" that you can write to get the cash advance.

- **APR:** The APR for cash advances may be higher than the APR for purchases.

---

example, if you have no previous balance, but you fail to pay the entire balance of new purchases by the payment due date, the issuer will compute the interest on the original balance that previously had been subject to an interest-free period. Read your agreement to find out if your issuer uses this approach and, if so, what specific two-cycle method is used.

How do these methods of calculating finance charges affect the cost of credit? Suppose your monthly interest rate is 1.5 percent, your APR is 18 percent, and your previous balance is $400. On the 15th day of your billing cycle, the card issuer receives and posts your payment of $300. On the 18th day, you make a $50 purchase:

- Using the average daily balance method (including new purchases), your finance charge would be $4.05.

- Using the average daily balance method (excluding new purchases), your finance charge would be $3.75.

- Using the average daily balance double cycle method (including new purchase and the previous month's balance), your finance charge would be $6.53.

- Using the adjusted balance method, your finance charge would be $1.50.

If you don't understand how your balance is calculated, ask your card issuer. An explanation also must appear on your billing statements.

Source: Excerpted from "Choosing a Credit Card: The Deal Is in the Disclosures," Federal Trade Commission, June 2008.

- **Fees:** The credit card company may charge a fee in addition to the interest you will pay on the amount advanced.

- **Limits:** Some credit cards limit cash advances to a dollar amount (for example, $200 per cash advance or $500 per week) or a portion of your credit limit (for example, 75% of your available credit limit).

- **How Payments Are Credited:** Many credit card companies apply your payments to purchases first and then to cash advances. Read your credit card agreement to learn how your payments will be credited.

How much is the credit limit?

The credit limit is the maximum total amount—for purchases, cash advances, balance transfers, fees, and finance charges—you may charge on your credit card. If you go over this limit, you may have to pay an "over-the-credit-limit fee."

What kind of card is it?

Most credit card companies offer several kinds of cards:

- Secured cards, which require a security deposit. The larger the security deposit, the higher the credit limit. Secured cards are usually offered to people who have limited credit records—people who are just starting out or who have had trouble with credit in the past.

- Regular cards, which do not require a security deposit and have just a few features. Most regular cards have higher credit limits than secured cards but lower credit limits than premium cards.

- Premium cards (gold, platinum, titanium), which offer higher credit limits and usually have extra features—for example, product warranties, travel insurance, or emergency services.

Does the card offer incentives and other features?

Many credit card companies offer incentives to use the card and other special features:

- Rebates (money back) on the purchases you make

- Frequent flier miles or phone-call minutes

- Additional warranty coverage for the items you purchase

- Car rental insurance

- Travel accident insurance or travel-related discounts

- Credit card registration, to help if your wallet or purse is lost or stolen and you need to report that all your credit cards are missing

Credit cards may also offer, for a price, services such as the following:

- Insurance to cover the payments on your credit card balance if you become unemployed or disabled, or die. Premiums are usually due monthly, making it easy to cancel if the payments are higher than you want to pay or you decide you don't need the insurance any longer.

- Insurance to cover the first $50 of charges if your card is lost or stolen. Under federal law, you are not responsible for charges over $50.

Before you sign up to pay for any of these features, think carefully about whether it will be useful for you. Don't pay for something you don't want or don't need.

How do I find information about credit cards?

You can find lists of credit card plans, rates, and terms on the internet, in personal finance magazines, and in newspapers. The Federal Reserve System surveys credit card companies every six months. You'll need to get the most recent information directly from the credit card company—by phoning the company, looking on the company's website, or reading a solicitation or application.

Under federal law, all solicitations and applications for credit cards must include certain key information, in a disclosure box similar to the one shown in Figure 29.1 (on page 292).

- **APR For Purchases:** The annual percentage rate you'll be charged if you carry over a balance from month to month. If the card has an introductory rate, you'll see both that rate and the rate that will apply after the introductory rate expires.

Annual percentage rate (APR) for purchases	2.9% until 11/1/09 after that, **14.9%**
Other APRs	Cash-advance APR: 15.9% Balance-transfer APR: 15.9% Penalty rate: 23.9% See explanation below. *
Variable-rate information	Your APR for purchase transactions may vary. The rate is determined monthly by adding 5.9% to the Prime Rate **
Grace period for repayment of balances for purchases	25 days on average
Method of computing the balance for purchases	Average daily balance (excluding new purchases)
Annual fees	None
Minimum finance charge	$.50
Transaction fee for cash advances: 3% of the amount advanced Balance-transfer fee: 3% of the amount transferred Late-payment fee: $25 Over-the-credit-limit fee: $25	
* Explanation of penalty. If your payment arrives more than ten days late two times within a six-month period, the penalty rate will apply. ** The Prime Rate used to determine your APR is the rate published in the *Wall Street Journal* on the 10th day of the prior month.	

Figure 29.1. Credit Card Disclosure Box.

- **Other APRs:** The APRs you'll be charged if you get a cash advance on your card, transfer a balance from another card, or are late in making a payment. More information about the penalty rate may be stated outside the disclosure box—for instance, in a footnote. In the example shown in Figure 29.1, if you make two payments that are more than ten days late within six months, the APR will increase to 23.9%.

- **Variable-Rate Information:** Information about how the variable rate will be determined (if relevant). More information may be stated outside the disclosure box—for instance, in a footnote.

- **Grace Period For Repayment Of Balances For Purchases:** The number of days you'll have to pay your bill for purchases in full without triggering a finance charge.

- **Method Of Computing The Balance For Purchases:** The method that will be used to calculate your outstanding balance if you carry over a balance and will pay a finance charge.

- **Annual Fees:** The amount you'll be charged each twelve-month period for simply having the card.

♣ It's A Fact!!
What if the item you purchase is damaged?

The federal Fair Credit Billing Act allows you to withhold payment on any damaged or poor-quality goods or services purchased with a credit card—even if you have accepted the goods or services—as long as you have made an attempt to solve the problem with the merchant.

The sale must have been for more than $50 and must have taken place in your home state or within 100 miles of your home address. You should notify the credit card company in writing and explain why you are withholding your payment.

You may withhold the payment while the credit card company investigates your claim. If you pay the charges for the goods on your credit card bill before the dispute is resolved, you will lose your right to make a claim.

Source: Federal Reserve Board, October 19, 2004.

- **Minimum Finance Charge:** The minimum, or fixed, finance charge that will be imposed during a billing cycle. A minimum finance charge usually applies only when a finance charge is imposed, that is, when you carry over a balance.

- **Transaction Fee For Cash Advances:** The charge that will be imposed each time you use the card for a cash advance.

- **Balance-Transfer Fee:** The fee that will be imposed each time you transfer a balance from another card.

- **Late-Payment Fee:** The fee that will be imposed when your payment is late.

- **Over-The-Credit-Limit Fee:** The fee that will be imposed if your charges exceed the credit limit set for your card.

What are your liability limits?

If your credit card is lost or stolen—and then is used by someone without your permission—you do not have to pay more than $50 of those charges. This protection is provided by the federal Truth in Lending Act. You do not need to buy "credit card insurance" to cover amounts over $50.

If you discover that your card is lost or stolen, report it immediately to your credit card company. Call the toll-free number listed on your monthly statement. The company will cancel the card so that new purchases cannot be made with it. The company will also send you a new card.

Make a list of your account numbers and the companies' phone numbers. Keep the list in a safe place. If your wallet or purse is lost or stolen, you'll have all the numbers in one place. Take the list of phone numbers—not the account numbers—with you when you travel, just in case a card is lost or stolen.

What can you do about billing errors?

The federal Fair Credit Billing Act covers billing errors. Examples of billing errors include the following:

- A charge for something you didn't buy
- A bill for an amount different from the actual amount you charged
- A charge for something that you did not accept when it was delivered
- A charge for something that was not delivered according to agreement
- Math errors
- Payments not credited to your account
- A charge by someone who does not have permission to use your credit card

If you think your credit card bill has an error, take the following steps:

- Write to the credit card company within 60 days after the statement date on the bill with the error. Use the address for "billing inquiries" listed on the bill. Tell the company your name and account number, that you believe the bill contains an error, and why you believe it's wrong, and the date and amount of the error (the "disputed amount").

- Pay all the other parts of the bill. You do not have to pay the "disputed amount" or any minimum payments or finance charges that apply to it.

If there is an error, you will not have to pay any finance charges on the disputed amount. Your account must be corrected.

If there is no error, the credit card company must send you an explanation and a statement of the amount you owe. The amount will include any finance charges or other charges that accumulated while you were questioning the bill.

Chapter 30

Other Plastic: Debit Cards, Prepaid Cards, Gift Cards, And More

Credit Vs. Debit Cards

Credit cards are a convenient form of borrowing. People generally use credit cards to purchase goods and services.

Credit cards provide a revolving line of credit. This means you can make an unlimited number of purchases, up to a pre-approved dollar limit. The limit might be $500, $1,000, $3,000, or much more.

You must pay at least a part of the bill every month. This is called a minimum payment. It is often a certain percentage of your balance.

Charge cards are used like credit cards, but you must pay the entire balance every month.

Debit cards are similar to credit cards except that they are tied to your checking account at a bank. When you use them to make a purchase or to take out money at an automated teller machine (ATM), the money is immediately taken out of your checking account. You need to be sure you have money in your checking account before you use a debit card.

About This Chapter: Excerpted from "Module 6: Charge It Right," *Money Smart for Young Adults*, a CD-based curriculum developed by the Federal Deposit Insurance Corporation (FDIC), March 2008.

Credit Cards

Payments: Buy now, pay later.

Interest Charges: Yes, if you carry a balance or your card offers no "grace period" (time to repay without incurring interest).

Other Potential Benefits: Freebies, such as cash rebates and bonus points good for travel deals. Some purchase protections.

Other Potential Concerns Fees And Penalties: Also not all cards offer grace periods. Overspending can cause debt problems.

Liability In The Event Of Unauthorized Transactions: Liability for unauthorized transactions capped at $50. The credit card company may voluntarily waive your liability.

Debit Cards

Payments: Buy now, pay now.

Interest Charges: No.

Other Potential Benefits: Easier and faster than writing a check. Avoid debt problems. More cards are now offering freebies. Some purchase protections.

Other Potential Concerns: Fees on certain transactions. You may overdraw your account if you don't record your debit card transactions.

Liability In The Event Of Unauthorized Transactions: Unauthorized transactions are immediately taken out of your checking account. Your liability is capped at $50 if you notify the bank within two business days after discovering the theft. Otherwise, you may be responsible for a larger amount.

Stored Value Cards

To use a stored value card, you deposit money upfront and the balance declines as you use the card. It works like a debit card, but it's not connected to your checking account. It has a limit like a credit card does. But since you deposit money ahead of time, you don't pay it back later. You can refresh the value of the card by depositing money into your stored value card account.

The following are examples of stored value cards:

- Telephone cards with prepaid minutes

- International gift cards that can be used anywhere the VISA, MasterCard, or American Express logo is displayed

- Payroll cards. These are cards that enable your employer to deposit your paycheck on the card, rather than issue you a paper check.

- Gift cards that you can purchase at retailers such as supermarkets, restaurants, department stores, etc.

- Cash cards

There are two major types of stored value cards: those that can only be used at one particular store or retailer (gift cards), and those that can be used at any merchant that accepts credit cards.

Depending on the type of card, stored value cards can have the following benefits:

- Reduce or eliminate check-cashing fees

- Offer 24-hour access to funds

- Make money transfers easy

- Offer the ability to make purchases using credit card networks

- Reduce the need to carry a lot of cash

One potential disadvantage of a stored value card is that your name may not be printed on the card and a refund may not be available if your card is lost or stolen. Ask if you can register your card with its issuer. Be sure to ask about any fees associated with a stored value card, such as monthly fees or inactivity fees. These lower the balance on your card.

Smart Cards

A smart card resembles a credit card in size and shape, but inside it is different. The inside of a smart card usually contains a microprocessor or computer chip. The chip is under a gold contact pad on one side of the card.

♣ It's A Fact!!
Gift Cards Are Great But
Beware Of Risks And Costs

You probably love getting gift cards for your birthday or other occasions so you can pick out exactly what you want at the store. Gift cards also are easy to buy and give to friends and relatives because they're widely available at stores and even at banks. But while gift cards may seem to be the perfect gift, they also can come with potential risks and costs. Whether you're giving or receiving a gift card, remember this:

Watch out for fees: You may be charged a fee for purchasing a gift card. You also may have fees deducted each time you use the card at a store or restaurant. Or, you may be charged fees for not using the card, perhaps $1 or more each month after going a year or so without making a purchase. "When a fee is deducted, that's less money for you to spend," says Janet Kincaid, Federal Deposit Insurance Commission (FDIC) Senior Consumer Affairs Officer.

Find out if there is an expiration date: "Gift cards aren't exactly like cash—they usually can't be used indefinitely," advises Kincaid. "You don't want to put gift cards away and forget about them because, if you let them expire, you could lose the entire balance on the card."

Immediately report a lost or stolen gift card to the card issuer: Some companies will replace a lost card (for a fee), others may not.

If you have a problem with a gift card that you can't solve by talking to a store employee, consider contacting your state government's consumer protection office, which will be listed in your local phone book or other directories.

Source: "Gift Cards Are Great But Beware of Risks and Costs," *FDIC Consumer News*, Federal Deposit Insurance Corporation, Summer 2006.

Think of the computer chip as replacing the usual magnetic strip on a credit card or debit card. It is used in some credit and cash cards, but also for security systems, wireless communication, and other technologies.

Some credit card companies are beginning to issue credit cards that are also smart cards. These may allow you to simply touch your card to a reader to make a payment, instead of having to swipe your card as in the past.

The most common smart card applications are include the following:

- Credit cards
- Electronic cash
- Computer security systems
- Wireless communication
- Banking
- Satellite TV
- Government identification
- Loyalty systems (like frequent flyer points)

Chapter 31

Installment Loans

What Is An Installment Loan?

An installment loan is a loan that is repaid in equal monthly payments or installments for a specific period of time, usually several years.

Types Of Loans

There are two types of installment loans:

• Secured loans

• Unsecured loans

Secured

A secured installment loan is one where the borrower offers collateral for the loan. The borrower gives up the collateral to the lender if the loan is not paid back as agreed.

Unsecured Installment Loans

Unsecured installment loans can be used for a variety of personal expenses such as education or medical expenses. Unsecured loans are sometimes called

About This Chapter: Excerpted from "Module 7: Paying for College and Cars," *Money Smart for Young Adults*, a CD-based curriculum developed by the Federal Deposit Insurance Corporation (FDIC), March 2008.

personal or signature loans. An unsecured loan is a loan that is not secured by collateral.

> **✎ What's It Mean?**
>
> Collateral: Collateral is security you provide a lender. Giving the lender collateral means that you promise an asset you own, such as your car, to the lender in case you cannot repay the loan. Generally, if the collateral is not enough to repay your loan, you are still responsible for the remaining balance and any fees and interest associated with the loan.

- There is no collateral requirement for an unsecured loan. The terms of the loan might range from one to five years.

- Since credit cards have become popular, the use of unsecured consumer installment loans has declined. However, some financial institutions still offer unsecured installment loans.

Benefits Of Unsecured Loans: Some benefits of unsecured installment loans include fast approval time and interest rates might be lower than credit card rates.

Loan Approval

The Four Cs Of Loan Decision Making

Lenders generally review the Four Cs to decide whether to make a loan to you. The Four Cs are capacity, capital, character, and collateral.

- Capacity refers to your present and future ability to meet your payment obligations. This includes whether you have enough income to pay your bills and other debts.

- Capital refers to the value of your assets and your net worth.

- Character refers to how you have paid bills or debts in the past. Your credit report is one tool lenders use to consider your willingness to repay your debts.

- Collateral refers to property or assets offered to secure the loan.

Tips About Unsecured Installment Loans

- You may find it beneficial to consolidate your loans. If you plan to use an unsecured installment loan to consolidate your other loans, make sure the new annual percentage rate (APR) is lower than your current APR.

- As with any other loan, you could become overwhelmed and unable to make the payments if you take on too much debt. If you have trouble paying your bills, you might consider getting credit counseling.

- Beware of debt consolidation traps. These are loans that you get in order to help pay off what you owe on several credit cards. They can be either secured loans, such as home equity loans, or unsecured loans.

- Beware of companies and websites that charge high rates and application fees. Look for hidden charges. Ask for references before signing an agreement.

- Choosing the wrong debt consolidation loan can make matters worse and put you further into debt. Shop around so that you have the information to decide on the debt consolidation loan that best meets your needs and budget. Research different lenders and collect quotes before deciding.

- Good credit counseling agencies can help you budget and negotiate with your lenders to make loan payments more manageable.

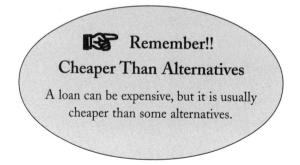

☞ Remember!!
Cheaper Than Alternatives
A loan can be expensive, but it is usually cheaper than some alternatives.

Chapter 32

Car Loans

Car Loans Vs. Car Leases

There are several factors that you need to consider when deciding between getting a car loan or a car lease. These include the following:

• Ownership potential

• Wear and tear

• Monthly payments

• Mileage limitations

• Auto insurance

• Cost

The minimum requirements for obtaining a car loan or lease vary. In general, you and/or the co-qualifier must be at least 18 years of age. The lender will ensure you have sufficient income to pay the loan, and will pull your credit report based on your Social Security number. The lender will also need to know how long you have held your present and past jobs, as well as how long you have been at your current and possibly past residences.

About This Chapter: Excerpted from "Module 7: Paying for College and Cars," *Money Smart for Young Adults*, a CD-based curriculum developed by the Federal Deposit Insurance Corporation (FDIC), March 2008.

Financing A Car

Getting a car loan is also referred to as financing a car. A car loan can be used to purchase a new or used car. Your car becomes your collateral for the loan, which means the lender will hold the car title until the loan is paid off. The title indicates who owns the car.

If you do not pay off the loan, the bank can take back the car and then sell it to get the remaining loan amount back. New car loans typically are for three to seven years and used car loans two to five years.

♣ **It's A Fact!!**
Where To Get Information

There are many decisions you must make before purchasing or leasing a car. You should know some points to consider when looking for a car.

The Federal Trade Commission (FTC) has many publications that can help you answer these questions so you can get a car at the best price. At the FTC website, http://www.ftc.gov, you can download many helpful brochures and articles.

A car loan might be one of the biggest expenses you have. Therefore, if you decide to purchase a car, you should know exactly how much you are paying for the car and exactly how much you need to borrow.

When shopping for a car, don't negotiate or make a decision based just on the monthly payment, even if the car dealer suggests that you do. The total amount you will pay depends on the price of the car you negotiate, the APR, and the length of the loan.

You decide to buy a used car and have saved $2,500 from your summer job for a down payment. You find a car you like and the monthly payment is

$225 for 60 months with your $2,500 down payment. The tax and registration fee is $575 and the APR is 12.10 percent. With this information you figure the total cost of the car as follows:

> $225 Monthly payment x 60 Number of payments = $13,500 Total of payments

> $13,500 Total of payments + $2,500 Down payment + $575 Tax and registration fee = $16,575 Total cost of car

Now, we can figure out how much the loan actually costs by comparing $16,575 to the cost of the car if you were to pay cash. If you pay cash for the car and do not take out a loan, the car dealer tells you he will give you a deal so that the car costs $12,595 plus tax and registration:

> $12,595 + $575 = $13,170

Now that you know the cost of the car if you paid cash and the cost of a 60-month loan, you can figure out the difference which would be the cost of your loan.

> $16,575 − $13,170 = $3,405 (the interest for the loan)

Financing Through Banks And Credit Unions

The financial institution where you already have an account is a good place to start when you need to finance a car. But, still be sure to shop around to make sure you are getting the best deal.

Most lenders can even pre-approve you for a car loan before you go car shopping. This means the financial institution calculates how much money you can borrow to buy your car. This is typically a free service and does not require you to accept a loan offer from the institution.

Financing Through The Car Dealer

Car dealers may also offer to finance your car loan. Dealers sometimes even offer low loan rates for specific cars. To get the lowest advertised rate, you might have to:

- make a large down payment;

- agree to a short loan term, usually three years or less;

- have an excellent credit history; or

- pay additional fees or purchase additional products that are not necessarily reflected in the APR.

Remember that a dealer offering a low interest rate is likely to be less willing to negotiate on the price of the car. Therefore, you may find that it's more affordable to negotiate a lower price on the car and finance through your own financial institution than it is to accept the dealer's offer of a low-interest rate loan.

> **♣ It's A Fact!!**
> **Where To Obtain A Car Loan**
>
> You can obtain a car loan from any of the following:
>
> - Banks
> - Credit unions
> - Thrifts
> - Finance companies
> - Car dealerships

CAUTION: Car Title Loans

Title loans are short-term (usually one month) loans that allow you to use your car as collateral to borrow money. They may sound like a good way to get quick cash, but they can be very costly.

Chapter 33

Education Loans

College is a large expense that will need a lot of planning and research. Some of you may not be attending college; you may be going on to vocational or trade school or be entering the workforce.

Calculate College Costs

When deciding on how to pay for college, tuition is not the only thing you will need to consider. There are many other costs such as books, fees, and housing that add up to a significant amount of money.

The cost of the college should be considered along with the academic programs of a school. College comparison shopping should include options such as two-year community colleges and schools close to home, which can help save on room and board.

Financial Aid Overview

The Free Application for Federal Student Aid (FAFSA) is the first step in the financial aid process. Use it to apply for federal student financial aid, such as the Pell grant, student loans, and college work-study. Most states and schools use FAFSA information to award their financial aid.

About This Chapter: Excerpted from "Module 7: Paying for College and Cars," *Money Smart for Young Adults*, a CD-based curriculum developed by the Federal Deposit Insurance Corporation (FDIC), March 2008.

How Is The FAFSA Used?

Your FAFSA responses are entered into a formula known as the Federal Methodology, which is required by the Higher Education Act of 1965. The result is your Expected Family Contribution, or EFC. The EFC is a number that measures your family's financial strength. It is subtracted from the cost of attendance at the school(s) you plan to attend which determines your eligibility for federal student aid.

Scholarships And Grants

A scholarship is money for college that you will not be expected to repay. Scholarships are definitely worth seeking!

Scholarships sponsored by colleges are often designated for students who fit a particular profile. For example, students who are from the college's home state, hold a specified grade point average, enroll in a particular major, or bring special talent, such as in athletics or in music. Other outside scholarships may be available to students whose parents work for a particular company or to

---

✔ Quick Tip
Tips To Getting Aid

Financial aid administrators and guidance counselors agree that the following tips speed up the application process:

Read The Instructions: Common words like "household," "investments," and even "parent" may have special meaning so make sure to read all instructions carefully. Many questions are asked specifically for purposes of student financial aid.

Apply Early: State and school deadlines will vary and tend to be early. Check to find out exact deadline dates. Your FAFSA will only be processed if it is received on or before the deadline.

Complete Your Tax Return: It is recommended that you and your parents (if you are a dependent student) complete your tax return before filling out your FAFSA. This will make completing the FAFSA easier because tax information is required.

File Electronically: Completing and submitting your FAFSA online is the fastest and most accurate way to apply for student aid.

Additional Forms: Many schools and states rely on the FAFSA as the single application for student aid. However, your school or state may require additional forms. Check with your state agency and the financial aid office at the school you plan to attend to find out if they require additional forms.

students who are eligible for scholarships sponsored by religious or civic organizations. You will need to check with each college to see what scholarships are available.

At the same time, though, be very wary of companies that guarantee or promise you scholarships, grants, or fantastic financial aid packages in exchange for a fee. Many of these are scams and you will simply lose your money and risk giving your personal information to a potentially unscrupulous business or individual.

Federal Loan Programs

You must complete the FAFSA before finding out what loan programs for which you are eligible. If you think you need a loan, do your homework and ask lots of questions before settling on one. Among the many options are federal government loan programs, including PLUS loans for parents and Perkins and Stafford loans for students.

There are also private loans. There are often big differences between private loans and federal student loans. A private lender likely will offer both types of loans, so be sure to ask questions to fully understand the pros and cons of any loan product.

Your state's department of education and the college's financial aid department are good resources when deciding on which type of loan is best for you. Don't completely depend on your school to pick the right loan or lender, though. Some colleges and private lenders have been scrutinized for conflicts of interest in steering students toward "preferred lenders." So, be sure to always do your own research and ask questions.

Repay Your Loan

After you graduate, leave school, or drop below half-time enrollment, you have a period of time before you must begin repayment. While you need to look carefully at correspondence from your lender for the exact repayment start date, the "grace period" will generally be six months for a Federal (FFEL) or Direct Stafford Loan and nine months for Federal Perkins Loans.

Exit Counseling

You'll receive information about repayment. Your loan provider will notify you when you have to start making loan payments. It is very important to make your full loan payment according to your repayment schedule. If you don't, you could end up in default, which has serious consequences. Student loans are real loans—just as real as car loans or mortgages. You have to pay back your student loans.

Depending on the type of loan you have, some graduates who get jobs in certain fields may even be eligible for special perks such as forgiveness of part of their student loan balance.

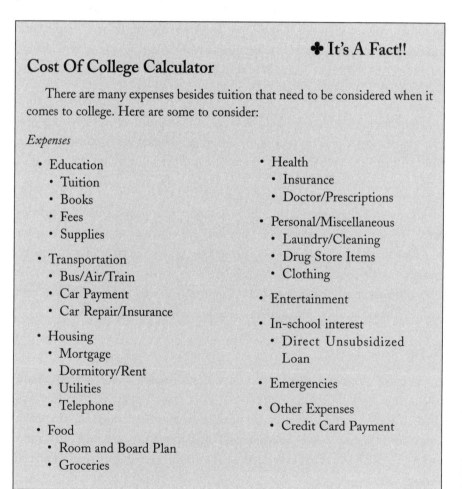

♣ It's A Fact!!

Cost Of College Calculator

There are many expenses besides tuition that need to be considered when it comes to college. Here are some to consider:

Expenses

- Education
  - Tuition
  - Books
  - Fees
  - Supplies

- Transportation
  - Bus/Air/Train
  - Car Payment
  - Car Repair/Insurance

- Housing
  - Mortgage
  - Dormitory/Rent
  - Utilities
  - Telephone

- Food
  - Room and Board Plan
  - Groceries

- Health
  - Insurance
  - Doctor/Prescriptions

- Personal/Miscellaneous
  - Laundry/Cleaning
  - Drug Store Items
  - Clothing

- Entertainment

- In-school interest
  - Direct Unsubsidized Loan

- Emergencies

- Other Expenses
  - Credit Card Payment

You can also explore options to manage your student loan payments after graduation, such as loan consolidation. But be sure to fully research the pros and cons of consolidation before signing any paperwork. Student loan consolidation can be used to reduce your monthly student loan payment or simplify your finances by making one payment per month.

Federal Pell Grant

A Federal Pell Grant, unlike a loan, does not have to be repaid. Pell Grants are awarded usually only to undergraduate students who have not earned a bachelor's or a professional degree. Pell Grants are considered a foundation of federal financial aid, to which aid from other federal and nonfederal sources might be added.

How much can I get?

The maximum Pell Grant award for the 2008–09 award year (July 1, 2008 to June 30, 2009) is $4,731. The maximum can change each award year and depends on program funding. The amount you get depends not only on your financial need, but also on your costs to attend school, your status as a full-time or part-time student, and your plans to attend school for a full academic year or less.

If I am eligible, how will I get the Pell Grant money?

Your school can apply Pell Grant funds to your school costs, pay you directly (usually by check), or combine these methods. The school must tell you in writing how much your award will be and how and when you'll be paid. Schools must disburse funds at least once per term (semester, trimester, or quarter). Schools that do not use semesters, trimesters, or quarters must disburse funds at least twice per academic year.

Federal Supplemental Educational Opportunity Grant (FSEOG)

The Federal Supplemental Educational Opportunity Grant (FSEOG) program is for undergraduates with exceptional financial need. Pell Grant recipients with the lowest expected family contributions (EFCs) will be considered first for a FSEOG. Just like Pell Grants, the FSEOG does not have to be repaid.

How much can I get?

You can receive between $100 and $4,000 a year, depending on when you apply, your financial need, the funding at the school you're attending, and the policies of the financial aid office at your school.

If I am eligible, how will I get the FSEOG money?

If you're eligible, your school will credit your account, pay you directly (usually by check), or combine these methods. Your school must pay you at least once per term (semester, trimester, or quarter). Schools that do not use semesters, trimesters, or quarters must disburse funds at least twice per academic year.

Academic Competitiveness Grant

The Academic Competitiveness Grant was made available for the first time for the 2006–2007 school year for first year college students who graduated from high school after January 1, 2006, and for second year college students who graduated from high school after January 1, 2005. The Academic Competitiveness Grant award is in addition to the student's Pell Grant award.

How much can a student receive?

An Academic Competitiveness Grant will provide up to $750 for the first year of undergraduate study and up to $1,300 for the second year of undergraduate study to full-time students who are eligible for a Federal Pell Grant and who had successfully completed a rigorous high school program, as determined by the state or local education agency and recognized by the Secretary of Education. Second year students must maintain a cumulative grade point average (GPA) of at least 3.0.

The National Science And Mathematics Access To Retain Talent Grant (National Smart Grant)

The National Science and Mathematics Access to Retain Talent Grant, also known as the National SMART Grant is available during the third and fourth years of undergraduate study to full-time students who are eligible for the Federal Pell Grant and who are majoring in physical, life, or computer sciences, mathematics, technology, or engineering, or in a foreign language determined critical to national security. The student must also have maintained a cumulative grade point average (GPA) of at least 3.0 in coursework required for the major. The National SMART Grant award is in addition to the student's Pell Grant award.

How much can a student receive?

A National SMART Grant will provide up to $4,000 for each of the third and fourth years of undergraduate study to full-time students who are eligible for a Federal Pell Grant and who are majoring in physical, life, or computer sciences, mathematics, technology, or engineering or in a foreign language determined critical to national security.

Institutional Grants

Colleges provide institutional grants to help make up the difference between college costs and what a family can be expected to contribute through income, savings, loans, and student earnings. Other institutional grants, known as merit awards or merit scholarships, are awarded on the basis of academic achievement. Some merit awards are offered only to students whose families demonstrate financial need; others are awarded without regard to a family's finances. Some grants come with special privileges or obligations. You'll want to find out about the types of grants awarded by each college you are considering.

Federal Work-Study (FWS)

Federal Work-Study (FWS) provides part-time jobs for undergraduate and graduate students with financial need, allowing them to earn money to help pay education expenses. The program encourages community service work and work related to the recipient's course of study.

Will I be paid the same as I would in any other job?

You'll be paid by the hour if you're an undergraduate. No FWS student may be paid by commission or fee. Your school must pay you directly (unless you direct otherwise) and at least monthly. Wages for the program must equal at least the current federal minimum wage but might be higher, depending on the type of work you do and the skills required. The amount you earn can't exceed your total FWS award. When assigning work hours, your employer or financial aid administrator will consider your award amount, your class schedule, and your academic progress.

What kinds of jobs are there in Federal Work-Study?

If you work on campus, you'll usually work for your school. If you work off campus, your employer will usually be a private nonprofit organization or a public agency, and the work performed must be in the public interest. Your school might have agreements with private for-profit employers for Federal Work-Study jobs. This type of job must be relevant to your course of study (to the maximum extent possible). If you attend a career school, there might be further restrictions on the jobs you can be assigned.

Federal Perkins Loans

A Federal Perkins Loan is a low-interest (five percent) loan for both undergraduate and graduate students with exceptional financial need. Federal Perkins Loans are made through a school's financial aid office. Your school is your lender, and the loan is made with government funds. You must repay this loan to your school. Your school will either pay you directly (usually by check) or apply your loan to your school charges. You'll receive the loan in at least two payments during the academic year.

How much can I borrow?

You can borrow up to $4,000 for each year of undergraduate study (the total you can borrow as an undergraduate is $20,000). The amount you receive depends on when you apply, your financial need, and the funding level at the school.

Other than interest, is there a charge for this loan?

No, there are no other charges. However, if you skip a payment, if it's late, or if you make less than a full payment, you might have to pay a late charge plus any collection costs.

When do I pay it back?

If you're attending school at least half time, you have nine months after you graduate, leave school, or drop below half-time status before you must begin repayment. This is called a "grace period." If you're attending less than half time, check with your college or career school to find out how long your grace period will be.

Stafford Loans (FFELS And Direct Loans)

In addition to Perkins Loans, the U.S. Department of Education administers the Federal Family Education Loan (FFEL) Program and the William D. Ford Federal Direct Loan (Direct Loan) Program. Both the FFEL and Direct Loan programs consist of what are generally known as Stafford Loans (for students) and PLUS Loans (for parents).

Schools generally participate in either the FFEL or Direct Loan program but sometimes participate in both. Under the Direct Loan Program, the funds for your loan come directly from the federal government. Funds for your FFEL will come from a bank, credit union, or other lender that participates in the program. Eligibility rules and loan amounts are identical under both programs, but repayment plans differ somewhat.

How can I get a FFEL or Direct Loan?

For either type of loan, you must fill out a FAFSA. After your FAFSA is processed, your school will review the results and will inform you about your loan eligibility. You also will have to sign a promissory note, a binding legal document that lists the conditions under which you're borrowing and the terms under which you agree to repay your loan.

Plus Loans (Parent Loans)

Parents can borrow a PLUS Loan to help pay your education expenses if you are a dependent undergraduate student enrolled at least half time in an eligible program at an eligible school. PLUS Loans are available through the Federal Family Education Loan (FFEL) Program and the William D. Ford Federal Direct Loan (Direct Loan) Program. Your parents can get either loan, but not both, for you during the same enrollment period. They also must have an acceptable credit history.

Part Five

Avoiding Financial Pitfalls

Chapter 34

Avoid Out-Of-Control Debt

Take Control Of Debt

Here's the definition of net worth (wealth):

$$\text{Assets} - \text{Liabilities} = \text{Net Worth}$$

Liabilities are your debts. Debt reduces net worth. Plus, the interest you pay on debt, including credit card debt, is money that cannot be saved or invested—it's just gone. Debt is a tool to be used wisely for such things as buying a house. If not used wisely, debt can easily get out of hand. For example, putting day-to-day expenses—like groceries or utility bills—on a credit card and not paying off the balance monthly can lead to debt overload.

Why People Get Into Trouble With Debt

Lots of people are mired in debt. In some cases, they could not control the causes of their debt. However, in some instances they could have.

Many people get into serious debt because they:

• Experienced financial stresses caused by unemployment, medical bills, or divorce.

About This Chapter: From "Building Wealth: A Beginner's Guide to Securing Your Financial Future," reprinted with permission from the Federal Reserve Bank of Dallas, www.dallasfed.org. © 2007.

- Could not control spending, did not plan for the future, and did not save money.

- Lacked knowledge of financial and credit matters.

Speaking Of Interest

When you take out a loan, you repay the principal, which is the amount borrowed, plus interest, the amount charged for lending you the money. The interest on your monthly balance is a good example of compound interest that you pay. The interest is added to your bill, and the next month interest is charged on that amount and on the outstanding balance. The bottom line on interest is that those who know about interest earn it; those who don't, pay it.

Avoid Credit Card Debt

> **✔ Quick Tip**
> **Tips For Controlling Debt**
>
> - Develop a budget and stick to it.
>
> - Save money so you're prepared for unforeseen circumstances.
>
> - You should have at least three to six months of living expenses stashed in your rainy day savings account, because as the poet Longfellow put it, "Into each life some rain must fall."
>
> - When faced with a choice of financing a purchase, it may be a better financial decision to choose a less expensive model of the same product and save or invest the difference.
>
> - Pay off credit card balances monthly.
>
> - If you must borrow, learn everything about the loan, including interest rate, fees and penalties for late payments or early repayment.
>
> Source: © 2007 Federal Reserve Bank of Dallas.

People who plan ahead rarely use credit cards. When they do, they pay off their balances every month. When a credit card balance is not paid off monthly, it means paying interest—often 20 percent or more a year—on everything purchased. So think of credit card debt as a high-interest loan.

Do you need to reduce your credit card debt? Here are some suggestions.

- Pay cash.

- Set a monthly limit on charging, and keep a written record so you don't exceed that amount.

- Limit the number of credit cards you have. Cut up all but one of your cards. Stash that one out of sight, and use it only in emergencies.

- Choose the card with the lowest interest rate and no (or very low) annual fee. But beware of low introductory interest rates offered by mail. These rates often skyrocket after the first few months.

- Don't apply for credit cards to get a free gift or a discount on a purchase.

- Steer clear of blank checks that financial services companies send you. These checks are cash advances that may carry a higher interest rate than typical charges.

- Pay bills on time to avoid late charges or increased interest rates.

Beware The Perils Of Payday Loans And Predatory Lenders

People can get deep in debt when they take out a loan against their paycheck. They write a postdated check in exchange for money. When they get paid again, they repay the loan, thus the name payday loan. These loans generally come with very high, double-digit interest rates. Borrowers who can't repay the money are charged additional fees for an extension, which puts them even deeper in debt. Borrowers can continue to pay fees to extend the loan's due date indefinitely, only to find they are getting deeper in debt because of the steep interest payments and fees.

Predatory lenders often target seniors and low-income people they contact by phone, mail or in person. After her husband died, 73-year-old Pauline got plenty of solicitations from finance companies. She was struggling to make ends meet on her fixed income. To pay off her bills, she took out a $5,000 home equity loan that carried a high interest rate and excessive fees. Soon she found she was even deeper in debt, so she refinanced the loan once, then again, and again, paying fees each time.

Pauline's children discovered her situation and paid off the loan. The lessons here are:

- Don't borrow from Peter to pay Paul.

- Never respond to a solicitation that makes borrowing sound easy and cheap.

- Always read the fine print on any loan application.

- Seek assistance from family members, local credit counseling services or others to make sure a loan is right for you.

Know What Creditors Say About You

Those who have used credit will have a credit report that shows everything about their payment history, including late payments.

✎ What's It Mean?
Legal Terms For Types Of Debt Actions

Bankruptcy: A legal declaration of insolvency. Bankruptcy will not fix credit record problems and will be part of your credit history for 10 years. You cannot necessarily walk away from your debts even with bankruptcy, as the law requires you to pay a portion of your unsecured debt if you are able to.

Foreclosure: A legal proceeding initiated by a creditor to take possession of collateral, for example a home that secured a defaulted loan.

Garnishment: A process by which a lender obtains directly from a third party, such as an employer, part of an employee's salary to satisfy an unpaid debt. Part of the employee's salary is taken each pay period until the debt is fully paid. This process must be authorized by a court order.

Judgment: A court order requiring a debtor to pay money to the creditor. The judgment places a security lien on the debtor's property until the judgment is satisfied (the debt is repaid).

Lien: A creditor's claim against property to secure repayment of a debt.

Repossession: Seizure of collateral that secured a loan in default.

Source: Excerpted from "Module 5: Borrowing Basics," *Money Smart for Young Adults*, a CD-based curriculum developed by the Federal Deposit Insurance Corporation (FDIC), March 2008.

The information in your credit report is used to create your credit score. A credit score is a number generated by a statistical model that objectively predicts the likelihood that you will repay on time. Banks, insurance companies, potential landlords and other lenders use credit scores.

Credit scores range from under 500 to 800 and above and are determined by payment history, the amount of outstanding debt, length of your credit history, recent inquiries on your credit report and the types of credit in use. Factors not considered in a credit score include age, race or ethnicity, income, job, marital status, education, length of time at your current address, and whether you own or rent your home.

A credit report that includes late payments, delinquencies or defaults will result in a low credit score and could mean not getting a loan or having to pay a much higher interest rate. The higher your score, the less risk you represent to the lender.

Review your credit report at least once a year to make sure all information is accurate. If you find an error, the Fair Credit Reporting Act requires credit reporting companies and those reporting information to them to correct the mistake. To start the process of fixing an error:

- Contact the credit reporting company online, by fax, or certified letter, identifying the creditor you have a dispute with and the nature of the error.

- Send the credit reporting company verifiable information, such as canceled checks or receipts, supporting your complaint.

- The credit reporting company must investigate your complaint within 30 days and get back to you with its results.

- Contact the creditor if the credit reporting company investigation does not result in correction of the error. When you resolve the dispute, ask the creditor to send the credit reporting company a correction.

If the issue remains unresolved, you have the right to explain in a statement that will go on your credit report. For example, if you did not pay a car repair bill because the mechanic didn't fix the problem, the unpaid bill may show up on your credit report, but so will your explanation.

Keep Your Good Name

Every month, go back to your budget and plan carefully to ensure your bills are paid before their due dates. For example, Betty makes sure she pays her bills on time. Betty gets paid twice a month. She has her paycheck set up for direct deposit so she doesn't have to scramble to get to the bank on payday. With her first paycheck each month, she pays her mortgage (which she has set up on auto debit), cable TV, and utility bills. Out of the second check, Betty makes her car payment (also on auto debit) and has a monthly deposit automatically made to her savings account. Betty has found that "autopilot" really simplifies budgeting and saving.

If you believe you are too deep in debt:

• Discuss your options with your creditors before you miss a payment.

• Seek expert help, such as Consumer Credit Counseling Services, listed in your local telephone directory.

• Avoid "credit repair" companies that charge a fee. Many of these are scams.

Save Money By Choosing The Right Loan

If you have good credit, you may want to take out a loan to purchase a house or to cover educational expenses—both are investments in the future. But regardless of how the money is spent, a loan is a liability, or debt, and decreases your wealth. So choose loans carefully. Shop and negotiate for the lowest interest rate. The interest you save can be invested to build wealth. Take a look at Table 34.1. In this example, it is obvious that Pixley Bank and Trust would charge the lowest interest over the term of the loan. What's not

Table 34.1. Interest Paid On A Sample $15,000 Care Loan For 5 Years

Lender	Interest Rate	Total Interest
Pixley Bank and Trust	6.5%	$2,609.53
XYZ Savings and Loan	7.5%	$3,034.15
Joe's Auto Sales	15%	$6,410.94

☞ Remember!!

Take Steps To Control Your Debt

As you can see, a big part of building wealth is making wise choices about debt. You need to maximize assets and minimize liabilities to maximize net worth. To manage debt, you need to know how much you have and develop strategies to control it.

When Bob decided to reduce his $3,000 credit card debt, he analyzed his debt and developed a strategy. He listed the balance, interest rate, and monthly interest on each credit card. He checked his credit score and shopped for the best rate on a new credit card. Then he transferred all his balances to that card. He cut up the old credit cards and used the interest he saved to pay toward the principal balance. He used the new card only for emergencies.

Source: © 2007 Federal Reserve
Bank of Dallas.

obvious is that your credit score may determine which interest rate you are offered. Use an online auto loan calculator to compare rates.

Save Money By Paying Off Loans Early

You can save interest expense by increasing your monthly payments or choosing a shorter payment term on your loan.

Let's use Betty as an example again. Betty, knew her new car would cost more than the sticker price because she would have to pay interest on the loan from the bank. After checking her options, she chose a shorter payment term with higher payments. Betty budgeted enough money each month to make the higher payments. By doing this, she will reduce the amount of interest she ultimately pays.

Table 34.2 (on page 328) shows how shorter terms with higher payments would affect the total amount and interest on Betty's $15,000 car loan.

Table 34.2. Interest Paid On A Sample $15,000 Car Loan at 8% Interest

	3-year	4-year	5-year
Number of payments	36	48	60
Payment	$470	$366	$304
Total paid	$16,922	$17,577	$18,249

Avoid the trap of getting "upside down"—owing more on the car than it is worth when you sell or trade it in. Betty's car will be paid for in three years, and she plans on driving it for at least eight years. Once her car is paid for, she will continue to budget for the car payment but will invest the money to further build her wealth.

Chapter 35

Watch Out For Predatory Lending Practices

A predator in the animal kingdom is one that hunts and zeros in on its prey before capturing it for dinner. A predator in the lending arena is one who zeros in on certain potential customers using deceptive or unfair tactics in order to make them a customer or charge them unfairly once they are a customer.

Predatory lending occurs when companies offer loan products using certain sales tactics or collection practices that are designed to frighten people and loan terms that deceive borrowers. Predatory lending has become a serious problem.

Abusive practices can occur in any sort of lending. We are going to talk about two common ones. It is also important to note that most of the problems are not caused by federally insured financial institutions.

Subprime Lending

Predatory lending often affects borrowers in the subprime market.

Subprime lenders charge higher interest rates and loan fees to offset the higher costs associated with lending to borrowers with credit history problems.

About This Chapter: Excerpted from "Module 5: Borrowing Basics," *Money Smart for Young Adults*, a CD-based curriculum developed by the Federal Deposit Insurance Corporation (FDIC), March 2008.

Most predatory loans are made to subprime borrowers, but not all subprime loans are predatory. Subprime lending can be beneficial, if performed in a fair, reasonable, and legal manner. A subprime loan may be the only alternative available to some borrowers.

Two Types Of Predatory Loans

Two types of predatory loans that you should be aware of are predatory payday loans and predatory mortgage loans.

> ✎ **What's It Mean?**
>
> Subprime Lending: Subprime lending involves giving credit to borrowers whose credit history shows late payments, collections, bankruptcy, etc. These types of borrowers are considered to be higher risk.
>
> Source: Federal Deposit Insurance Corporation (FDIC), March 2008.

Predatory Payday Loans

The first type of predatory loan is a payday loan made using predatory practices. Payday loans are small cash advances, usually of $500 or less. To get a loan, these steps are involved:

- A borrower gives a payday lender a postdated personal check or an authorization for automatic withdrawal from the borrower's bank account.

- In return, the borrower receives cash, minus the lender's fees.

Assume you go to a payday lender and borrow $200. The payday lender will usually make a two-week loan and might charge a fee of $30. You will write a postdated check to the lender for $230, dated after your next payday. The payday lender holds the check for two weeks.

When the loan is due, you can repay it by letting the lender cash the check, or you can give the lender the full amount due in cash.

The annual percentage rate (APR) for this transaction is 390 percent. An APR for a typical payday loan may be even higher than this example.

Most payday lenders allow you to "roll over" or renew your loan. The lender will charge an additional fee. In this case, you would write another postdated check, this time for $260 ($230 + $30 additional fee).

Remember that payday loans should only be used for emergencies. If you cannot fully repay the loan within a few pay periods, you should consider a longer term loan from a financial institution.

♣ **It's A Fact!!**

The federal Truth in Lending Act treats payday loans like other types of credit: the lenders must disclose the cost of the loan. Payday lenders must give you the finance charge (a dollar amount) and the annual percentage rate (APR—the cost of credit on a yearly basis) in writing before you sign for the loan. The APR is based on several things, including the amount you borrow, the interest rate and credit costs you're being charged, and the length of your loan.

A payday loan—that is, a cash advance secured by a personal check or paid by electronic transfer is—very expensive credit. How expensive? Say you need to borrow $100 for two weeks. You write a personal check for $115, with $15 the fee to borrow the money. The check casher or payday lender agrees to hold your check until your next payday. When that day comes around, either the lender deposits the check and you redeem it by paying the $115 in cash, or you roll-over the loan and are charged $15 more to extend the financing for 14 more days. If you agree to electronic payments instead of a check, here's what would happen on your next payday: the company would debit the full amount of the loan from your checking account electronically, or extend the loan for an additional $15. The cost of the initial $100 loan is a $15 finance charge and an annual percentage rate of 391 percent. If you roll-over the loan three times, the finance charge would climb to $60 to borrow the $100.

Source: Excerpted from "Payday Loans Equal Very Costly Cash: Consumers Urged to Consider Alternatives," *FTC Consumer Alert*, Federal Trade Commission, March 2008.

Catch Phrases Of Abusive Lenders

There are some catch phrases that should alert you to potential predatory practices. You may have already heard some of these in advertisements or seen them in mail, or on billboards. Beware when you hear the following:

- "125 percent of your home/car's value": It can be dangerous to borrow more than your home or car is worth. If you stop making payments, you can lose your house or vehicle and still owe money.

✔ Quick Tip
Indicators Of Possible Predatory Practices

Predatory Payday Lending

1. The company advertises terms that it does not actually offer.

2. You are not given disclosures listing terms, such as the finance charge and APR.

3. There is no "cooling off" or waiting period between the time you repay a payday loan and the time you are allowed to obtain another loan.

4. You can get a payday loan even if you currently owe payday loans to other companies at the same time.

5. You can obtain as many payday loans as you want each year.

6. You can get a payday loan to finance unpaid interest and fees.

7. The company threatens to prosecute you criminally for writing a bad check even though it knew you had insufficient funds in your account to pay the check and you paid it a payday loan fee.

Indicators Of Predatory Mortgage Lending

1. Excessive fees: Points and fees are costs not directly reflected in interest rates. Because these costs can be financed, they are easy to disguise or downplay. On predatory loans, fees totaling more than five percent of the loan amount are common.

2. Abusive prepayment penalties: Borrowers with higher interest subprime loans have a strong incentive to refinance as soon as their credit improves.

- "Incredibly low monthly payment": There is no disclosure as to how the lender intends to calculate monthly payments. There is a possibility the lender might have you pay only interest and not the principal, so you will never pay off the loan.

- "No upfront fees": Be careful of loans that promise no upfront fees. This does not mean there are no fees. Many times, there are expensive fees added on to the cost of the loan and you will pay interest on these

However, most subprime mortgages carry a prepayment penalty—a fee for paying off a loan early. Be careful of prepayment penalties that last more than three years and/or cost more than six months' interest.

3. Kickbacks to brokers: When brokers deliver a loan with an inflated interest rate (that is, higher than the rate acceptable to the lender), the lender often pays the broker a fee known as a "yield spread premium." This payment makes the loan more costly to the borrower. You can avoid this by shopping around for the best rate.

4. Loan flipping: A lender "flips" a loan by refinancing it several times within a short time frame to generate fee income without providing any net tangible benefit to the borrower. Flipping can quickly drain borrower equity and increase monthly payments—sometimes on homes that had been previously owned free of debt.

5. Unnecessary products: Sometimes borrowers may pay more than necessary because lenders sell and finance unnecessary insurance or other products along with the loan.

6. Asset-based lending: Predatory lenders may approve a loan based on the value of a customer's equity in the home instead of his or her ability to repay the loan. The lender may later encourage the customer to default so the lender can get ownership of the home.

7. Steering and targeting: Predatory lenders may steer borrowers into subprime mortgages, even when the borrowers could qualify for a less expensive, typical loan. Vulnerable borrowers may face aggressive sales tactics and sometimes outright fraud.

Source: Federal Deposit Insurance Corporation (FDIC), March 2008.

loan fees. This can be very costly. For example, if a $5,000 loan fee is added into the amount you borrow, you are paying $5,000 plus interest on the $5,000 over the life of the loan.

- "Even if you have a bad credit history…": Beware of lenders who promise you loans even if you have a bad credit history. If you have a bad credit history, you will most likely pay higher interest rates and more

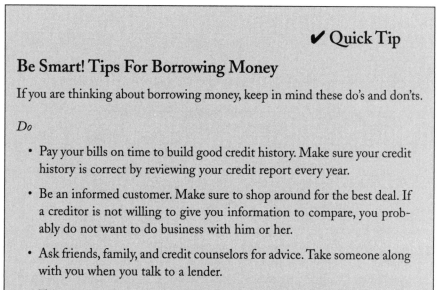

✔ Quick Tip

Be Smart! Tips For Borrowing Money

If you are thinking about borrowing money, keep in mind these do's and don'ts.

Do

- Pay your bills on time to build good credit history. Make sure your credit history is correct by reviewing your credit report every year.

- Be an informed customer. Make sure to shop around for the best deal. If a creditor is not willing to give you information to compare, you probably do not want to do business with him or her.

- Ask friends, family, and credit counselors for advice. Take someone along with you when you talk to a lender.

- Take your time before deciding on the best loan or lender.

- Be careful of lenders who tell you they do not care about your credit history or how much you earn. Many of these lenders charge higher interest rates and higher fees.

Don't

- Do not let lenders pressure you into a decision before you are ready.

- Do not respond to advertisements that make lending sound cheap and easy.

- Do not respond to offers to refinance your loan shortly after you just refinanced it. Make sure you really need the loan or the loan makes economic sense for you.

Source: Federal Deposit Insurance Corporation (FDIC), March 2008.

expensive loan origination fees. All lenders take your credit history into account. Be aware that while some predatory lenders have been known to target low-income communities for high-cost, high-interest loans, no one is immune from their deceptive offers.

- "It's free and you have nothing to lose": If it sounds too good to be true, it probably is. Even though the initial loan evaluation is free, there are other ways predatory lenders will take money from you. There might be hidden fees.

- "Act now, this is a limited-time offer": Beware of "limited-time offers." Many predatory lenders try to pressure you into acting fast, even though you are not comfortable with the loan conditions.

The True Cost Of Alternative Financial Services

Many lenders advertise "easy money." These types of loans are generally easier to obtain but also cost significantly more. Getting credit is not cheap. However, getting a bank loan is usually less expensive than other alternatives. We are going to look at two of these alternatives: Rent-to-own services and refund anticipation services.

Rent-To-Own

Rent-to-own services let you use an item for a period of time by making monthly or weekly payments. If you want to purchase the item, the store will set up a plan for you to rent it until you pay enough to own it. The store is the legal owner of the item until you make the final payment. If you miss a payment, the store can take the item back. If this happens, you will not own the item, and you will not get your money back. Rent-to-own agreements are technically not loans, so no interest is charged. However, the difference between the cash price and your total payment is like the interest you pay on a loan. Generally, using rent-to-own services is more expensive than getting a consumer installment loan to buy the item outright.

Refund Anticipation

Refund anticipation loans are short-term loans secured by your expected income tax refund. Although the business preparing your income tax return will give you the money, you are actually receiving a loan from a bank or finance company. Because you do not have to pay any fees associated with obtaining a refund anticipation loan at the time you receive the money, you may not realize how much this loan is really costing you.

Example: Your refund is $1,500.

• The fees associated with filing your income tax return with the tax preparation service and getting the refund anticipation loan equal $300.

• So, you will receive a check for $1,200. You are paying $300 in fees to obtain your income tax refund.

It is important to remember that the paperwork you sign to receive a refund anticipation loan will legally obligate you to repay a $1,500 loan. So, if your actual refund is only $800, you are responsible for repaying $700, plus interest to the lender that made the refund anticipation loan. And the higher the loan amount, the higher the refund anticipation loan fee.

Here are some typical costs associated with getting a refund anticipation loan.

• Tax preparation fee: $100

• Refund anticipation fee: $75

• Electronic filing fee: $40

• Document preparation: $33

• Total Cost: $248

When you electronically file (e-file) your tax return and request direct deposit, your refund is often deposited in your bank account within two weeks. Sometimes refund anticipation loans take just as long, yet cost you substantially more money. Many organizations host Volunteer Income Tax Assistance (VITA) sites. VITA is an IRS-coordinated program that provides free income tax assistance and e-filing. Income eligibility restrictions apply. Contact the IRS for a location near you.

Chapter 36

If Your Credit, ATM, Or Debit Cards Are Lost Or Stolen

Many people find it easy and convenient to use credit cards and automated teller machine (ATM) or debit cards. The Fair Credit Billing Act (FCBA) and the Electronic Fund Transfer Act (EFTA) offer procedures for you to use if your cards are lost or stolen.

Limiting Your Financial Loss

Report the loss or theft of your credit cards and your ATM or debit cards to the card issuers as quickly as possible. Many companies have toll-free numbers and 24-hour service to deal with such emergencies. It's a good idea to follow up your phone calls with a letter. Include your account number, when you noticed your card was missing, and the date you first reported the loss.

You also may want to check your homeowner's insurance policy to see if it covers your liability for card thefts. If not, some insurance companies will allow you to change your policy to include this protection.

Credit Card Loss Or Fraudulent Charges (FCBA): Your maximum liability under federal law for unauthorized use of your credit card is $50. If

About This Chapter: "Credit, ATM and Debit Cards: What to Do If They're Lost or Stolen," Federal Trade Commission (www.ftc.gov), June 2002.

you report the loss before your credit cards are used, the FCBA says the card issuer cannot hold you responsible for any unauthorized charges. If a thief uses your cards before you report them missing, the most you will owe for unauthorized charges is $50 per card. Also, if the loss involves your credit card number, but not the card itself, you have no liability for unauthorized use.

After the loss, review your billing statements carefully. If they show any unauthorized charges, it's best to send a letter to the card issuer describing each questionable charge. Again, tell the card issuer the date your card was lost or stolen, or when you first noticed unauthorized charges, and when you first reported the problem to them. Be sure to send the letter to the address provided for billing errors. Do not send it with a payment or to the address where you send your payments unless you are directed to do so.

ATM Or Debit Card Loss Or Fraudulent Transfers (EFTA): Your liability under federal law for unauthorized use of your ATM or debit card depends on how quickly you report the loss. If you report an ATM or debit card missing before it's used without your permission, the EFTA says the card issuer cannot hold you responsible for any unauthorized transfers. If unauthorized use occurs before you report it, your liability under federal law depends on how quickly you report the loss.

For example, if you report the loss within two business days after you realize your card is missing, you will not be responsible for more than $50 for unauthorized use. However, if you don't report the loss within two business days after you discover the loss, you could lose up to $500 because of an unauthorized transfer. You also risk unlimited loss if you fail to report an unauthorized transfer within 60 days after your bank statement containing unauthorized use is mailed to you. That means you could lose all the money in your bank account and the unused portion of your line of credit established for overdrafts. However, for unauthorized

> **✔ Quick Tip**
>
> If unauthorized transfers show up on your bank statement, report them to the card issuer as quickly as possible. Once you've reported the loss of your ATM or debit card, you cannot be held liable for additional unauthorized transfers that occur after that time.

transfers involving only your debit card number (not the loss of the card), you are liable only for transfers that occur after 60 days following the mailing of your bank statement containing the unauthorized use and before you report the loss.

Protecting Your Cards

The best protections against card fraud are to know where your cards are at all times and to keep them secure. For protection of ATM and debit cards that involve a personal identification number (PIN), keep your PIN a secret. Don't use your address, birthdate, phone or Social Security number as the PIN and do memorize the number.

The following suggestions may help you protect your credit card and your ATM or debit card accounts.

For Credit And ATM Or Debit Cards

- Be cautious about disclosing your account number over the phone unless you know you're dealing with a reputable company.

- Never put your account number on the outside of an envelope or on a postcard.

- Draw a line through blank spaces on charge or debit slips above the total so the amount cannot be changed.

- Don't sign a blank charge or debit slip.

- Tear up carbons and save your receipts to check against your monthly statements.

- Cut up old cards—cutting through the account number—before disposing of them.

- Open monthly statements promptly and compare them with your receipts. Report mistakes or discrepancies as soon as possible to the special address listed on your statement for inquiries. Under the FCBA (credit cards) and the EFTA (ATM or debit cards), the card issuer must investigate errors reported to them within 60 days of the date your statement was mailed to you.

- Keep a record—in a safe place separate from your cards—of your account numbers, expiration dates, and the telephone numbers of each card issuer so you can report a loss quickly.

- Carry only those cards that you anticipate you'll need.

For ATM Or Debit Cards

- Don't carry your PIN in your wallet or purse or write it on your ATM or debit card.

- Never write your PIN on the outside of a deposit slip, an envelope, or other papers that could be easily lost or seen.

- Carefully check ATM or debit card transactions before you enter the PIN or before you sign the receipt; the funds for this item will be fairly quickly transferred out of your checking or other deposit account.

- Periodically check your account activity. This is particularly important if you bank online. Compare the current balance and recent withdrawals or transfers to those you've recorded, including your current ATM and debit card withdrawals and purchases and your recent checks. If you notice transactions you didn't make, or if your balance has dropped suddenly without activity by you, immediately report the problem to your card issuer. Someone may have co-opted your account information to commit fraud.

♣ It's A Fact!! Buying A Registration Service

For an annual fee, companies will notify the issuers of your credit card and your ATM or debit card accounts if your card is lost or stolen. This service allows you to make only one phone call to report all card losses rather than calling individual issuers. Most services also will request replacement cards on your behalf.

Purchasing a card registration service may be convenient, but it's not required. The FCBA and the EFTA give you the right to contact your card issuers directly in the event of a loss or suspected unauthorized use.

If you decide to buy a registration service, compare offers. Carefully read the contract to determine the company's obligations and your liability. For example, will the company reimburse you if it fails to notify card issuers promptly once you've called in the loss to the service? If not, you could be liable for unauthorized charges or transfers.

Chapter 37

Identity Theft And Identity Fraud

What Are Identity Theft And Identity Fraud?

"But he that filches from me my good name/Robs me of that which not enriches him/And makes me poor indeed." - Shakespeare, Othello, act iii. Sc. 3.

The short answer is that identity theft is a crime. Identity theft and identity fraud are terms used to refer to all types of crime in which someone wrongfully obtains and uses another person's personal data in some way that involves fraud or deception, typically for economic gain. The information in this chapter is intended to explain why you need to take precautions to protect yourself from identity theft. Unlike your fingerprints, which are unique to you and cannot be given to someone else for their use, your personal data—especially your Social Security number, your bank account or credit card number, your telephone calling card number, and other valuable identifying data—can be used, if they fall into the wrong hands, to personally profit at your expense. In the United States and Canada, for example, many people have reported that unauthorized persons have taken funds out of their bank or financial accounts, or, in the worst cases, taken over their identities altogether,

About This Chapter: Excerpted from "Identity Theft and Identify Fraud," an undated document produced by the U.S. Department of Justice, available online at http://www.usdoj.gov/criminal/fraud/websites/idtheft.html; accessed July 1, 2008 and contact information verified in February 2009.

running up vast debts and committing crimes while using the victims' names. In many cases, a victim's losses may include not only out-of-pocket financial losses, but substantial additional financial costs associated with trying to restore his reputation in the community and correcting erroneous information for which the criminal is responsible.

What Are The Most Common Ways To Commit Identity Theft Or Fraud?

Many people do not realize how easily criminals can obtain our personal data without having to break into our homes. In public places, for example, criminals may engage in "shoulder surfing"—watching you from a nearby location as you punch in your telephone calling card number or credit card number—or listen in on your conversation if you give your credit-card number over the telephone to a hotel or rental car company.

Even the area near your home may not be secure. Some criminals engage in "dumpster diving"—going through your garbage cans or a communal dumpster or trash bin—to obtain copies of your checks, credit card or bank statements, or other records that typically bear your name, address, and even your telephone number. These types of records make it easier for criminals to get control over accounts in your name and assume your identity.

If you receive applications for "preapproved" credit cards in the mail, but discard them without tearing up the enclosed materials, criminals may retrieve them and try to activate the cards for their use without your knowledge. (Some credit card companies, when sending credit cards, have adopted security measures that allow a card recipient to activate the card only from his or her home telephone number but this is not yet a universal practice.) Also, if your mail is delivered to a place where others have ready access to it, criminals may simply intercept and redirect your mail to another location.

In recent years, the internet has become an appealing place for criminals to obtain identifying data, such as passwords or even banking information. In their haste to explore the exciting features of the internet, many people respond to "spam"—unsolicited e-mail—that promises them some benefit but requests identifying data, without realizing that in many cases, the requester has no intention of keeping his promise. In some cases, criminals reportedly have used computer technology to obtain large amounts of personal data.

With enough identifying information about an individual, a criminal can take over that individual's identity to conduct a wide range of crimes: for example, false applications for loans and credit cards, fraudulent withdrawals from bank accounts, fraudulent use of telephone calling cards, or obtaining

☞ Remember!!
How do thieves steal an identity?

Identity theft starts with the misuse of your personally identifying information such as your name and Social Security number, credit card numbers, or other financial account information. For identity thieves, this information is as good as gold.

Skilled identity thieves may use a variety of methods to get hold of your information, including the following:

- **Dumpster Diving:** They rummage through trash looking for bills or other paper with your personal information on it.

- **Skimming:** They steal credit/debit card numbers by using a special storage device when processing your card.

- **Phishing:** They pretend to be financial institutions or companies and send spam or pop-up messages to get you to reveal your personal information.

- **Changing Your Address:** They divert your billing statements to another location by completing a change of address form.

- **Old-Fashioned Stealing:** They steal wallets and purses; mail, including bank and credit card statements; pre-approved credit offers; and new checks or tax information. They steal personnel records, or bribe employees who have access.

- **Pretexting:** They use false pretenses to obtain your personal information from financial institutions, telephone companies, and other sources.

Source: Excerpted from "About Identity Theft: Deter. Detect. Defend. Avoid ID Theft," Federal Trade Commission (www.ftc.gov).

other goods or privileges which the criminal might be denied if he were to use his real name. If the criminal takes steps to ensure that bills for the falsely obtained credit cards, or bank statements showing the unauthorized withdrawals, are sent to an address other than the victim's, the victim may not become aware of what is happening until the criminal has already inflicted substantial damage on the victim's assets, credit, and reputation.

What Should I Do To Avoid Becoming A Victim Of Identity Theft?

To reduce or minimize the risk of becoming a victim of identity theft or fraud, there are some basic steps you can take. For starters, just remember the word "SCAM":

S: Be Stingy about giving out your personal information to others unless you have a reason to trust them, regardless of where you are.

At home, start by adopting a "need to know" approach to your personal data. Your credit card company may need to know your mother's maiden name, so that it can verify your identity when you call to inquire about your account. A person who calls you and says he's from your bank, however, doesn't need to know that information if it's already on file with your bank; the only purpose of such a call is to acquire that information for that person's personal benefit. Also, the more information that you have printed on your personal bank checks—such as your Social Security number or home telephone number—the more personal data you are routinely handing out to people who may not need that information.

♣ It's A Fact!!

To victims of identity theft and fraud, the task of correcting incorrect information about their financial or personal status, and trying to restore their good names and reputations, may seem as daunting as trying to solve a puzzle in which some of the pieces are missing and other pieces no longer fit as they once did. Unfortunately, the damage that criminals do in stealing another person's identity and using it to commit fraud often takes far longer to undo than it took the criminal to commit the crimes.

Source: U.S. Department of Justice.

If someone you don't know calls you on the telephone and offers you the chance to receive a "major" credit card, a prize, or other valuable item, but asks you for personal data—such as your Social Security number, credit card number or expiration date, or mother's maiden name—ask them to send you a written application form. If they won't do it, tell them you're not interested and hang up. If they will, review the application carefully when you receive it and make sure it's going to a company or financial institution that's well-known and reputable. The Better Business Bureau can give you information about businesses that have been the subject of complaints.

If you're traveling, have your mail held at your local post office, or ask someone you know well and trust—another family member, a friend, or a neighbor—to collect and hold your mail while you're away.

If you have to telephone someone while you're traveling, and need to pass on personal financial information to the person you're calling, don't do it at an open telephone booth where passersby can listen in on what you're saying; use a telephone booth where you can close the door, or wait until you're at a less public location to call.

C: Check your financial information regularly, and look for what should be there and what shouldn't.

If you have bank or credit card accounts, you should be receiving monthly statements that list transactions for the most recent month or reporting period. If you're not receiving monthly statements for the accounts you know you have, call the financial institution or credit card company immediately and ask about it.

If you're told that your statements are being mailed to another address that you haven't authorized, tell the financial institution or credit card representative immediately that you did not authorize the change of address and that someone may be improperly using your accounts. In that situation, you should also ask for copies of all statements and debit or charge transactions that have occurred since the last statement you received. Obtaining those copies will help you to work with the financial institution or credit card company in determining whether some or all of those debit or charge transactions were fraudulent.

If someone has gotten your financial data and made unauthorized debits or charges against your financial accounts, checking your monthly statements carefully may be the quickest way for you to find out. Too many of us give those statements, or the enclosed checks or credit transactions, only a quick glance, and don't review them closely to make sure there are no unauthorized withdrawals or charges.

If someone has managed to get access to your mail or other personal data, and opened any credit cards in your name or taken any funds from your bank account, contact your financial institution or credit card company immediately to report those transactions and to request further action.

A: Ask periodically for a copy of your credit report. Your credit report should list all bank and financial accounts under your name, and will provide other indications of whether someone has wrongfully opened or used any accounts in your name.

M: Maintain careful records of your banking and financial accounts. Even though financial institutions are required to maintain copies of your checks, debit transactions, and similar transactions for five years, you should retain your monthly statements and checks for at least one year, if not more. If you need to dispute a particular check or transaction—especially if they purport to bear your signatures—your original records will be more immediately accessible and useful to the institutions that you have contacted.

What Should I Do If I've Become A Victim Of Identity Theft?

If you think you've become a victim of identity theft or fraud, act immediately

> **☞ Remember!!**
> Even if you take all suggested precautionary steps, it's still possible that you can become a victim of identity theft. Records containing your personal data—credit-card receipts or car-rental agreements, for example—may be found by or shared with someone who decides to use your data for fraudulent purposes.
>
> Source: U.S. Department of Justice.

to minimize the damage to your personal funds and financial accounts, as well as your reputation. Here's a list—based in part on a checklist prepared by the California Public Interest Research Group (CalPIRG; http://www.calpirg.org/issues/identity-theft-prevention) and the Privacy Rights Clearinghouse—of some actions that you should take right away:

Contact the Federal Trade Commission (FTC) to report the situation, whether online (www.ftc.gov), by telephone toll-free at 877-ID THEFT (877-438-4338) or TDD at 202-326-2502, or by mail to Consumer Response Center, FTC, 600 Pennsylvania Avenue, N.W., Washington, DC 20580.

Under the Identity Theft and Assumption Deterrence Act, the Federal Trade Commission is responsible for receiving and processing complaints from people who believe they may be victims of identity theft, providing informational materials to those people, and referring those complaints to appropriate entities, including the major credit reporting agencies and law enforcement agencies. For further information, please check the FTC's identity theft web pages (http://www.ftc.gov/bcp/edu/microsites/idtheft). You can also call your local office of the FBI or the U.S. Secret Service to report crimes relating to identity theft and fraud.

You may also need to contact other agencies for other types of identity theft:

- Your local office of the Postal Inspection Service if you suspect that an identity thief has submitted a change-of-address form with the Post Office to redirect your mail, or has used the mail to commit frauds involving your identity.

- The Social Security Administration if you suspect that your Social Security number is being fraudulently used (call 800-269-0271 to report the fraud).

- The Internal Revenue Service if you suspect the improper use of identification information in connection with tax violations (call 1-800-829-0433 to report the violations).

Call the fraud units of the three principal credit reporting companies:

- Equifax: To report fraud, call (800) 525-6285 or write to P.O. Box 740250, Atlanta, GA 30374-0250.

- Experian (formerly TRW): To report fraud, call (888) EXPERIAN or (888) 397-3742, fax to (800) 301-7196, or write to P.O. Box 1017, Allen, TX 75013.

- Trans Union: To report fraud, call (800) 680-7289 or write to P.O. Box 6790, Fullerton, CA 92634.

♣ It's A Fact!!
Warning: Identity Thieves Target Young People, Too

You've probably heard or read about "identity theft," which happens when someone learns enough private information about another person to be able to withdraw money from a bank account or obtain a new credit card in that other person's name and use it for purchases that will not be paid for. But did you know that adults aren't the only people whose identity is being used by ID thieves?

Crooks target young people like you even though you may be too young to have a checking account or credit card on your own. They can use your name, address, and Social Security number to open accounts.

While we don't want to scare you, we do want to help you protect yourself and your family from ID theft.

Be extra careful with your full name and address, date of birth, Social Security number, bank account information, phone number, and your mother's maiden name. This is personal information that banks and other businesses use to confirm your identity, which can be very valuable to an ID thief wanting to pose as you to commit fraud.

Don't give out personal information in response to an incoming call or e-mail from a stranger or an advertisement on the internet. For example, beware of what law enforcement officials call "phishing," a type of identity theft in which criminals use fake websites and e-mails to "fish" for valuable personal information.

In the typical phishing scam, you receive an e-mail supposedly from a company you may do business with or even from a government agency. The e-mail

To opt out of pre-approved offers of credit and marketing lists, call (800) 680-7293 or (888) 5OPTOUT or write to P.O. Box 97328, Jackson, MS 39238.

Contact all creditors with whom your name or identifying data have been fraudulently used. For example, you may need to contact your long-distance telephone company if your long-distance calling card has been stolen or you find fraudulent charges on your bill.

---

describes a reason you must "resubmit" bank account numbers or other personal information. If you follow their instructions, the thieves hiding behind what you think is a legitimate website or e-mail can use the information to withdraw or spend money in your name.

"Identity thieves are very good at pretending to be legitimate business people and government officials so they can convince others to share personal information or even send money," says Michael Benardo, manager of the Federal Deposit Insurance Corporation (FDIC)'s financial crimes section.

That's why you should never provide personal information in response to a phone call, e-mail, or a pop-up ad on the web, no matter how official it may appear to be.

Never share your passwords or ID numbers for your computer with friends or strangers. Be especially suspicious of new "friends" you've met through the internet, such as through a website where people can post information about themselves and can contact others through that site. These people could be fraud artists.

Don't leave your birth certificate or documents with your Social Security number unprotected at home, at school or anywhere else. For example, while you may need to provide your birth certificate as proof of your age when you sign up for a sports league or get your learner's permit, you shouldn't leave your birth certificate in your locker at school or any other place that may not be safe.

Source: From "Warning: Identity Thieves Target Young People, Too," *FDIC Consumer News*, Federal Deposit Insurance Corporation, Summer 2006.

Contact all financial institutions where you have accounts that an identity thief has taken over or that have been created in your name but without your knowledge. You may need to cancel those accounts, place stop-payment orders on any outstanding checks that may not have cleared, and change your automated teller machine (ATM) card, account, and personal identification number (PIN).

Contact the major check verification companies (listed in the CalPIRG-Privacy Rights Clearinghouse checklist) if you have had checks stolen or bank accounts set up by an identity thief. In particular, if you know that a particular merchant has received a check stolen from you, contact the verification company that the merchant uses:

- CheckRite: 800-766-2748
- ChexSystems: 800-428-9623 (closed checking accounts)
- CrossCheck: 800-552-1900
- Equifax: 800-437-5120
- National Processing Co. (NPC): 800-526-5380
- SCAN: 800-262-7771
- TeleCheck: 800-710-9898

Chapter 38

Con Artists Want Your Money: Avoid These Scams And Schemes

Sweepstakes And Lotteries Scams

Congratulations, it's your lucky day! You've just won $5,000!

If you get a phone call or a letter with a message like this, be skeptical. Scam artists often use the promise of a valuable prize or award to entice consumers to send money, buy overpriced products or services, or contribute to bogus charities. People who fall for their ploys may end up paying more and more for the products—if they ever get them at all.

How To Avoid Prize And Sweepstakes Fraud

The next time you get a "personal" telephone call or letter telling you "it's your lucky day," remember:

About This Chapter: This chapter includes information from the following documents produced by the Federal Trade Commission (www.ftc.gov): "Sweepstakes and Lotteries Scams," undated; "Charities and Fundraising Phone Fraud," undated; "Work-at-Home Schemes," March 2001; "'Net Based Business Opportunities: Are Some Flop-portunities?" June 2002; "Costly Coupon Scams," August 1997; "Multilevel Marketing Plans," (produced in cooperation with the North American Securities Administrators Association), November 1996; and "Take This Scheme and Stuff It: Avoiding Envelope-Stuffing Rip-Offs." Despite the older dates of some of these documents, the information still provides appropriate guidance regarding potential fraudulent activities. Additional information from Investopedia ULC is cited separately within the chapter.

♣ It's A Fact!!

Fake Check Scams

It's your lucky day! You just won a foreign lottery! The caller says so. And they are sending a cashier's check to cover the taxes and fees. All you have to do to get your winnings is deposit the check and wire the money to the sender to pay the taxes and fees. You're guaranteed that when they get your payment, you'll get your prize.

There's just one catch: this is a scam. The check is no good, even though it appears to be a legitimate cashier's check. The lottery angle is a trick to get you to wire money to someone you don't know. If you were to deposit the check and wire the money, your bank would soon learn that the check was a fake. And you would be out the money: The money you wired can't be recovered, and you're responsible for the checks you deposit—even though you don't know they're fake.

Source: "Sweepstakes and Lotteries Scams, FTC, undated, online at http://www.ftc.gov/bcp/edu/microsites/phonefraud/sweepstakes.shtml; accessed October 31, 2008.

- Don't pay to collect sweepstakes winnings. If you have to pay to collect your winnings, you're not winning—you're buying. Legitimate sweepstakes don't require you to pay "insurance," "taxes", or "shipping and handling charges" to collect your prize.

- Hold on to your money. Scammers pressure people to wire money through commercial money transfer companies because wiring money is the same as sending cash. When the money's gone, there's very little chance of recovery. Likewise, resist any push to send a check or money order by overnight delivery or courier. Con artists recommend these services so they can get to your money before you realize you've been cheated.

- Phone numbers can deceive. Some con artists use internet technology to call you. It allows them to disguise their area code: although it may look like they're calling from your local area, they could be calling from anywhere in the world.

How To Recognize A Reloader

[Note: A "reloader" is a double scammer—someone who targets victims of telemarketing fraud and tries to scam them again.]

- Their offer requires a "recovery fee." Legitimate organizations, like national, state, and local consumer enforcement agencies and non-profit organizations, do not charge or guarantee results for their services to help you get your money back from a telemarketing fraud.

- Their offer requires you to wire money or send it by a courier.

- They contact you several times to urge you to buy more merchandise to increase your chances of winning so-called valuable prizes.

Charities And Fundraising Phone Fraud

Charities perform a variety of valuable services in our society. Many are facing increases in costs and demands and decreases in funding. To meet these financial challenges, charities are asking for larger contributions from more donors—and they're asking more often than they used to, often using telemarketing and direct mail solicitations to raise funds for their causes. At the same time, fraudsters are using the phone and the mail to solicit for fraudulent charities.

Consider the following precautions to ensure that your donation dollars benefit people and organizations you want to help. They're good practices whether you're contacted by an organization's employees, volunteers, or professional fund-raisers, soliciting donations by phone, mail, or in person.

How To Avoid Charity And Fundraising Fraud

- Donate to recognized charities with a history. Look up the organization at the Better Business Bureau's Wise Giving Alliance (http://www.give.org), Charity Navigator (http://www.charitynavigator.org), or the American Institute of Philanthropy (http://www.charitywatch.org). Ask the caller "Are you calling on behalf of a charity? What is the name of your organization?"

- Look closely at charities with names similar to well-known organizations. Some phony charities try to gain your trust by using names that sound or look like legitimate organizations. Ask the caller "Can you point me to a website or another resource for more information about your organization?"

♣ **It's A Fact!!**

International Lottery Scams

"Congratulations! You may receive a certified check for up to $400,000 U.S. CASH! Tax free! Your odds to WIN are 1-6." "Hundreds of U.S. citizens win every week using our secret system! You can win as much as you want!"

Sound great? It's a fraud.

Scam operators are using the telephone to entice U.S. consumers to buy chances in high-stakes foreign lotteries from as far away as Australia and Europe. These lottery solicitations violate U.S. law, which prohibits the cross-border sale or purchase of lottery tickets by phone or mail.

The FTC has these words of caution for consumers who are thinking about responding to a foreign lottery:

- If you play a foreign lottery—on the telephone or through the mail—you're violating federal law.

- There are no secret systems for winning foreign lotteries. Your chances of winning more than the cost of your tickets are slim to none.

- If you purchase one foreign lottery ticket, expect many more bogus offers for lottery or investment "opportunities." Your name will be placed on "sucker lists" that fraudulent telemarketers buy and sell.

- Keep your credit card and bank account numbers to yourself. Scam artists often ask for them during an unsolicited sales pitch.

- The bottom line: Ignore all phone solicitations for foreign lottery promotions. If you receive what looks like lottery material from a foreign country, give it to your local postmaster.

Source: "Sweepstakes and Lotteries Scams, FTC, undated, online at http://www.ftc.gov/bcp/edu/microsites/phonefraud/sweepstakes.shtml; accessed October 31, 2008.

♣ **It's A Fact!!**

Telemarketers who make calls across state lines on behalf of charitable organizations must comply with certain federal standards:

- They must make their calls between 8:00 a.m. and 9:00 p.m.

- They must promptly identify the charity they represent and that they are calling to ask for money.

- They may not lie or mislead you to get a contribution.

- They may not call you again if you asked them not to.

Source: "Charities and Fundraising Phone Fraud," FTC, undated, online at http://www.ftc.gov/bcp/edu/microsites/phonefraud/publicsafety.shtml; accessed October 31, 2008.

- Avoid giving cash gifts. They can be lost or stolen. For security and tax purposes, it's best to pay by check, made payable to the charity, not the solicitor. Ask, "Can you give me a receipt showing the amount of my contribution and stating that it is tax deductible?"

- Be skeptical if someone thanks you for a pledge you don't remember making. If you have any doubts about whether you've made a pledge or previously contributed, check your records.

- Reject high pressure appeals. Legitimate fund-raisers don't put you on the spot to give. Ask, "Can you mail me more information about the charity and how it works?"

- Do not do business with any charity offering to send a courier or overnight delivery service to collect your donation.

- Consider the costs. When you buy merchandise or tickets for special events, or get "free" goods in exchange for giving, remember that part of your contribution was used to pay for it.

- Be cautious of promises of guaranteed sweepstakes winnings in exchange for a contribution. According to U.S. law, you never have to give a donation to be eligible to win a sweepstakes.

- A special word about appeals that tug at your heart strings, especially pleas involving patriotism and current events: Before you give, make sure the organization has the infrastructure to deliver the help it is claiming to provide.

- After receiving a call asking for a donation, call the charity in question to find out whether it is aware of the solicitation and has authorized the use of its name.

Work-At-Home Schemes

Be part of one of America's Fastest Growing Industries!

Earn thousand of dollars a month—from your home—Processing Medical Billing Claims.

You can find ads like this everywhere—from the street light and telephone pole on your corner

♣ It's A Fact!!
Facts About Fire, Police, Or Military Fundraisers

- Simply having the words "police" or "firefighter" in an organization's name doesn't mean police or firefighters are members of the group or will benefit from the funds raised.

- An organization may claim it has ties with local police or firefighters, but that doesn't mean contributions will be used locally or for public safety. Call your local organization to verify the connection.

- Many solicitations for police and fire service organizations are made by professional fund-raisers who are paid to do the job.

- Donations to some police or firefighter groups may not be tax deductible.

- The Department of Defense does not endorse specific war-related charities. Visit www.army.mil/operations/oif/FAQ.shtml a for more information about legitimate military relief societies that provide assistance to U.S. Service members and their families.

Source: "Charities and Fundraising Phone Fraud," FTC, undated, online at http://www.ftc.gov/bcp/edu/microsites/phonefraud/publicsafety.shtml; accessed October 31, 2008.

to your newspaper and PC. While you may find these ads appealing, especially if you can't work outside your home, proceed with caution. Not all work-at-home opportunities deliver on their promises.

Many ads omit the fact that you may have to work many hours without pay. Or they don't disclose all the costs you will have to pay. Countless work-at-home schemes require you to spend your own money to place newspaper ads, make photocopies, or buy the envelopes, paper, stamps, and other supplies or equipment you need to do the job. The companies sponsoring the ads also may demand that you pay for instructions or "tutorial" software. Consumers deceived by these ads have lost thousands of dollars, in addition to their time and energy.

Classic Work-At-Home Schemes

Medical Billing: Ads for pre-packaged businesses—known as billing centers—are in newspapers, on television and on the internet. If you respond, you'll get a sales pitch that may sound something like this: There's "a crisis" in the health care system, due partly to the overwhelming task of processing paper claims. The solution is electronic claim processing. Because only a small percentage of claims are transmitted electronically, the market for billing centers is wide open.

The promoter also may tell you that many doctors who process claims electronically want to "outsource" or contract out their billing services to save money. Promoters will promise that you can earn a substantial income working full or part time, providing services like billing, accounts receivable, electronic insurance claim processing, and practice management to doctors and dentists. They also may assure you that no experience is required, that they will provide clients eager to buy your services or that their qualified salespeople will find clients for you.

The Reality: You will have to sell. These promoters rarely provide experienced sales staff or contacts within the medical community.

The promoter will follow up by sending you materials that typically include a brochure, application, sample diskettes, a contract (licensing agreement), disclosure document, and in some cases, testimonial letters, videocassettes, and reference lists. For your investment of $2,000 to $8,000, a promoter will promise software, training, and technical support. And the company will encourage you to call its references. Make sure you get many names from which to chose. If only one or two names are given, they may be "shills"— people hired to give favorable testimonials. It's best to interview people in person, preferably where the business operates, to reduce your risk of being mislead by shills and also to get a better sense of how the business works.

Few consumers who purchase a medical billing business opportunity are able to find clients, start a business, and generate revenues—let alone recover their investment and earn a substantial income. Competition in the medical

---

✔ **Quick Tip**

Where To Complain

If you have spent money and time on a work-at-home program and now believe the program may not be legitimate, contact the company and ask for a refund. Let company representatives know that you plan to notify officials about your experience. If you can't resolve the dispute with the company, file a complaint with these organizations:

- The Federal Trade Commission works for the consumer to prevent fraud and deception. Call 877-FTC-HELP (877-382-4357) or log on to http://www.ftc.gov.

- The Attorney General's office in your state or the state where the company is located. The office will be able to tell you whether you're protected by any state law that may regulate work-at-home programs.

- Your local consumer protection offices.

- Your local Better Business Bureau.

- Your local postmaster. The U.S. Postal Service investigates fraudulent mail practices.

- The advertising manager of the publication that ran the ad. The manager may be interested to learn about the problems you've had with the company.

Source: FTC, 2001.

billing market is fierce and revolves around a number of large and well-established firms.

Envelope Stuffing: Promoters usually advertise that, for a "small" fee, they will tell you how to earn money stuffing envelopes at home. Later—when it's too late—you find out that the promoter never had any employment to offer. Instead, for your fee, you're likely to get a letter telling you to place the same "envelope-stuffing" ad in newspapers or magazines, or to send the ad to friends and relatives. The only way you'll earn money is if people respond to your work-at-home ad.

Assembly Or Craft Work: These programs often require you to invest hundreds of dollars in equipment or supplies. Or they require you to spend many hours producing goods for a company that has promised to buy them. For example, you might have to buy a sewing or sign-making machine from the company, or materials to make items like aprons, baby shoes, or plastic signs. However, after you've purchased the supplies or equipment and performed the work, fraudulent operators don't pay you. In fact, many consumers have had companies refuse to pay for their work because it didn't meet "quality standards."

Unfortunately, no work is ever "up to standard," leaving workers with relatively expensive equipment and supplies—and no income. To sell their goods, these workers must find their own customers.

Questions To Ask

Legitimate work-at-home program sponsors should tell you—in writing—what's involved in the program they are selling. Here are some questions you might ask a promoter:

- What tasks will I have to perform? (Ask the program sponsor to list every step of the job.)
- Will I be paid a salary or will my pay be based on commission?
- Who will pay me?
- When will I get my first paycheck?
- What is the total cost of the work-at-home program, including supplies, equipment and membership fees? What will I get for my money?

The answers to these questions may help you determine whether a work-at-home program is appropriate for your circumstances, and whether it is legitimate.

You also might want to check out the company with your local consumer protection agency, state Attorney General, and the Better Business Bureau,

---

✔ Quick Tip
Advice From The Federal Trade Commission

The Federal Trade Commission (FTC) offers this advice to consumers considering an internet-related business opportunity:

- Consider the promotion carefully. If it claims buyers can earn a certain income, then it also must give the number and percentage of previous purchasers who achieved the earnings. If an earnings claim is there—but the additional information isn't—the business opportunity seller is probably violating the law.

- Get earnings claims in writing. If the business opportunity costs $500 or more, then the promoter must back up the earnings claim in a written document. It should include the earnings claim, as well as the number and percentage of recent clients who have earned at least as much as the promoter suggested. If it's a work-at-home or other business opportunity that involves an investment of under $500, ask the promoter to put the earnings information in writing.

- Study the business opportunity's franchise disclosure document. Under the FTC Franchise Rule, many business opportunity promoters are required to provide this document to potential purchasers. It includes information about the company, including whether it has faced any lawsuits from purchasers or lawsuits alleging fraud. Look for a statement about previous purchasers. If the document says there have been no previous purchases but the seller offers you a list of references, be careful: the references probably are phonies.

- Interview each previous purchaser in person, preferably where their business operates. The FTC requires most business opportunity promoters to give potential purchasers the names, addresses, and phone numbers of at least ten previous purchasers who live the closest to the potential not only where the company is located, but also where you live. These organizations can tell you whether they have received complaints about the work-at-home program that interests you. But be wary: the absence of complaints doesn't necessarily mean the company is legitimate. Unscrupulous companies may settle complaints, change their names, or move to avoid detection.

purchaser. Interviewing them helps reduce the risk of being misled by phony references.

- Contact the attorney general's office, state or county consumer protection agency and Better Business Bureau both where the business opportunity promoter is based and where you live to find out whether there is any record of unresolved complaints. While a complaint record may indicate questionable business practices, a lack of complaints doesn't necessarily mean that the promoter and the business opportunity don't have problems. Unscrupulous dealers often change names and locations to hide a history of complaints.

- If the business opportunity involves selling products from well-known companies, call the legal department of the company whose merchandise would be promoted. Find out whether the business opportunity and its promoter are affiliated with the company. Ask whether the company has ever threatened trademark action against the business opportunity promoter.

- Consult an attorney, accountant or other business advisor before you put any money down or sign any papers. Entering into a business opportunity can be costly, so it's best to have an expert check out the contract first. If the promoter requires a deposit, ask your attorney to establish an escrow account where the deposit can be maintained by a third party until you make the deal.

- Take your time. Promoters of fraudulent business opportunities are likely to use high-pressure sales tactics to get you to buy in. If the business opportunity is legitimate, it'll still be around when you're ready to decide.

Source: FTC, June 2002.

'Net Based Business Opportunities: Are Some Flopportunities?

Whether it's recruiting people to sell so-called internet-access devices, placing kiosks with internet access in public places, or dealing in other internet-related activities, consumers are being lured to the vast commercial potential of the web by business promoters.

However, the Federal Trade Commission (FTC) says that many of these business opportunities are scams that promise more than they can possibly deliver. The scam artists lure would-be entrepreneurs with false promises of big earnings for little effort. They pitch their fraudulent offerings on the web, in e-mail solicitations, through infomercials, classified ads and newspaper and magazine "advertorials," and in flyers, telemarketing pitches, seminars, and direct-mail solicitations.

✔ Quick Tip
Reporting Possible Fraud

If you suspect a business opportunity promotion is fraudulent, report it to the following agencies:

• The state attorney general's office in the state where you live and in the state where the business opportunity promoter is based.

• Your county or state consumer protection agency. Check the blue pages of the phone book under county and state government.

• The Better Business Bureau in your area and the area where the promoter is based.

• The FTC. File a complaint online at http://www.ftc.gov/ or call toll free 877-FTC-HELP (877-382-4357).

Source: FTC, June 2002.

Here are a few examples of internet-related business opportunities that didn't live up to their promises:

Providing TV Access To The Internet

The Pitch: The promoter promises that you can earn thousands of dollars a month by recruiting people to sell devices that provide television access to the internet.

The Problem: The program claims to pay participants based on how many people they recruit into the program, not on their product sales. That makes the program a pyramid scheme—not a legitimate multi-level marketing plan. Pyramid schemes are illegal. Mathematically, nearly everyone who participates in them loses their money. When there are no new recruits, the pyramid collapses.

Selling Walk-Up Internet Access

The Pitch: The promoter claims you can earn big money by selling machines or kiosks that provide walk-up internet access—for a fee—in places like airports, hotels and shopping malls. The machines cost thousands of dollars, but the promoter says the cost can be recovered because the machines generate "amazing" earnings. And, the company promises to help find profitable locations for the machines.

The Problem: Rather than the high-traffic locations that the promoter promises, the buyer's machines get placed where demand for internet access is low. As a result, a would-be entrepreneur can't possibly make the promised earnings.

Giving Seminars On Making Money On The Internet

The Pitch: The promoter advertises that you can earn more than $150,000 as an "internet consultant" who sponsors free seminars to teach other consumers how to make money on the internet.

The Problem: The seminars really feature high-pressure sales pitches for the promoter's internet yellow pages or internet advertising. And, even though the promoter promises to provide internet and sales training to buyers—for a fee of several thousand dollars—the buyers never get the promised training. In the end, they never earn the promised amounts.

Costly Coupon Scams

Cents-off coupons are providing big bucks for scam artists who offer business opportunity and work-at-home schemes featuring coupon certificate booklets and coupon clipping services. Using the internet to market these so-called opportunities, fraudulent promoters are promising entrepreneurs, charity groups, and consumers earnings of "hundreds per week" and "thousands per month" simply by selling coupon certificate booklets or cutting coupons at home. The fact is that consumers and manufacturers are getting clipped in these costly—and deceptive—coupon capers.

There's only one legitimate way to use a coupon: Cut it out of the newspaper or other source and use it toward the purchase of the designated product. A coupon is meant to be used only by the consumer who buys the product for which the coupon is printed. Selling or transferring coupons to a third party violates most manufacturers' coupon redemption policies—and usually voids the coupon.

Coupons are big business. More than 3,000 manufacturers distribute nearly 330 billion coupons—worth an estimated $280 billion—every year in an effort to help consumers save money. Indeed, it is thought that 77 percent of American households use some eight billion coupons to save $4.7 billion on their grocery bills.

Yet, fraudulent promoters are making money marketing and misrepresenting coupon-based business opportunities to unwary consumers and even savvy organizations.

Among the victims are would-be entrepreneurs trying to run a business from home, people with otherwise limited income opportunities, and people just trying to make a living, who are losing savings and time and effort; charity groups, lured into selling coupon certificate booklets as fundraisers; and consumers who are dealing with complicated forms involving difficult procedures and handling fees to receive the same coupons manufacturers give away for free.

How The Coupon Scams Work

Coupon Certificate Booklet Scams: A promoter sells an investor a business opportunity selling coupon certificate booklets. The investor is supposed to sell the booklets to consumers for $20 to $50 each. The booklets contain 20 to 50 certificates, each of which can be redeemed for $10 worth of grocery coupons. That makes each booklet "worth" between $200 and $500 in coupons. To redeem the certificates for coupons, the consumer must complete and mail a form, select 30 to 50 products from a list and include a self-addressed, stamped envelope and a processing fee.

In theory, the investor should make big profits selling the booklets to consumers. And consumers should save big money by using the coupons when they buy the groceries. In reality, though, the promoter is the only one who makes money.

Investors who spend several hundred to several thousand dollars to buy the certificate booklet distributorship lose money because inflated earnings claims never pan out. Consumers who pay out substantial processing fees and postage for coupons lose money because they can clip coupons for themselves from their newspaper. To redeem $500 worth of certificates, for example, a consumer might pay postage and processing fees of over $100. And everyone loses on false claims that coupons have no expiration date: Only a tiny share of coupons issued by manufacturers have no expiration date.

Coupon Clipping Scam: A related scam centers on coupon clipping. Promoters make overblown promises about the income or profit potential for consumers working at home clipping coupons. These claims certainly sound appealing, but they are unsubstantiated at best and bold lies at worst. Making money—particularly "hundreds per week" and "thousands per month"—isn't that easy. Success generally requires hard work.

Sometimes, fraudulent promoters use coupons clipped by consumers to fill orders from other consumers who redeem the coupon certificates. Many manufacturers have policies that do not allow coupons to be transferred. That is, the coupons that are being sold may not be redeemed by the retailer or manufacturer.

Coupon Scheme Clues

You can avoid losing your money to a bogus work-at-home coupon opportunity. Listen for these tell-tale tactics:

- Guarantees of big profits, high income or amazing savings in a short time.

- Claims that no risk is involved.

- Lots of pressure to act now.

- Claims that this is a hot, "can't miss" opportunity.

Still tempted to get involved in a coupon clipping venture through an ad in the newspaper, a magazine or on the internet? Exercise caution. Ask questions—and make sure the answers add up. [See the Quick Tip box on pages 360–361, Advice From The Federal Trade Commission for some questions to get you started.]

Multilevel Marketing Plans

Multilevel marketing plans, also known as "network" or "matrix" marketing, are a way of selling goods or services through distributors. These plans typically promise that if you sign up as a distributor, you will receive commissions—for both your sales of the plan's goods or services and those of other people you recruit to join the distributors. Multilevel marketing plans usually promise to pay commissions through two or more levels of recruits, known as the distributor's "downline."

If a plan offers to pay commissions for recruiting new distributors, watch out! Most states outlaw this practice, which is known as "pyramiding." State laws against pyramiding say that a multilevel marketing plan should only pay commissions for retail sales of goods or services, not for recruiting new distributors.

Why is pyramiding prohibited? Because plans that pay commissions for recruiting new distributors inevitably collapse when no new distributors can be recruited. And when a plan collapses, most people—except perhaps those at the very top of the pyramid—lose their money.

The Federal Trade Commission cannot tell you whether a particular multilevel marketing plan is legal. Nor can it give you advice about whether to join such a plan. You must make that decision yourself. However, the FTC suggests that you use common sense, and consider these seven tips when you make your decision:

- Avoid any plan that includes commissions for recruiting additional distributors. It may be an illegal pyramid.

- Beware of plans that ask new distributors to purchase expensive inventory. These plans can collapse quickly—and also may be thinly-disguised pyramids.

- Be cautious of plans that claim you will make money through continued growth of your "downline"—the commissions on sales made by new distributors you recruit—rather than through sales of products you make yourself.

☞ Remember!!

The absence of complaints doesn't necessarily mean the promotion is legitimate. Unscrupulous promoters may settle complaints, change their names, or move to avoid detection.

FTC, December 2003.

- Beware of plans that claim to sell miracle products or promise enormous earnings. Just because a promoter of a plan makes a claim doesn't mean it's true! Ask the promoter of the plan to substantiate claims with hard evidence.

- Beware of shills—"decoy" references paid by a plan's promoter to describe their fictional success in earning money through the plan.

- Don't pay or sign any contracts in an "opportunity meeting" or any other high-pressure situation. Insist on taking your time to think over a decision to join. Talk it over with your with someone you trust such as your parents, a knowledgeable adult friend, an accountant, or lawyer.

- Do your homework! Check with your local Better Business Bureau and state Attorney General about any plan you're considering—especially when the claims about the product or your potential earnings seem too good to be true.

Take This Scheme And Stuff It: Avoiding Envelope-Stuffing Rip-Offs

$550 to $3,000 weekly. Ten dollars for each circular you mail...Free Postage...Free Circulars...No Newspaper Ads...No Magazine Ads...No Bulletin Board Ads! Paychecks mailed to you every week! Advance paycheck forms included in your package!!

Sound familiar? Of course. Ads for envelope-stuffing "opportunities" seem to be everywhere—from your mailbox to your newspaper to your e-mail inbox. Promoters usually advertise that, for a "small" fee, they will tell you how to earn big money stuffing envelopes at home. They claim that they'll pay you a certain amount of money for each envelope stuffed, resulting in hundreds or thousands of dollars for you each week.

These ads may seem appealing, especially if you are looking for a home-based business. But according to the Federal Trade Commission (FTC), the nation's consumer protection agency, ads like these don't tell the whole story because the promoters aren't really offering a job.

Instead, say FTC attorneys, after you send your money, you're likely to get a letter telling you to place the same "envelope-stuffing" ad in newspapers or magazines, or to send the ad to friends and relatives. The only way you'll earn money is if people respond to your ad; in fact, the government says, the promoters themselves rarely pay anyone.

If you're tempted by an envelope stuffing "opportunity," here are some questions to ask the promoters before you send any money or sign up to receive more information:

- Who will pay me?
- When will I get my first paycheck?
- Will I be paid a salary or will my pay be based on commission?
- What tasks will I have to perform?
- What is the total cost of the envelope-stuffing program, including supplies, equipment, and membership fees? What will I get for my money?

The answers to these questions may help you determine whether an envelope-stuffing opportunity is appropriate for your circumstances and whether it's legitimate. It also may help to check out the company with your local consumer protection agency, state Attorney General, and the Better Business Bureau in the community where the company is located as well as the community where you live. These organizations can tell you whether they have received complaints about the promotion that interests you.

What Is A Pyramid Scheme?

By Reem Heakal. "What Is a Pyramid Scheme" is reprinted with permission from Investopedia ULC. © 2008 Investopedia.com.

A pyramid scheme is a fraudulent investing plan that has unfortunately cost many people worldwide their hard-earned savings. The concept behind the pyramid scheme is simple and should be easy to identify; however, it is often presented to potential investors in a disguised or slightly altered form. For this reason, it is important to not only understand how pyramid schemes work, but also to be familiar with the many different shapes and sizes they can take.

The Scheme

As its name indicates, the pyramid scheme is structured like a pyramid. It starts with one person—the initial recruiter—who is on top, at the apex of the pyramid. This person recruits a second person, who is required to "invest" $100 which is paid to the initial recruiter. In order to make his or her money back, the new recruit must recruit more people under him or her, each of whom will also have to invest $100. If the recruit gets ten more people to invest, this person will make $900 with just a $100 investment.

The ten new people become recruiters and each one is in turn required to enlist an additional ten people, resulting in a total of 100 more people. Each of those 100 new recruits is also obligated to pay $100 to the person who recruited him or her; recruiters get a profit of all of the money received minus the initial $100 paid to the person who recruited them. The process continues until the base of the pyramid is no longer strong enough to support the upper structure (meaning there are no more recruits).

The Fraud

The problem is that the scheme cannot go on forever because there is a finite number of people who can join the scheme (even if all the people in the world join). People are deceived into believing that by giving money they will make more money ("with an investment of just $100, you will receive $900 in return"). But no wealth has been created; no product has been sold; no investment has been made; and no service has been provided.

The fraud lies in the fact that it is impossible for the cycle to sustain itself, so people will lose their money somewhere down the line. Those who are most vulnerable are those towards the bottom of the pyramid, where it becomes impossible to recruit the number of people required to pay off the previous layer of recruiters. This kind of fraud is illegal in the Unites States and most countries throughout the world. It is estimated that 90% of people who get involved in a pyramid scheme will lose their money.

☞ Remember!!

It is easy to see how a pyramid scheme can work, but participating in it (regardless of the form in which it is presented) involves deception and fraud because not everyone will receive the money that is promised in return.

As with any other investment plan you consider entering, it is important to ask the right questions. How will this money be invested? What is the rate of return? Who will be investing it? Talk to professionals and do your research before placing your money anywhere. And always remember that if a plan promises you'll get rich quick with no risk or doesn't tell you how your money will be invested, you should raise a red flag and exercise caution before getting on board.

Source: From "What Is a Pyramid Scheme," reprinted with permission from Investopedia ULC. © 2008 Investopedia.com.

Fraud Disguised

Because people are attracted to the idea of making a quick buck with very little effort, many different forms of disguised pyramid schemes have succeeded in fooling people. Despite the illusion of legality presented by these revamped schemes, they are still illegal. It is thus important to recognize the characteristics of such so-called investment plans.

Many schemes will adopt the guise of gift-giving or loans that take place in investment clubs because none of these activities are technically illegal. However, the practice of donating a gift (tax free up to $12,000 in the U.S.) to someone (the recruiter), then having to recruit people into the club in order to receive a return on your investment (or your gift, rather) is essentially a pyramid scheme in disguise.

Multi-Level Marketing (MLM)

Legal multi-level marketing (MLM) involves being recruited in order to sell a product or service that actually has some inherent value. As a recruit, you can make a profit from the sales of the product or service, so you don't necessarily have to recruit more salespeople below you. And while you may be encouraged to recruit other salespeople whose sales would give you more profit, you can stick to just selling the product directly to the consumer if you choose.

A pyramid scheme MLM, however, will most likely sell a product with no independent value. The product could take the form of reports of some kind, for example, or mailing lists. In this kind of pyramid scheme, you would be required to recruit new members into the MLM in order to make a profit and keep the MLM alive. Joining the MLM is the only reason anyone would buy the products sold by this pyramid scheme.

Ponzi Schemes

Named after Charles Ponzi, who ran such a plot from 1919–1920, the Ponzi scheme is a fraudulent investment plan. It is not necessarily a pyramid, which is hierarchical. In a Ponzi scheme, there is one person who takes people's money as an "investment" and does not necessarily tell them how their returns will be generated. As such, the people's return on investment could be generated by anything; it could come from money taken from new investors—which means new investors essentially pay off the old investors—or even from money made by gambling in Las Vegas.

Chain Letters

Chain letters can be received electronically or through snail mail and are not illegal on their own. However, they take on the form of a pyramid scheme when the letter asks you to donate a certain amount of money (even just $0.05) to the people on a list, then delete the name of the first person on the list, add your name, and forward the letter to a certain number of other people. The next people receiving the letter are then asked to do the same thing, so that you can receive your money as well. By forwarding the letter, you are asking people to give money with the promise of making money.

Chapter 39

Avoid Modeling Scams

What could be more flattering? Someone approaches you at the mall and says, "You could be a model. You've got the 'look' we're after. Here's my card. Give me a call to set up an appointment." People have always said you're good looking. Now, visions of glamour, travel, and money flash before your eyes.

It's true that some successful models have been discovered in everyday places like malls, boutiques, clubs, and airports. But the vast majority of would-be models knock on door after agency door before work comes their way.

It's All An Act

If and when you make that follow-up appointment, you'll probably find yourself in an office filled with lots of other model and actor hopefuls. Then the spiel starts. What you thought was a job interview with a talent agency turns into a high-pressure sales pitch for modeling or acting classes, or for "screen tests" or "photo shoots" that can range in price from several hundred to several thousand dollars.

Man, woman, or child—it makes no difference to bogus model and talent scouts. Often, these scouts are after one thing—your money—and will

About This Chapter: "If You've Got The Look, Look Out! Avoiding Modeling Scams," Federal Trade Commission (www.ftc.gov), May 1999. Despite the older date of this document, the cautions it provides are still pertinent.

say just about anything to get it. But what they say isn't always what they mean.

What They Say Vs. What They Mean

Unscrupulous model and talent scouts have their acts down pat. Listen carefully to read between their lines.

"We're scouting for people with your 'look' to model and act."

I need to sign up as many people as possible. My commission depends on it.

"Your deposit is totally refundable."

Your deposit is refundable only if you meet very strict refund conditions.

"You must be specially selected for our program. Our talent experts will carefully evaluate your chances at success in the field and will only accept a few people into our program."

We take almost everyone.

"There's a guaranteed refund if you're not accepted into the program."

Everyone's accepted into the program. Forget the refund.

"You can't afford our fees? No problem. You can work them off with the high-paying jobs we'll get you."

We demand payment, whether or not you get work.

"Commissions from our clients are our major source of income."

Our income comes from the fees we charge you.

Pose-itioning Yourself

To break into the business, you—the talent—need professional photos. There are two types of standard photographs—a "head shot" and a "composite card."

> ### ✔ Quick Tip
> ### Talent Tips
>
> • Steer clear of modeling companies that require you to use a specific photographer. Compare fees and the work quality of several photographers.
>
> • Be suspicious if a company requires an up-front fee to serve as your agent.
>
> • Be cautious if the school has a special referral relationship with a specific modeling agency. The two could be splitting your fees, or the agency may not be suited to your needs.

• The typical marketing tool for an actor, experienced or not, is the head shot, usually an 8" x 10" black and white photo of the face, with your resume printed on the back.

• A "comp card," the typical marketing tool for the experienced model or the wannabe, usually features several shots on the same sheet, showing off the talent in different attire or settings.

Agencies and schools offer separate and distinct services. Make sure you know the difference.

• Modeling (or talent) agencies secure employment for experienced models and actors. Some agents require that you sign up exclusively with them; others may allow you to register with them as well as with other agencies in town.

• Modeling and acting schools claim to provide instruction—for a fee— in poise, posture, diction, skin care, make-up application, the proper walk, and more. Modeling schools do not necessarily act as agents or find work for you—after you take their classes, you may be on your own.

Avoiding A Model Rip-Off

• Ask yourself, "why me?" Don't let your emotions—and the company's flattery—take control. Think carefully and critically about how you were approached: if it was in a crowded mall, think how many others also may have been approached.

• Avoid high-pressure sales tactics. Never sign a document without reading and understanding it first. In fact, ask for a blank copy of the contract to take home and review with someone you trust. If the company refuses, walk away.

- Be leery of companies that only accept payment in cash or by money order. Read it as a strong signal that the company is more interested in your money than your career.

- Be wary of claims about high salaries. Successful models in small markets can earn $75 to $150 an hour, but the work is irregular.

- Ask for the names, addresses, and phone numbers of models and actors who have secured successful work—recently—based on the company's training.

✔ **Quick Tip**
Where To
Complain

If you've think you've been scammed by a bogus model or talent scout, contact your local consumer protection agency, state Attorney General, or Better Business Bureau. They're in your local directory assistance.

- Check out client claims. If an agency says it has placed models and actors in specific jobs, contact the companies to verify that they've hired models and actors from the agency.

- Be skeptical of local companies claiming to be the "biggest" agency or a "major player" in the industry, especially if you live in a smaller city or town.

- Realize that different parts of the country have different needs. For example, New York is recognized for fashion modeling; the Washington/Baltimore area is known for industrial or training films.

- Ask if the company/school is licensed or bonded, if that's required by your state. Verify this information with the appropriate authorities, such as your local consumer protection agency or state Attorney General. Make sure the license is current.

- Ask your local Better Business Bureau, consumer protection agency and state Attorney General if there are any unresolved consumer complaints on file about the company.

- Get everything in writing, including any promises that have been made orally.

- Keep copies of all important papers, such as your contract and company literature, in a safe place.

Chapter 40

Travel Fraud: Avoiding A Spring Break Bust

Avoid A School Break Bust

Planning a school break trip? A sunny beach? A foreign country? Skiing? If you're using a special tour package, you may think everything's taken care of. How sure are you?

Before you show up at the airport with your boogie board, passport, or skis, review the tour package carefully and investigate the operator. Lots of students don't get the trip they expect; others lose out completely. They didn't take the time to carefully read the fine print, evaluate the promotion, and make sure it's not run by a fly-by-night company peddling a first-class scam.

Flights for many school break trips are by public charter, which have different rules than commercial flights. Before you dot the "i"s and cross the "t"s on your contract, do some homework and take a good look at the package. The Federal Trade Commission (FTC) and the American Society of Travel Agents (ASTA) offer the following tips and information to help you avoid a school break bust.

About This Chapter: This chapter includes "Avoid a School Break Bust," July 1999, and "Telemarketing Travel Fraud," August 2000, Federal Trade Commission (www.ftc.gov). Despite the older date of these documents, the cautions provided are still pertinent.

✔ Quick Tip
How To Gear Up For A Great Trip

Whether you're off to see the sights, ski the slopes, or sunbathe on the sand, it pays to be an informed travel shopper. To help you avoid vacation frustration, the Federal Trade Commission (FTC), the nation's consumer protection agency, offers these tips.

- Buy your vacation package from a business you have confidence in. Ask family and friends to recommend a company with a good track record. Think twice if you can't get a person on the phone to answer your questions or if the ad doesn't give the company's street address. Contact the state Attorney General, consumer protection agency and Better Business Bureau where you live and where the company is based to see if there is a history of complaints on file.

- Be on the alert for the telltale signs of a travel scam. Unsolicited faxes or e-mails for deeply discounted travel packages promise the world. But the fraudsters behind these offers will leave you at the gate.

- Verify and clarify. Call to verify your reservations and arrangements. Get the details behind vague promises that you'll be staying at a "five-star" resort or sailing on a "luxury" cruise ship. When you have the names, addresses, and telephone numbers of the airlines, car rental companies, and hotels you'll be using, confirm all arrangements for yourself.

- Put it on paper. Get the details of your vacation in writing. Get a copy of the company's cancellation and refund policies, and ask "What if...?" Consider whether some form of travel cancellation insurance may be appropriate.

- Use a credit card to make your purchase. If you don't get what you paid for, you may be able to dispute the charges with your credit card company. However, don't give your account number to any business until you've verified that it is reputable.

- Avoid a travel club flub. Ask questions before joining a travel club. Sometimes, a "free trial" membership can result in unauthorized charges on your credit card. Find out what you'll get for your money and how you can cancel.

- Won a "free" vacation? Not so fast. Scam artists may tell you you've won a "free" vacation, but then claim to need your credit card number for "verification." Tell 'em to take a hike. If the promotion is legit, you never need to pay for a prize.

Source: "Travel Tips: How to Gear Up for a Great Trip," Federal Trade Commission (www.ftc.gov), February 2006.

- **Check Out The Operator:** Avoid high-pressure sales pitches for a school break package. Ask the operator to send you information about the business and the names of satisfied customers. Ask friends who have used the operator about their experience. Check with local travel agents to see if they know if the operator is legitimate, or call ASTA's Consumer Affairs Department (703-739-8739). If the trip involves a charter flight, call the Department of Transportation (DOT) Public Charter Licensing Division (202-366-2396) to make sure the charter operator has properly filed to operate charter flights from your departure city to your destination. Charter packages cannot be sold until the charter filing is approved by the DOT.

- **Read The Fine Print:** Get a copy of the operator/participant contract. This will tell you the conditions under which the operator can change flight schedules (usually charters can be canceled for any reason by the operator up until ten days before the trip), hotel accommodations (operators may put you up in an alternate hotel listed in the operator contract that is not as nice as the hotel advertised in the package materials), and the rules and penalties for cancellation. Ask about cancellation insurance. Rules state that an operator cannot ask for or accept your payment until you have signed and returned the contract.

- **Understand Your Rights:** According to DOT rules, you have a right to cancel a charter package without penalty if the operator makes a "major change." Major changes include a change of departure or return date or city, a hotel substitution to a property not named in the charter operator/participant contract, or a package price increase of more than ten percent.

- **Pay By Credit Card:** It gives you more protection than cash or a check. If you pay by check for a charter package, make sure it is payable to an escrow account (as required by federal law for charters) and call the bank handling the escrow account to verify its validity. Be wary of charter operators who are reluctant to provide escrow bank information—they may be selling another firm's space—or who tell you they'll send a courier to pick up your money.

- **Expect Flight Delays:** They're common on charter flights. DOT rules allow for a charter flight to be delayed up to 48 hours if mechanical difficulties occur. And the operator is not obligated to provide alternate transportation or compensate you for your expenses if such a delay occurs. Check the contract to see if the operator will cover any costs (lodging, car rental, etc.) associated with flight delays not related to mechanical difficulties.

Telemarketing Travel Fraud

Hello...you have been specially selected to receive our SPECTACULAR LUXURY DREAM VACATION offer!

Have you ever been tempted to sign up to win a "free" trip at a fair, trade show, or restaurant? If so, you may get a phone call, letter, unsolicited fax, e-mail, or postcard telling you that you've won a vacation. Be careful. It may be a "trip trap." The vacation that you've "won" likely isn't free. And the "bargain-priced" travel package you're offered over the telephone or internet may not fit your idea of luxury.

While some travel opportunities sold over the phone or offered through the mail, internet, or by fax are legitimate, many are scams that defraud consumers out of millions of dollars each month. The word "offer" can be a clue to hidden charges. When you get the phone call, or place the call in response to a postcard, letter, fax or internet ad, you also get a sales pitch for a supposedly luxurious trip—one that you could pay dearly for.

The salesperson may ask for your credit card number to bill your account for the travel package. Once you pay, you receive the details of the "package," which usually include instructions for making trip reservation requests. Your request often must be accompanied by yet another fee. In addition, many offers require you to pay upgrade costs to receive the actual destinations, accommodations, cruises, or dates you were promised. Some offers may require you to pay more for port charges, hotel taxes, or service fees.

See a pattern developing? New charges are being added every step of the way. You may never get your "bargain" trip because your reservations may not be confirmed or because you must comply with hard-to-meet hidden or expensive "conditions."

Telemarketing travel scams usually originate out of "boiler rooms." Skilled salespeople, often with years of experience selling dubious products and services over the phone, pitch travel packages that may sound legitimate, but often are not. These pitches usually include the following characteristics:

- **Oral Misrepresentations:** Particular schemes vary, but all fraudulent telemarketers promise you a "deal" they can't possibly deliver. Unfortunately, you won't know it until your money's gone.

- **High Pressure/Time Pressure Tactics:** Scam operators often say they need your commitment to buy immediately or that the offer won't be available much longer. They typically brush aside questions or concerns with vague answers or assurances.

- **"Affordable" Offers:** Unlike fraudulent telemarketers who try to persuade people to spend thousands of dollars on an investment scheme, fraudulent travel telemarketers usually pitch club membership or vacation offers in a lower price range. The offers sound reasonable and are designed to appeal to anyone who is looking for a getaway.

- **Contradictory Follow-up Material:** Some companies may agree to send you written confirmation of your deal. However, it usually bears little resemblance to the offer you accepted over the phone. The written materials often disclose additional terms, conditions, and costs.

How To Protect Yourself

Unpleasant surprises can ruin a vacation, especially when they cost money. That's why it pays to investigate a travel package before you buy. But it can be difficult to tell a legitimate sales pitch from a fraudulent one. Consider these travelers' advisories:

- Be wary of "great deals" and low-priced offers. Few legitimate businesses can afford to give away products and services of real value or substantially undercut other companies' prices.

- Don't be pressured into buying. A good offer today usually will be a good offer tomorrow. Legitimate businesses don't expect you to make snap decisions.

- Ask detailed questions. Find out exactly what the price covers and what it doesn't. Ask about additional charges. Get the names of the hotel, airports, airlines and restaurants included in your package. Consider contacting these businesses directly to verify arrangements. Ask about cancellation policies and refunds. If the salesperson can't give you detailed answers, hang up.

- If you decide to buy, find out the name of the travel provider—the company that is getting your reservations and tickets. This company usually is not the telemarketer.

- Get all information in writing before you agree to buy. Once you receive the written information, make sure it reflects what you were told over the phone and the terms you agreed to.

- Don't buy part of the package—the air fare or hotel stay—separately from the rest. If the deal is not what you expected, it may be difficult to get your money back for the part of the package you purchased.

> ✔ **Quick Tip**
> **Where To Complain**
>
> Several organizations can provide additional information and help you with complaints. Your state Attorney General or the Attorney General in the state where the company is located probably has a division that deals with consumer protection issues.
>
> The American Society of Travel Agents, Consumer Affairs, at 1101 King Street, Alexandria, VA 22314, may be able to mediate your dispute with an ASTA member.

- Don't give your credit card number or bank information over the phone unless you know the company. One easy way for a scam operator to close a deal is to get your credit card number and charge your account. Sometimes fraudulent telemarketers say they need the number for verification purposes only. Don't believe them.

- Don't send money by messenger or overnight mail. Some scam artists may ask you to send them a check or money order immediately. Others may offer to send a messenger to pick up your payment. If you pay with cash or a check, rather than a credit card, you lose your right to dispute fraudulent charges under the Fair Credit Billing Act. If you charged your trip to a credit card, you may dispute the charges by writing to your credit card issuer at the address provided for billing disputes. If possible, do this as soon as you receive your statement. In any case, the law gives you up to 60 days after the bill's statement date to dispute the charge.

- Check out the company before you buy. Contact the Attorney General in your state or where the company is located to see if any complaints have been lodged against the travel firm or the travel provider. Be aware that fraudulent businesses often change their names to avoid detection.

- If in doubt, say "no." Trust your instincts. It's less risky to turn down the offer and hang up the phone.

Chapter 41

Gambling: Don't Bet On Winning

It doesn't take a math whiz to know that if you gamble—if you play poker with your friends, get your big sis to buy you a lottery ticket, or make a bet on your favorite basketball team—you're probably going to end up losing money.

After all, gambling is a multibillion-dollar industry—they're raking it in, not giving it away. Why do you think your bookie is taking your bets instead of placing his own?

"Say you bet $100," says Drew, who started gambling on sports when he was 14 and taking his friends' bets at 16. "If you win, you win $100. But if you lose, you can lose $110 to $125, depending on the juice the book wants to charge. And if you bet and win that $100, most likely you are going to roll that over into some other bets. I have never seen someone win more than they lose."

A Losing Prospect

OK, Drew isn't dumb, and neither are most teens. But millions of them still gamble every year. A study by the University of Florida shows that most people have placed bets by the time they reach their 12th birthday—that's earlier than the age most people first try drinking or smoking cigarettes. Between half and three-quarters of underage teens—about seven million nationwide— gamble. They know the odds are stacked against them. So why do they keep throwing their hard-earned cash down the drain?

Drew, who plays basketball, thinks athletes and other competitive kids bet on sports because it makes the game more exciting for them—almost like the rush they get when they're playing. Plus, they see their friends doing it, and they don't always get the straight story on how tough it can be. "You rarely ever hear of the guys going to pay the book money," he says, "but they will always tell you of the time they went to collect their money from the book."

Most people can gamble for fun and never have a problem with it. It helps if you're "legal," of course—check the laws where you live, but in most states it's 18 or 21, depending on the type of game you're playing. (Also, if you're not sticking to state-sanctioned gambling, like in casinos—if you're placing bets with a bookie—you're participating in a criminal enterprise and could be arrested!) Chad, for example, lost $40 on a scratch-off lottery ticket on his 18th birthday, and now occasionally bets $10 or $20 on darts. He'll never have a problem, he says, because he hates losing so much he'll never bet more money than that.

Not Just Fun And Games

Many teens do have a problem, though. Four percent of the teens in

> ### ♣ It's A Fact!!
>
> Here are reasons experts say people gamble:
>
> - **Everyone Else Is Doing It:** Even Mom, Dad, and Principal Skinner! Gambling is pretty socially acceptable these days. Some schools even sponsor events like after-prom casino nights. And most people start gambling with their families.
>
> - **The Self-Esteem Boost:** Everyone loves a winner, and sometimes even losers feel cool when they're waving around $20 bills.
>
> - **Escape From Other Problems:** Like drugs and alcohol, gambling can offer a temporary reprieve from depression or just a way to take your mind off your parent's divorce or your recent breakup.

the Florida study were problem, or pathological, gamblers, and that can be as much of a problem as drug or alcohol addiction. And it can happen to anyone. The average teen who has problems with gambling is super-smart, involved in lots of activities, successful, and motivated—at least until the addiction starts to get in the way. Then, the person's likely to stop being interested in friends or activities, sell a prized CD collection to get more cash, or suddenly become moody, tired, and angry.

✔ Quick Tip

If you think you or a friend might have a problem with gambling, there are ways to get help. Check out the National Council on Problem Gambling website (http://www.ncpgambling.org), or call its help line at 800-522-4700. Because really, there are lots of better ways to spend your hard-earned dough!

Part Six

If You Need More Information

Chapter 42

Online Money Management Tools

Calculators

Alliance for Investor Education (AIE)
Savings Calculator
Website: http://www.investoreducation.org/cindex2.cfm

Bankrate.com
Mortgage, Auto, Credit Card, Home Equity, Investment, Retirement, Personal Finance, Savings, and Tax Calculators
Website: http://www.bankrate.com/brm/rate/calc_home.asp

Bureau of the Public Debt
Growth, Savings, and Tax Advantage Calculators
Website: http://www.treasurydirect.gov/indiv/tools/tools_estimationcalc.htm

Calculators—Financial.com
Home Financing, Personal Financing, Investment, Retirement, and Lease Calculators
Website: http://calculators-financial.com

About This Chapter: The websites in this chapter are listed in alphabetical order. Inclusion on this list does not mean endorsement. All websites were verified in July of 2008.

CCH Financial Planning

Mortgage, Credit Cards and Debt, Investment, Tax, Personal Finance, Loan, Automobile, Retirement Savings, Savings, and Business Calculators
Website: http://www.finance.cch.com/tools/calcs.asp

Choose to Save

American Savings Education Council (ASEC)
Auto, Bond, Budget, College, Credit Card, Home, Insurance, Life Expectancy, Mutual Funds, Paycheck Planning, Retiree Health, Retirement, Roth IRA, Savings, Social Security, Stock, and Tax Calculators
Website: http://www.asec.org/tools/ycalcs.htm

Consumer and Family Economics

University of Illinois Extension
Credit Card and Savings Calculators
Website: http://www.ace.uiuc.edu/cfe/calculators.html

Credit Union National Association, Inc.

Mortgage, Auto, Savings, and Loans Calculators
Website: http://cucalc.cuna.org

FinAid

College Costs and Savings, Integrated Saving/Borrowing, Trust Funds, Needs Analysis, Loans, Budgeting, and Insurance Calculators
Website: http://www.finaid.org/calculators

Financial Calculators Inc.

Cash Flow, College, Credit, Home and Mortgage, Tax, Insurance, Paycheck and Benefits, Qualified Plans, Retirement, Saving, Investment Calculators
Website: http://www.financialcalculators.com

Money Management International

Budget, Auto, and Home Calculators
Website: http://www.moneymanagement.org/FinancialTools

Money Matters To Me
Loan, General Interest, Mortgage, and Repayments Calculators
Website: http://www.moneymatterstome.co.uk/Interactive-Tools

My Money
College Planning, Group Life Insurance, Home Buying, Investing, Mortgage, Saving Bonds, Social Security, Tax Withholding, and Thrift Savings Plan Calculators
Website: http://www.mymoney.gov/calculators.shtml

Smart About Money
National Endowment for Financial Education (NEFE)
Retirement and Mutual Fund Cost Calculator
Website: http://www.smartaboutmoney.org/nefe/pages/content.asp?page=1710#HelpfulTools

U.S. Securities and Exchange Commission
Mutual Fund, Tax Comparison, College Savings, Loan, Savings, Social Security Retirement, Ballpark Estimate Retirement, and 529 College Savings Plan Expense Calculator
Website: http://www.sec.gov/investor/tools.shtml

Wachovia Securities
IRA, Retirement, and Savings Calculators
Website: http://www.agedwards.com

Young Consumers
Loan, Repayments, and Interest Calculator
Website: http://www.gov.im/youngconsumers/tools

Financial Quizzes

Acción
Financial Self Assessment Quiz
Website: http://yourmoney.accion.org/site/c.cqLMI2OGKrF/b.1626171/k.C9B7/Test_Your_Financial_Literacy__Financial_Literacy_Quiz.htm

Centre For Flexible Learning
Financial Terms Quiz
Website: http://cfl-x.uwindsor.ca/artsadmin/quiz/aboutQuiz.html

Florida State University
Fundamental of Financial Planning: Check Your Financial IQ
Website: http://learningforlife.fsu.edu/course/fp101/quiz.htm

Money Management International
The Credit Game Quiz
Website: http://www.moneymanagement.org/FinancialTools/Quizzes/
CreditGame.asp

Rutgers
Financial Fitness, Identity Theft Risk Assessment, Investment Risk
Tolerance, and Personal Resiliency Resources Assessment Quizzes
Website: http://njaes.rutgers.edu/money

Smart About Money
National Endowment for Financial Education (NEFE)
Financial Assessment Quiz
Website: http://www.smartaboutmoney.org/nefe/pages/
content.asp?page=1410

U.S. Securities and Exchange Commission (SEC)
Test Your Money $marts Quiz
Website: http://www.sec.gov/investor/tools/quiz.htm

Games

Ernest & Young's Moneyopolis
Website: http://www.moneyopolis.com

Investopedia Simulator
Website: http://simulator.investopedia.com

It All Adds Up
Website: http://www.italladdsup.org

LavaMind's Gazillionaire
Website: http://www.gazillionaire.com

NEFE High School Financial Planning Program
Success Street Game
Website: http://hsfpp.nefe.org/students/
channels.cfm?chid=53&tid=3&deptid=15

Planet Orange
Website: http://www.orangekids.com

Stock Market Game
Foundation for Investor Education
Website: http://www.smg2000.org

Stock-Trak
Website: http://www.stocktrak3.com

StocksQuest.com
Website: http://investsmart.coe.uga.edu/C001759/stocksquest/
mystocks.htm

Virtual Stock Exchange
Website: http://www.virtualstockexchange.com

Chapter 43

Resources For Financial Information

Budgeting and Financial Information

American Bankers Association
1120 Connecticut Avenue, N.W.
Washington, DC 20036
Toll-Free: 800-BANKERS
(226-5377)
Phone: 202-663-5000
Fax: 202-663-7543
Website: http://www.aba.com

**American Financial Services
Association (AFSA)
Education Foundation**
919 18th Street, N.W.
Washington, DC 20006
Phone: 202-466-8611
Fax: 202-223-0321
Website: http://www.afsaef.org
E-mail: info@afsaef.org

**American Institute of
Certified Public Accountants**
Personal Financial Planning
Division
1211 Avenue of the Americas
New York, NY 10036
Toll-Free: 888-777-7077
Website: http://www.aicpa.org or
http://www.360financialliteracy.org

**American Savings Education
Council**
1100 13th Street, N.W., Suite 875
Washington, DC 20005
Phone: 202-659-0670
Fax: 202-775-6312
Website: http://www.asec.org
E-mail: info@asec.org

About This Chapter: The organizations in this chapter are listed alphabetically by topic.
All contact information was verified in July of 2008.

Asset Builders of America

1213 North Sherman Ave., Suite 195
Madison, WI 53704
Toll-Free: 866-3040-6896
Phone: 608-663-6332
Fax: 608-441-6902
Website: http://
www.assetbuilders.org
E-mail: info@assetbuilders.org

Bloomberg News Service

Phone: 212-318-2000
Fax: 917-369-5000
Website: http://www.bloomberg.com

Certified Financial Planner Board of Standards

Communication and Consumer
Services
1425 K Street, N.W., Suite 500
Washington, DC 20005
Toll-Free: 800-487-1497
Phone: 202-379-2299
Fax: 202-379-2299
Website: http://www.CFP-Board.org
E-mail: mail@cfp-board.org

Choose To Save

American Savings Education
Council
1100 13th Street, N.W., Suite 875
Washington, DC 20005
Phone: 202-659-0670
Fax: 202-775-6312
Website: http://www.choosetosave.org
E-mail: info@choosetosave.org

Cooperative State Research, Education, and Extension Service

U.S. Department of Agriculture
Cooperative State Research,
Education, and Extension Service
800 9th Street S.W.
Washington, DC 20024
Phone: 202-720-4423
Website: http://
www.csrees.usda.gov

Federal Citizen Information Center

Toll-Free: 800-FED-INFO
(333-4636)
Website: http://www.pueblo.gsa.gov

Federal Deposit Insurance Corporation (FDIC)

Phone: 877-ASK-FDIC (275-3342)
TDD: 800-925-4618
Website: http://www.fdic.gov

Federal Reserve Education

Website: http://
www.federalreserveeducation.org

Federal Trade Commission

Consumer Response Center
600 Pennsylvania Avenue, N.W.
Washington, DC 20580
Toll-Free: 877-382-4357
TDD/TTY: 866-653-4261
Website: http://www.ftc.gov

Financial Literacy Two Thousand and Ten

Website: http://www.fl2010.org

Financial Planning Association

4100 E. Mississippi Avenue
Suite 400
Denver, CO 80246-3053
Toll free: 800-647-6340
or 800-322-4237
Fax: 303-759-0749
Website: http://www.fpanet.org
E-mail: fpa@fpanet.org

InCharge Education Foundation

2101 Park Center Dr. Suite 310
Orlando FL 32835
Phone: 407-291-7770
Website: http://
www.inchargefoundation.org

Institute for Financial Literacy

P.O. Box 1842
Portland, ME 04104
Toll-Free: 866-662-4932
Phone: 207-221-3600
TTY: 866-662-4937
Fax: 207-221-3691
Website: http://
www.financiallit.org

Internal Revenue Service (IRS)

General Information: 800-829-1040
Automated Refund Information:
800-829-4477
Taxpayer Advocate Service:
877-777-4778
TDD Toll-Free: 800-829-4059
Website: http://www.irs.gov

Iowa State University Cooperative Extension

2150 Beardshear Hall
Ames, IA 50011-2046
Phone: 515-294-6675
Fax: 515-294-4715
Website: http://
www.extension.iastate.edu/finances

Jump$tart Coalition for Personal Financial Literacy

919 18th Street, N.W., Suite 300
Washington, DC 20006
Toll-Free: 888-45-EDUCATE
(453-382289)
Fax: 202-223-0321
Website: http://www.jumpstart.org
E-mail: info@jumpstartcoalition.org

Junior Achievement, Inc.

JA Worldwide
1 Education Way
Colorado Springs, CO 80906
Phone: 719-540-8000
Fax: 719-540-6299
Website: http://www.ja.org

Kiplinger
1729 H Street N.W.
Washington, DC 20006
Phone: 202-887-6426
Website: http://
www.kiplinger.com

MoneyCentral
Website: http://
moneycentral.msn.com/home.asp

MoneyWi$e
Website: http://
www.money-wise.org

Morningstar
Phone: 312-384-4000
Website: http://
www.morningstar.com

Motley Fool
2000 Duke Street, 4th Floor
Alexandria, VA 22314
Phone: 703-838-3665
Fax: 703-254-1999
Website: http://www.fool.com

Myvesta
P.O. Box 8587
Gaithersburg, MD 20898-8587
Website: http://www.dca.org

National Association of Personal Financial Advisors
3250 North Arlington Heights Rd.
Suite 109
Arlington Heights, IL 60004
Toll-Free: 800-366-2732
Phone: 847-483-5400
Fax: 847-483-5415
Website: http://www.napfa.org
E-mail: info@napfa.org

National Council on Economic Education
1140 Avenue of the Americas
Suite 202
New York, NY 10036
Toll-Free: 800-338-1192
Phone: 212-730-7007
Fax: 212-730-1793
Website: http://www.ncee.net
E-mail: info@ncee.net

National Endowment for Financial Education
5299 DTC Boulevard, Suite 1300
Greenwood Village, CO 80111
Phone: 303-741-6333
Website: http://www.nefe.org

Native Financial Education Coalition
Website: http://www.nfec.info

Office of Financial Education
U.S. Treasury Department
Website: http://www.treas.gov

Operation Hope: Banking on Our Future

Website: http://www.operationhope.org

Practical Money Skills

Website: http://www.practicalmoneyskills.com

Profit Sharing/401(k) Society of America

20 N. Wacker Drive, Suite 3700
Chicago, IL 60606
Phone: 312-419-1863
Website: http://www.401k.org

Rutgers Cooperative Extension

Website: http://www.investing.rutgers.edu

Securities Industry and Financial Markets Association Foundation for Investor Education (SIFMA)

120 Broadway, 35th Floor
New York, NY 10271-0080
Phone: 212-313-1200
Fax: 212-313-1301
Website: http://www.sifma.org

Society of Financial Service Professionals

17 Campus Boulevard, Suite 201
Newtown Square, PA 19073-3230
Phone: 610-526-2500
Fax: 610-527-1499
Website: http://www.financialpro.org

Sovereign Bank's KidsBank.com

Website: http://www.kidsbank.com

Standard and Poor's

55 Water Street
New York, NY 10041
Phone: 212-438-1000
or 212-438-2000
Website: http://www.standardandpoors.com

U.S. Financial Literacy and Education Commission

Website: http://www.mymoney.gov

U.S. Securities and Exchange Commission

100 F Street, N.E.
Washington, DC 20549
Phone: 202-942-8088
Website: http://www.sec.gov
E-mail: help@sec.gov

U.S. Treasury's Page for Kids

Website: http://www.treas.gov/kids

USAA Educational Foundation
Website: http://
www.usaaedfoundation.org

Wi$eUp
JFK Federal Building
Government Center, Room 525 A
Boston, MA 02203
Phone: 800-827-5335
Phone: 617-565-1988
Website: http://
wiseupwomen.tamu.edu

Consumer Information and Insurance

American Council of Life Insurers
101 Constitution Ave. N.W., Suite 700
Washington, DC 20001-2133
Phone: 202-624-2000
Toll free: 800-942-4242
Fax: 202-624-2319
Website: http:www.acli.com

Consumer Action
717 Market Street, Suite 310
San Francisco, CA 94103
Phone: 415-777-9635
or 213-624-8327
Fax: 415-777-5267
Website: http://
www.consumer-action.org
E-mail: info@consumer-action.org

Consumer Checkbook
1625 K Street, N.W., 8th Floor
Washington, DC 20006
Toll-Free: 800-213-7283
Website: http://www.checkbook.org

Consumer Debit Resource
AboutChecking and Education
Consumer Outreach
C/O 4900 N Scottsdale Road
Suite 1000
Scottsdale, AZ 85251
Toll-Free: 800-428-9623
Fax: 602-659-2197
Website: http://
www.consumerdebit.com

Consumer Federation of America

1620 I Street, N.W., Suite 200
Washington, DC 20006
Phone: 202-387-6121
Website: http://
www.consumerfed.org
E-mail: cfa@consumerfed.org

Consumer Reports Online

Website: http://
www.consumerreports.org

Consumer World

Website: http://
www.consumerworld.org

Institute of Consumer Financial Education's Children and Money

Website: http://
www.financial-education-icfe.org/
children_and_money/index.asp

Insurance Information Institute

110 William Street
New York, NY 10038
Phone: 212-346-5500
Website: http://www.iii.org

National Consumer Law Center, Inc.

Website: http://
www.consumerlaw.org

National Consumers League

1701 K Street, N.W., Suite 1200
Washington, DC 20006
Phone: 202-835-3323
Fax: 202-835-0747
Website: http://www.nclnet.org
E-mail: info@nclnet.org

U.S. Consumer Gateway and Federal Consumer Information Center

Website: http://www.consumer.gov

Credit Reporting and Credit Scoring Agencies and Information

Annual Credit Report Request Service
P. O. Box 105281
Atlanta, GA 30348-5281
Toll-Free: 877-322-8228
Website: https://
www.annualcreditreport.com

CardTrack
Website: http://www.cardtrak.com

Credit Union National Association
P.O. Box 431
Madison, WI 53701-0431
Toll-Free: 800-356-9655
Fax: 608-231-4127
Website: http://www.cuna.org

Equifax
P.O. Box 740241
Atlanta, GA 30374-0241
Toll-Free: 800-685-1111
Website: http://www.equifax.com

Experian
P.O. Box 1017
Allen, TX 75013-0949
Toll-Free: 888-397-3742
Website: http://www.experian.com

Freddie Mac
Credit Smart Program
Website: http://
www.freddiemac.com/creditsmart

National Association of Professional Insurance Agents
400 North Washington Street
Alexandria, VA 22314
Phone: 703-836-9340
Fax: 703-836-1279
Website: http://www.pianet.com
E-mail: web@pianet.org

Springboard Credit Education
Website: http://www.credit.org

TransUnion
P.O. Box 2000
Chester, PA 19022
Toll-Free: 800-916-8800
Website: http://
www.transunion.com

Information about Debt Management, Collection Practices, and Bankruptcy

American Association of Credit and Collection Officials

Website: http://
www.acainternational.org

Borrower Services at the Direct Loan Servicing Center

Federal Student Aid
Toll-Free: 800-848-0979
TTY: 800-848-0983
Website: http://www.dl.ed.gov

Debtors Anonymous

General Service Office
P.O. Box 920888
Needham, MA 02492-0009
Phone: 781-453-2743
Fax: 781-435-2745
Website: http://
www.debtorsanonymous.org
E-mail:
webmaster@debtorsanonymous.org

Direct Loan Consolidation Center

Federal Student Aid
Toll-Free: 800-557-7392
TTY 800-557-7395
Website: http://
www.loanconsolidation.ed.gov

"Don't Borrow Trouble" Campaign

Freddie Mac
Website: http://
www.dontborrowtrouble.com

Gamblers Anonymous

International Service Office
P.O. Box 17173
Los Angeles, CA 90017
Phone: 213-386-8789
Fax: 231-386-0030
Website: http://
www.gamblersanonymous.org
E-mail:
isomain@gamblersanonymous.org

National Foundation for Credit Counseling

801 Roeder Road, Suite 900
Silver Spring, MD 20910
Toll-Free: 800-388-2227
Phone: 301-589-5600
Website: http://www.nfcc.org

U.S. Trustee Program Credit Counseling

Phone: 202-514-4100
Website: http://www.usdoj.gov/ust
E-mail: ust.cc.help@usdoj.gov

Index

Index

Page numbers that appear in *Italics* refer to illustrations. Page numbers that have a small 'n' after the page number refer to information shown as Notes at the beginning of each chapter. Page numbers that appear in **Bold** refer to information contained in boxes on that page (except Notes information at the beginning of each chapter).

A

Acción, website address 393
ACH *see* Automated Clearing House
Adams, John **8**
adjusted balance, credit cards **288–89**
advance fee loans, described 263–64
advertisements
 abusive lenders 332–35
 computer purchases 227–28
 hyperlinks **226**
 impulse buying 165–69
 used cars 239–41
 work-at-home schemes 356–61
AFSA *see* American Financial
 Services Association
age factor
 credit cards **284**
 identity theft 348–49
 insurance coverage **147**
 work hours **29**
 work requirements **24, 28**
Alliance for Investor Education,
 website address 391
allowance, overview 19–22
"All That Glitters ... How to Buy
 Jewelry" (FTC) 229n

American Association of Credit and
 Collection Officials, website address
 405
American Bankers Association,
 contact information 397
American Council of Life Insurers,
 contact information 402
American Financial Services
 Association (AFSA), Education
 Foundation, contact information
 397
American Institute of Certified Public
 Accountants, contact information 397
American Savings Education Council,
 contact information 392, 397
America's Charities, website address 158
Annual Credit Report Request Service,
 contact information 404
annual percentage rate (APR)
 automobile purchases 237–38
 cash advances 289
 credit applications 255
 credit cards 285, 291–93
 fixed *versus* variable rate **286**
 payday loans 330
 truth in lending disclosure 276–79

annual percentage yield (APY)
  calculations 68
  defined 72
  described 68–69
Annuit Coeptis 8
APR *see* annual percentage rate
APY *see* annual percentage yield
as is sale, used vehicles 210
Asset Builders of America, contact
  information 398
Association of Young Latino
  Entrepreneurs, website address 50
ATM *see* automated teller machines
ATM cards
  checking accounts 132–34
  described 90–91
  fraudulent use 338–39
  identity theft 350
  purchases 183
  savings accounts 118
  see also debit cards
"Auction Guides: Not So Hot
  Properties" (FTC) 237n
auctions
  used car purchases 241–42
  used vehicles 242
Automated Clearing House (ACH)
  payment options 185
  website address 190
automated teller machines (ATM)
  checking accounts 124, 131–33
  deposits 137–38
  described 91
  savings accounts 118
automatic deposit
  described 119
  savings accounts 118–19
automobile insurance *see* insurance
  coverage
automobile purchases
  loans *versus* leases 305
  other costs 238
  overview 237–42
  service contracts 208–14
"Auto Service Contracts" (FTC) 201n
average daily balance, credit cards
  288–89
"Avoid a School Break Bust" (FTC)
  377n

"Avoiding Costly Banking Mistakes: No
  Trivial Pursuit" (FDIC) 101n
"Avoiding Legal Business Hassles" (US
  Small Business Administration) 37n

B

balance
  bank accounts 87–88
  debit cards 101–2
bank accounts
  described 90
  error prevention 101–11
  see also electronic banking
banking mistakes
  overview 101–11
  quick tips 102
bank loans
  checking accounts 122
  entrepreneurs 46
Bank of America, savings accounts
  publication 113n
bankruptcy
  credit records 263
  debt-relief services 261
  defined 324
banks
  described 86
  overview 85–92
  see also electronic banking
bank statements
  checking account review 140
  unauthorized transfers 338
Barton, William 8
Benardo, Michael 349
Better Business Bureau (BBB), Wise
  Giving Alliance Standards for Charity
  Accountability, website address 157
"Big Print. Little Print. What's the
  Deal?" (FTC) 221n
billing errors
  consumer rights 192
  credit cards 294
Bloomberg News Service, contact
  information 398
bonds, defined 72
bonus, defined 59
Borrower Services at the Direct Loan
  Servicing Center, contact information 405

borrowing money
  barriers **274**
  overview 273–82
  repayments **278**
  responsibilities **276–77**
  smart tips **334**
bouncing checks
  described **143**
  extra fees 101–2
Boys and Girls Clubs of America,
  website address 49
Boy Scouts of America, website address 49
budget box system, described 82
budgets
  cell phone plans 215
  computer purchase 222
  credit records 261
  overview 77–84
  shopping strategies **168–69**
"Building Wealth: A Beginner's Guide
  to Securing Your Financial Future"
  (Federal Reserve Bank of Dallas) 321n
Bureau of the Public Debt, website
  address 391
business ownership, investments 74
business plans
  described **39**
  entrepreneurs 43–44
  website address **45**
"Buying A Used Car" (FTC) 237n
buying clubs, overview 243–49
"Buy It Or Not?" (Northwestern Mutual
  Foundation) 165n

C

Calculators - Financial.com, website
  address 391
capacity
  credit decisions 279–80
  loan decisions 302
capital
  credit decisions 280–81
  loan decisions 302
"Car Ads: Reading Between the Lines"
  (FTC) 237n
carats, described 233
  see also karats
CardTrack, website address 404

car loans, overview 305–8
  see also automobile purchases
car purchases see automobile purchases
car title loans 308
cash advances, credit cards 288–90
Castle Works, Inc., shopping information
  publication 171n
CCH Financial Planning, website
  address 392
CD see certificates of deposit
cell phones
  cramming, described **218**
  etiquette **220**
  overview 215–20
Centre For Flexible Learning, website
  address 394
certificates of deposit (CD)
  defined **72**
  described 116
Certified Financial Planner Board of
  Standards, contact information 398
"$$$ Cha-Ching: Money Matters" (US
  Small Business Administration) 37n
chain letters 372
changes of address, identity theft **343**
character
  credit decisions 281–82
  loan decisions 302
charge cards, defined **254**
  see also credit cards; debit cards
Charitable Choices, website address 158
"Charities and Fundraising Phone Fraud"
  (FTC) 351n
charity
  allowances 22
  fundraising phone fraud 353–55
  overview 153–61
  quick tips **154**, **161**
Chase, Salmon P. 9
checkbook, described 128
check-clearing system, described **95**
checking accounts
  accurate balances **143**
  bank loans **122**
  bank statement review **140**
  cash back **138**
  defined **90**
  described 90
  features **125**

checking accounts, continued
  overview 121–44
  reconciliation form sample *142*
  types, described 123–24
  voided checks **130**
checklists
  entrepreneurs 43
  international shopping **182**
check register
  accuracy 103
  described 127–28, 131
  sample form *128*
checks
  purchases 184–85
  sample form *130*
  savings accounts 119
check writing, described 129–31
Choose To Save
  contact information 398
  website address 392
"Choosing a Credit Card"
  (Federal Reserve Board) 283n
chores, allowances **20**
club account, defined **72**
Coinage Act (1792) **10**
coins
  commemoratives **13**
  described 10–14
  faces and backs, listed **14**
  minting process, described **12**
collateral
  credit decisions 282
  described **302**
  loan decisions 302
college
  cost calculator **312**
  education loans 309–18
commemorative coins, described **13**
commission, defined **59**
compensation, defined **59**
complaint letter sample *198*
complaints
  credit card purchases **293**
  credit records 262–63
  mail order buying clubs **249**
  modeling scams **376**
  online shopping 180–81
  shopping strategies 191–200
  work-at-home programs **358**

compound interest
  annual percentage yield 68
  savings accounts **115**, 117
computers
  bill payments 188–89
  personal finance programs 82
  purchase information 221–28
con artists, overview 351–72
Consumer Action, contact
  information 402
Consumer and Family Economics,
  website address 392
Consumer Checkbook, contact
  information 402
Consumer Debit Resource, contact
  information 402
Consumer Federation of America,
  contact information 403
consumer installment loans, described
  273–74
Consumer Reports Online, website
  address 403
Consumer World, website address 403
continuity plans, described 247–50
"Continuity Plans: Coming to
  You Like Clockwork" (FTC)
  243n
contributions *see* charity
Cooling-Off Rule 193–96
Cooperative State Research, Education,
  and Extension Service, contact
  information 398
copyrights, described 41
corporations, described 40
"Costly Coupon Scams" (FTC) 351n
counseling
  credit records 261–63
  entrepreneurs 48
  student loans 312–13
counterfeit currency
  described 5–6, 16–18
  quick tips **17**
Counterfeit Currency Detection
  Act (1992) 17
coupon scams, described 364–66
coverage, defined **146**
cramming, described **218**
Creative Education Foundation,
  website address **42**

credit
    overall costs 275–79
    overview 253–71
    see also borrowing money
"Credit, ATM and Debit Cards:
    What to Do If They're Lost or
    Stolen" (FTC) 337n
credit card payments
    late payments 105–6
    minimum amounts 106–7
    words of advice **106**
credit cards
    age factor **284**
    balance computations **288–89**
    damaged items **293**
    versus debit cards 295–96
    debt management 322–23
    defined **254**
    described 273
    disclosure box sample *292*
    fixed *versus* variable
        rates **286**
    keeping track 258–59
    overview 283–94
    purchases 185–86
    unauthorized transactions **185**
    see also stolen credit cards
credit denial, described **262**
credit history
    bank deposits 86
    entrepreneurs 47
credit reports
    debt management 324–25
    free access 265–71
    identity theft 345
    periodic reviews 108–9
    website address **47**, **266**
credit scores
    described **256**
    new credit cards **108**
credit scoring agencies
    contact information 268, 404
    website address **47**, **266**
Credit Union National
    Association, Inc.
    contact information 404
    website address 392
credit unions, described **86**
cubic Zirconia **234**

currency
    amount in circulation **15**
    circulation process 14–15
    faces and backs, listed **10**
    overview 3–18
    printing process, described **5**

D

daily spending diary *83*, **166**
damaged paper money **16**
Daniels, Kirk 105–6
days in term, described **68**
debit cards
    checking accounts 132–34
    versus credit cards 295–96
    defined **254**
    described 90–91
    fraudulent use 338–39
    purchases 186–88
    savings accounts 118
    unauthorized transactions **185**
    see also ATM cards
debt collection, avoidance **260**
debt management
    overview 321–28
    quick tips **322**, **327**
Debtors Anonymous, contact
    information 405
debt-relief services, fraud **261**
Department of Justice (DOJ)
    see US Department of Justice
deposit accounts, described 90
deposits
    bank accounts 87
    checking accounts 135–39
deposit slips
    bank accounts 87
    cash back **138**
    sample *135*
desktop computers 221–22
diamonds
    imitations **234**
    overview 233–34
diaries, daily spending *83*, **166**
direct deposit
    checking accounts 139
    described 189–90
    savings accounts 118–19

Direct Load Consolidation Center,
  contact information 405
Direct Loan Program 317
disability insurance *see* insurance coverage
dispute resolution
  automobile service contracts 213–14
  jewelry purchase 235–36
  warranties 204–5
dispute resolution programs, consumer
  rights 199
Distributive Education Clubs of
  America, website address 49
diversification, defined **72**
dividends
  described **73**
  tax information 58–59
DOJ *see* US Department of Justice
"Dollars and Cents" (Federal Reserve
  Bank of Atlanta) 3n
donations *see* charity
do not call list 161
"Don't Borrow Trouble" Campaign,
  website address 405
door-to-door sales, consumer rights
  193–96
double-cycle balances, credit cards
  288–89
W.E.B. Dubois Scholars Institute,
  website address 48
dumpster diving, described 342, **343**

E

earning money, overview 23–30
ECOA *see* Equal Credit Opportunity Act
EDIE *see* Electronic Deposit Insurance
  Estimator
Edison, Thomas **13**
education loans
  application process tips **310**
  overview 309–18
EFC *see* expected family contribution
EFT *see* electronic funds transfers
EFTA *see* Electronic Fund Transfer Act
electronic banking
  bill payments 134
  overview 93–99
Electronic Deposit Insurance Estimator
  (EDIE) **88**, 123

electronic funds transfers (EFT)
  described 93–94
  error corrections **96**
Electronic Fund Transfer Act (EFTA)
  94–98, **185**, 337–39
"Electronic Fund Transfers"
  (Federal Reserve Board) 93n
electronic scanning, pricing accuracy
  176–77
employment
  credit reports 271
  internships 31–36
  summer jobs 31–36
endorsement, defined **136**
engraved intaglio steel plate method,
  described **5**
Entrepreneur.com, website address **42**
Entrepreneur Magazine, website address **50**
entrepreneurs, overview 37–50
Entrepreneurship Education, website
  address **42**
Entrepreneur U, website address **50**
envelope stuffing schemes 359, 368–69
E Pluribus Unum **8**
Equal Credit Opportunity Act
  (ECOA) 279
Equifax, contact information 268, 404
equity
  defined **72**
  home loans 274–75
Ernest and Young's Moneyopolis,
  website address 394
expected family contribution (EFC) 310
expense envelope system, described 82–83
expenses
  budgets 78–80
  described **80**
Experian, contact information 268, 404

F

FACT Act *see* Fair and Accurate
  Credit Transactions Act
FAFSA *see* Free Application for
  Federal Student Aid
Fair and Accurate Credit Transactions
  Act (FACT Act) 265, 270
Fair Credit Billing Act (FCBA) **192**, **293**,
  337–38

Fair Credit Reporting Act (FCRA) **47**, 265–71
Fair Isaac score (FICO) **256**
Fair Labor Standards Act (FLSA) **24, 28**
fake check scams, described **352**
FCBA *see* Fair Credit Billing Act
FCRA *see* Fair Credit Reporting Act
FDIC *see* Federal Deposit Insurance Corporation
Federal Bureau of Investigation (FBI)
  Internet Crime Complaint Center **180**
  online fraud publication 179n
Federal Citizen Information Center, contact information 398
Federal Deposit Insurance Corporation (FDIC)
  contact information 398
  publications
    bank information 85n
    banking mistakes 101n
    borrowing basics 273n
    budgets 77n
    car loans 305n
    charge cards 295n
    checking accounts 121n
    education loans 309n
    installment loans 301n
    predatory lending issues 329n
  website address **104**
Federal Family Education Loan (FFEL) 317
federal Pell Grant *see* Pell Grant
Federal Perkins Loans 316–17
Federal Reserve Act 3
Federal Reserve Bank of Atlanta, publications
  currency overview 3n
  website address **18**
Federal Reserve Bank of Chicago, payment options publication 183n
Federal Reserve Bank of Dallas, debt control publication 321n
Federal Reserve Board, publications
  credit card choices 283n
  electronic fund transfers 93n
Federal Reserve Districts
  described **4**
  listed **4**
Federal Reserve Education, website address 398

Federal Reserve notes, described 3–4
Federal Student Aid, contact information 405
Federal Supplemental Educational Opportunity Grant (FSEOG) 313–14
Federal Trade Commission (FTC)
  contact information **177**, 398
  fraud prevention **205**
  publications
    advertisements 221n
    automobile purchase 237n
    credit overview 253n
    error resolutions 191n
    jewelry purchases 229n
    lost charge cards 337n
    mail order buying clubs 243n
    modeling scams 373n
    scams 351n
    service contracts 201n
    stolen charge cards 337n
    travel fraud 377n
    warranties 201n
Federal Work-Study (FES) 315–16
fees
  bank accounts 88, 104–5
  bounced checks 101–2
  checking accounts 124–25
  cost of credit 275
  credit applications 255
  credit cards 185, 287–88, 292–93
  insufficient funds 102–3
  late payments 105–6
fellowships, tax information 59–63
FFEL *see* Federal Family Education Loan
FICO *see* Fair Isaac score
50 States Quarters Program Act (1997) 13
FinAid, website address 392
finance charges
  credit cards 286–87, **288–89**, 293
  truth in lending disclosure 276–77
financial aid, education loans 309–18
Financial Calculators, Inc., website address 392
financial goals, budgets 78
Financial Literacy Two Thousand and Ten, website address 399
financial management
  checking accounts 122
  entrepreneurs 44–45

Financial Planning Association,
contact information 399
"Finding A Summer Job Or Internship"
(Nemours Foundation) 31n
fine print
cell phone plans 218
computer purchases 225–28
credit applications 255–57
travel fraud 379
fixed expenses, defined **80**
fixed rate, described 275, **286**
flexible expenses, defined **80**
Florida State University, website
address 394
FLSA *see* Fair Labor Standards Act
William D. Ford Federal Direct Loan
Program 317
foreclosure, defined **324**
foreign lottery scams, described **354**
4-H, website address 50
four C's
credit decisions 279–82
loan decisions 302–3
401(k) retirement plan, defined **72**
403(b) retirement plan, defined **72**
franchises, described 40
Franklin, Benjamin **8**, **10**
fraud
advance fee loans 263–64
cell phone plans 220
charitable giving 159–61
online shopping 179–82
overview 351–72
reporting process **362**
fraud prevention, quick tips **194–95**
Freddie Mac, website address 404
Free Application for Federal Student
Aid (FAFSA) 309–10
free credit reports *see* credit reports
"Frequently Asked Questions" (US
Small Business Administration) 37n
FSEOG *see* Federal Supplemental
Educational Opportunity Grant
FTC *see* Federal Trade Commission
Fulbright grant 60
fundraisers, fraud 353–56, **356**
Future Business Leaders of America,
website address 49
FWS *see* Federal Work-Study

G

Gamblers Anonymous, contact
information 405
gambling
overview 385–87
reasons **386**
"Gambling: Don't Bet on
Winning" (PPFA) 385n
garnishment, defined **324**
gemstones
overview 231–33
treatments **232**
"Getting Credit: What You Need to
Know about Credit" (FTC) 253n
gift cards
described 296–97
risks **298**
gifts *see* charity
Girl Scouts of America,
website address 49
"Going Wireless" (National
Consumers League) 215n
gold, overview 229–30
gold certificates, described 4
gold purchases, karats, described **230**
Gottesburen, Lynne **284**
grace period
credit applications 255
credit cards 285–86, 292
Grant, Ulysses S. **10**
grants, college finances 310–11
Great Seal of the United States,
US currency **8**
gross income, defined **79**

H

Hamilton, Alexander **10**
Heakal, Reem 369
health insurance *see* insurance coverage
"Health Insurance: Protecting Health and
Paying for Treatment" (Northwestern
Mutual Foundation) 145n
home loans, described 274–75
see also mortgages
home ownership, investments 71
Horwitz, Paul **178**
"How to Right a Wrong" (FTC) 191n

I

"Ideas for Your Business" (US Small
Business Administration) 37n
identity theft
age factor 348–49
filing complaints 259
methods, described 343
overview 341–50
prevention 259–61, 267
Identity Theft and Assumption
Deterrence Act 347
"Identity Theft and Identity Fraud"
(DOJ) 341n
"If You've Got The Look, Look Out!
Avoiding Modeling Scams" (FTC) 373n
implied warranties
described 203
used vehicles 210
impostor websites, described 266
impulse buying, described 165–69
InCharge Education Foundation,
contact information 399
income
budgets 78–79
described 79
individual retirement account (IRA),
defined 73
individual taxpayer identification
number (ITIN) 89, 126
installment loans, overview 301–3
Institute for Financial Literacy,
contact information 399
Institute of Consumer Finance Education's
Children and Money, website
address 403
institutional grants, described 315
insufficient funds
checking accounts 124–25
described 101–3
insurance coverage
age factor 147
bank deposits 85–86, 86, 88
checking accounts 122–23
entrepreneurs 40
higher costs 149
overview 145–51
savings accounts 69
stolen credit cards 337

Insurance Information Institute,
contact information 403
interest
checking accounts 124
cost of credit 275
described 68
savings accounts 116
tax information 57–59
see also annual percentage yield;
compound interest
interest rates
credit cards 186
debt management 322–23
savings accounts 116–17
Internal Revenue Service (IRS)
contact information 399
tax information publication 51n
website address 48
international lottery scams,
described 354
"Internet Fraud" (FBI) 179n
internships, overview 31–36
interview, employment 35–36
investment income, tax
information 57–59
investment products, described 71
investments
choices 71
defined 73
described 69–70
pay yourself first, described 75
Investopedia Simulator, website
address 394
Iowa State University Cooperative
Extension, contact information
399
IRA see individual retirement account
iridium 230–31
IRS see Internal Revenue Service
It All Adds Up, website address 395
ITIN see individual taxpayer
identification number

J

Jackson, Andrew 10
JA Titan, website address 42
Jefferson, Thomas 8, 10, 13, 14
jewelry purchases, overview 229–36

jobs
   entrepreneurs 37–50
   internships 31–36
   listed **26–27**
   overview 23–30
   worst **34**
judgment, defined **324**
Jump$tart Coalition for Personal Financial
   Literacy, contact information 399
Junior Achievement
   contact information 399
   website address 49

K

karats, described 229–30
   see also carats
Kennedy, John F. **14**
Kincaid, Janet 106–7, 109, **169**, **178**
Kiplinger, contact information 400

L

LavaMind's Gazillionaire, website
   address 395
lemon laws **210**
"Let's Talk Allowances" (Northwestern
   Mutual Foundation) 19n
liabilities, described 321
lien, defined **324**
life insurance *see* insurance coverage
"Life Insurance: Protecting the Family
   Income" (Northwestern Mutual
   Foundation) 145n
Lincoln, Abraham **10**, 13, **14**
liquidity, defined **73**
loan consolidation, described 303
loans *see* bank loans; borrowing money;
   education loans; payday loans
lottery scams, described **354**

M

mail orders
   complaints **249**
   consumer rights 191–93
managing credit, quick tips **280**
"Managing Your Savings Account"
   (Bank of America) 113n

Marshall, John **13**
Marshall, Mira 109–11
matrix marketing 366
Medicare tax, defined **54**
mentors, entrepreneurs 38, 48
minimum balances
   checking accounts 124
   savings accounts 115
mints, US coins 11–12
miracle of compounding
   see compound interest
MMDA *see* money market
   deposit account
modeling scams
   overview 373–76
   talent tips **375**
"Module 1: Bank On It" (FDIC) 85n
"Module 2: Check It Out" (FDIC) 121n
"Module 3: Setting Financial Goals"
   (FDIC) 77n
"Module 4: Pay Yourself First"
   (FDIC) 67n
"Module 5: Borrowing Basics"
   (FDIC) 273n, 329n
"Module 6: Charge It Right"
   (FDIC) 295n
"Module 7: Paying for College and
   Cars" (FDIC) 301n, 305n, 309n
money, growth strategies 67–75
   see also currency
MoneyCentral, website address 400
money management *see* financial
   management
Money Management International,
   website address 392, 394
money market accounts
   debit cards 118
   defined **73**
   described 116
money market deposit account
   (MMDA), described 124
Money Matters To Me, website
   address 393
Money Smart for Young Adults (FDIC)
   banking information 85n, 121n
   budgeting information 67n, 77n
   credit information 273n, 295n, 329n
   loan information 301n, 305n, 309n
MoneyWi$e, website address 400

monthly payment calendar *84*
monthly payment schedules, described
  81–82
"More About ... Giving Wisely"
  (SIFMA) 153n
Morningstar, contact information 400
mortgages, additional costs 110–11
Motley Fool
  contact information 400
  earning money publication 23n
multilevel marketing plans 366–67,
  369–72
"Multilevel Marketing Plans"
  (FTC) 351n
mutual funds, defined **73**
My Money, website address 393
Myvesta, contact information 400

N

National Academy Foundation,
  website address 48
National Association of Personal
  Financial Advisors, contact
  information 400
National Association of Professional
  Insurance Agents, contact
  information 404
National Bank notes, described 4
National Collegiate Inventors and
  Innovators Alliance, website
  address **42**
National Consumer Law Center,
  Inc., website address 403
National Consumers League
  cell phone plans publication 215n
  contact information 403
National Council on Economic
  Education, contact information 400
National Council on Problem Gambling,
  contact information **387**
National Credit Union Administration
  (NCUA), described **88**
National Endowment for Financial
  Education, contact information 400
National Foundation for Credit
  Counseling, contact information 405
National Mentoring Partnership, website
  address 48

National Science and Mathematics
  Access to Retain Talent Grant 314–15
National Smart Grant 314–15
National White Collar Crime Center,
  described **180**
Native Financial Education
  Coalition, website address 400
NCUA *see* National Credit Union
  Administration
negative option plans, described
  243–47, **246**
negotiable order of withdrawal
  (NOW) account 124
Nemours Foundation, summer jobs
  publication 31n
"Net Based Business Opportunities:
  Are Some Flop-portunities?"
  (FTC) 351n
net income, defined **79**
Network for Good, website address 158
network marketing 366
newspaper carriers, tax information 57
non-sufficient funds (NSF)
  see insufficient funds
Northwestern Mutual Foundation,
  publications
  allowances 19n
  insurance coverage 145n
  smart shopping 165n
notebook computers 221–22
Novus Ordo Seclorum 8
NOW account, described 124
NSF (non-sufficient funds)
  see insufficient funds

O

Office of Financial Education,
  website address 400
online fraud
  advice **360–61**
  credit cards 181
  described 362–64
  statistics **180**
Operation Hope: Banking on Our
  Future, website address 401
opportunity cost, described 30
Ory, Vince 221n
osmium 230–31

overdrafts
  bank accounts 88
  checking accounts 124–25, 144
  described 103–4
  savings accounts 119
  see also insufficient funds

P

palladium 230–31
paperless money transfers
  see electronic funds transfers
paper money
  damaged **16**
  described 3–9
parents
  allowances 19–20
  automobile insurance 149
  chores **20**
  college loans 317–18
  job interview advice **35**
  life insurance 150
partnerships, described 40
patents, described 40
payday loans
  described 323–24, **331**
  overview 330–31
payroll taxes
  defined **54**
  rates **54**
pay yourself first
  described 29, **75**
  savings accounts **119**
pearls, overview 234–35
Pell Grants 61, 313
penalty APR
  credit cards 285
  truth in lending disclosure 277–79
Perkins Loans *see* Federal Perkins Loans
personal identification number (PIN)
  checking accounts 132
  described 91, 94
  identity theft 350
  safety considerations **132**, 339–40
pewter 231
phishing, described **343**, 348–49
PIN *see* personal identification number
planchets, described **12**
Planet Orange, website address 395

Planned Parenthood Federation of
  America (PPFA), gambling publication
  385n
plastic cards *see* ATM cards; credit cards;
  debit cards
platinum, described 230–31
PLUS loans 317–18
point-of-sale transactions (POS)
  checking accounts 131–32
  described 94
Ponzi schemes 371–72
POS *see* point-of-sale transactions
PPFA *see* Planned Parenthood
  Federation of America
Practical Money Skills, website
  address 401
preauthorized transfers, described 94,
  98–99
precious metals, overview 229–31
predatory lending practices
  described 323–24
  indicators **332–33**
  overview 329–36
premiums, defined **146**
"Prenotification Negative Option Plans"
  (FTC) 243n
Prenotification Negative Option Rule 244
pretexting, described **343**
previous balance, credit cards **288–89**
principal, described **68**
privacy
  bank accounts 92
  debit cards 134
Profit Sharing/401(k) Society of America,
  contact information 401
property insurance *see* insurance coverage
"Protecting Autos: The Vehicles and the
  People in Them" (Northwestern Mutual
  Foundation) 145n
"Protecting Property: Replacing and
  Repairing the Things You Own"
  (Northwestern Mutual Foundation) 145n
"Protecting Your Income: When You
  Cannot Work and Earn" (Northwestern
  Mutual Foundation) 145n
"Purchase Options for Consumers"
  (Federal Reserve Bank of Chicago) 183n
"Putting It in Writing" (US Small Business
  Administration) 37n

pyramid schemes
  described **370**
  overview 366–67, 369–72

R

rebates
  computer purchases 226–27
  credit cards 290
  described **174**
recordkeeping
  checking accounts 139–43
  identity theft 346
  tax information **62**
refund anticipation loans,
  described 335–36
registration services, lost/stolen
  credit cards **340**
Regulation E **185**
reloaders, described 353
rent-to-own, described 335
repossession, defined **324**
résumés, described 32
retirement accounts, described 70–71
  see also 401(k) retirement plan; 403(b)
    retirement plan; individual
    retirement accounts
rhodium 230–31
risk, investments 75
risk *versus* return, defined **73**
Roosevelt, Franklin D. 13, **14**
rule of 72, described **70**, 74
Rutgers, website address 394
Rutgers Cooperative Extension,
  website address 401
ruthenium 230–31

S

Sacagawea **14**
"Safeguarding Your Money"
  (Northwestern Mutual
  Foundation) 145n
safety considerations
  bank deposits 85–86
  cell phones **220**
  checking accounts 122–23
  debit cards 134
  online purchases **188**

salaries
  defined **59**
  described 51
sales
  comparison shopping **172**
  overview 171–78
savings
  opportunity cost 30
  smart shopping 170
savings accounts
  defined **90**
  described 69–70, 90
  overview 113–20
savings action plans, described 74–75
savings and loan associations, described **86**
savings banks, described **86**
savings bonds, described **74**
savings register sample *114*
SBA *see* US Small Business
  Administration
scams *see* fraud
scholarships
  college finances 310–11
  tax information 59–63
SEC *see* US Securities
  and Exchange Commission
secured loans, described 301
Securities and Exchange Commission
  (SEC) *see* US Securities and Exchange
  Commission
Securities Industry and Financial Markets
  Association Foundation for Investor
  Education (SIFMA)
  charity information publication 153n
  contact information 401
security features, currency 6–7
self-employment income, tax
  information 56–57
service contracts
  cell phones 215–20
  complaints **212**
  described 202–3
  overview 206–14
  versus warranties **207**
"Service Contracts" (FTC) 201n
shares, defined **73**
shopping strategies
  budgets **168–69**
  comparisons **172**

shopping strategies, continued
  consumer rights 191–200
  international purchases **182**
  need *versus* want **178**
  online shopping 179–82
  overview 165–70
  payment options 183–90
  rebates **174**
  sale merchandise 171–78
SIFMA *see* Securities Industry and
  Financial Markets Association
  Foundation for Investor Education
signature card, described 126
silver, described 230–31
silver certificates, described 4
skimming, described **343**
Smart About Money, website address
  393, 394
smart cards, described 297–99
SMART Grant 314–15
"Smart Shopping" (Northwestern
  Mutual Foundation) 165n
Social Security number (SSN) 89, 126, 261
Social Security tax, defined **54**
Society of Financial Service Professionals,
  contact information 401
software, personal finance programs 82
sole proprietorships, described 39
Sovereign Bank's KidsBank.com,
  website address 401
"Spending Smarts: Surfing the Sales"
  (Castle Works, Inc.) 171n
"Spending Smarts: Ten Super Shopping
  Tips" (Castle Works, Inc.) 171n
spoken warranties, described **202**
Springboard Credit Education, website
  address 404
SSN *see* Social Security number
Standard and Poor's, contact information 401
statement savings, defined **73**
statistics, online fraud **180**
Stock Market Game, website address 395
stocks, defined **73**
Stock-Trak, website address 395
stolen credit cards
  credit applications 255–57
  described **264**
  liability limits 186
  overview 337–40

stop-payment fees, checking accounts 125
stop payments, preauthorized items **99**
stored value cards, described **91**, 296–97
students
  education loans 309–18
  tax information 51–63
Students In Free Enterprise, website
  address 49
subprime lending
  defined **330**
  described 329–30
summer jobs, *versus* internships 31–36
"Sweepstakes and Lotteries Scams"
  (FTC) 351n

T

"Take This Scheme and Stuff It:
  Avoiding Envelope-Stuffing Rip-offs"
  (FTC) 351n
"Taxable Income for Students" (IRS)
  51n
tax-exempt bonds, tax information 58
tax forms
  W-2 form *52*, 55, **55**
  W-4 form **55**, *56*
tax information
  charitable giving 155–57
  overview 51–63
  recordkeeping **62**
telemarketers
  fraud 159–61, 351–53
  restrictions **355**
  travel fraud 380–83
"Telemarketing Travel Fraud"
  (FTC) 377n
telephone orders, consumer rights
  191–93
telephone transfers, described 94
term, described **72**
text messaging, wireless internet
  service **217**
theft, electronic funds transfers 95–97
Thompson, Charles **8**
thrifts, described **86**
time limits, unauthorized
  transactions **185**
tip income, defined **59**
tips, tax information 51–55

"Tips for Buying a Computer"
  (Ory) 221n
total payments, truth in lending
  disclosure 277
trademarks, described 41
trade secrets, described 41
transferring funds, savings accounts
  118–19
  see also electronic funds transfers
TransUnion, contact information 268,
  404
travel fraud, preparations **378**
travel schemes, overview 377–83
Treasury bills, described **74**
Treasury bonds, described **74**
Treasury notes, described **74**
Truth in Lending Act **331**
truth in savings disclosures,
  described 69, 275–79
tuition programs, tax information 61
  see also education loans
two-cycle balances, credit cards
  288–89

U

universal default, truth in lending
  disclosure 279
universal product code (UPC),
  pricing accuracy **176–77**
unordered merchandise, consumer
  rights 193
unsecured installment loans,
  described 301–3
unsolicited items, described **159**
UPC *see* universal product code
USAA Educational Foundation,
  website address 402
US Bonds, defined **74**
US Consumer Gateway and Federal
  Consumer Information Center,
  website address 403
US Department of Justice (DOJ),
  identity theft publication 341n
US Department of Labor, website
  address 48
used car purchases *see* automobile
  purchases
used vehicles, warranties **210**

US Financial Literacy and Education
  Commission, website address 401
US Patent and Trade Office, website
  address 48
US Securities and Exchange
  Commission (SEC)
  contact information 401
  website address 393, 394
US Small Business Administration
  (SBA), entrepreneurs publication 37n
US Treasury Securities, defined **74**
US Treasury's Page for Kids, website
  address 401
US Trustee Program Credit Counseling,
  contact information 405

V

value, allowances 21–22
VantageScore **256**
variable rate, described 275, **286**
vermeil 231
Villafranca, Eloy 102, **108**
Virtual Stock Exchange, website
  address 395
volunteer activities, described 154–55

W

Wachovia Securities, website address 393
wages
  defined **59**
  described 51
warranties
  credit cards 291
  overview 201–5
  versus service contracts **207**
  used vehicles **210**
"Warranties" (FTC) 201n
Washington, George **10**, **14**
"Ways to Save and Make Money"
  (Motley Fool) 23n
"What Is a Pyramid Scheme?"
  (Heakal) 369
"What's It Worth?" (Northwestern
  Mutual Foundation) 165n
wireless internet service, text
  messaging **217**
wireless telephone service *see* cell phones

Wi$eUp, contact information 402
withdrawal, bank accounts 87
withdrawal slip sample *117*
withholding taxes
  described **53**
  tips 53–55
work-at-home schemes
  complaints **358**
  described 356–61
"Work-at-Home Schemes" (FTC) 351n

worksheets, monthly income, expenses **81**
written warranties, described 201–2

Y

Young America's Business Trust,
  website address 50
Young Consumers, website address 393
"Your Business Buddy List" (US Small
  Business Administration) 37n